The Sale of Works of Art

THE SALE OF WORKS OF ART

A Study based on the Times-Sotheby Index

GERALDINE KEEN

NELSON

THOMAS NELSON AND SONS LTD
36 Park Street London W1
P.O. Box 2187 Accra
P.O. Box 25012 Nairobi
P.O. Box 21149 Dar es Salaam
77 Coffee Street San Fernando Trinidad

THOMAS NELSON (AUSTRALIA) LTD
597 Little Collins Street Melbourne 3000

THOMAS NELSON AND SONS (CANADA) LTD
81 Curlew Drive Don Mills Ontario

THOMAS NELSON (NIGERIA) LTD
P.O. Box 336 Apapa Lagos

THOMAS NELSON AND SONS (SOUTH AFRICA) (PTY) LTD
51 Commissioner Street Johannesburg

Contents

Illustrations

8

Preface

In 1967 I was asked by *The Times* to help them set up a project which was under discussion with Sotheby's–the construction of an art price index. A statistician by training and a journalist by trade, I represented *The Times* side of the project, while Ian Bennett and Charlotte Prest worked on it for Sotheby's.

For over a year we devoted ourselves to digging through old records and working out how a price index could be constructed in each of the fields we had set ourselves to cover. In each field we had the backing of Sotheby's experts to help us assess what prices were comparable and help us to set our ever-growing file of old records into logical order.

It was the research that went into this project which lies behind this book. To an outsider, the criteria which determine that one painting is more desirable than another in market terms were mysterious and fascinating, as also were the reasons for one field being more fashionable among collectors than another. It is this that led me to try and set out in book form how the considerations of art history, decorative appeal, availability, collecting traditions, and the structure of the international market combine to determine a market price for priceless works of art.

The opinions expressed in this book are entirely my own and undoubtedly specialists will find much to criticize. My excuse must be the size of the field I have tried to tackle. I have tried to trace the market forces over a very wide field, and no doubt will have stumbled on points of detail. I am, however, tremendously indebted to Sotheby's for the help they have so generously given me, not only in the original construction of the Index, but also in my attempt to seek out the forces that lay behind the figures and charts which we constructed, and for saving me from making too many mistakes in trying to find my way in the curious and complicated highways and by-ways of the art market. My thanks are particularly due to my companions and associates Ian Bennett and Charlotte Prest.

All references to the Times-Sotheby Index in this book are

limited to the period 1951 to July 1969. Figures for the level of the Index for the full year 1969 are not available as this book goes to press. In general, the record prices quoted refer also to the highest prices paid at auction before July 1969. Prices quoted of works sold at auction outside England do not include sales tax.

Acknowledgements

The author wishes to acknowledge with gratitude the assistance of the following auctioneers in providing the illustrations for this book: Étude Ader et Picard; Paul Brandt; Christie Manson and Woods Ltd; Gallerie Motte; the Museum of Fine Arts, Boston; the National Gallery of Art, Washington, DC; Etude Rheims et Laurin; and Sotheby & Co. The Walker Art Gallery, Liverpool, have also very kindly supplied photographs.

Her thanks are also due to the following galleries and individuals who have agreed to the reproduction of works that they purchased at Sotheby's:

London: Thomas Agnew & Son; H. Blairman & Sons; H. M. Calmann; Hallsborough Gallery; James Hanson; Leonard Koetser; Leger Galleries; Leggatt Bros; Frank Partridge & Sons; Edward Speelman.

New York: Bodley Gallery; Nathan Cummings; Leonard Hutton Galleries; Sydney Janis; and Selected Artists Galleries Inc.

Collection Deder, Rhineland, Germany; Galleria Internationale, Milan, Italy; David M. Koetser Gallery, Zürich, Switzerland; Kornfeld and Klipstein, Bern, Switzerland; R. E. Lewis Inc., San Francisco, California; Lotar Neumann, Switzerland; The Norton Simon Foundation, Norton Simon Inc. Museum of Art, and Mr and Mrs Norton Simon, Fullaton, California; and Captain T. Rogers, Airlie, Lucan, Co. Dublin, Eire.

Acknowledgements are also made to the following for permission to reproduce works in their possession: King's College, Cambridge (page 79); Mr and Mrs Paul Mellon (facing pages 198 and 204); the Metropolitan Museum of Art, New York (page 74; page 121, Rogers Fund 1964; facing page 199); and the Trustees of the National Gallery, London (pages 76, 80, 171).

CHAPTER 1

Money and Art

The art market flourished as never before in the 1960s. There were more people collecting than at any other period in history, and collecting over a wider spectrum of works of art. Both buyers and sellers were continually asking themselves the question: 'What is this worth?' And harassed auctioneers and dealers were continually trying to guess the answer–for values in the art market are never clearly defined.

But another question should surely be posed first: 'Why is it worth anything at all?' This is the question which this book seeks to answer, by looking into the relation between money and art. The answer is partly as old as time, for most of the great art of the past, which is now venerated, studied and considered a precious heritage, came into existence following the normal economic laws of supply and demand. And partly the answer lies in our present-day society and its values. Here the springboard for this survey is the Times-Sotheby Index of fine-art prices. The Index, which measures the extent to which prices have risen for works of art over the two decades 1950–1970, is based on the prices realized by paintings, drawings, prints and other art works at international auctions. In the chapters that follow an attempt will be made not only to review the ever-shifting levels of auction prices, but also to explain the factors that determine the auction price of a 'priceless' work of art. First, however, it is necessary to look at some of the fundamental reasons why money and art come to be connected.

The market in art exists because of the very natural pleasure that most people take in possessing beautiful things, and it is aided by the equally natural pleasure afforded to others by ostentation. From the moment that two people want to possess the same picture, a market for that picture exists. And in the nature of things there is usually a middleman to play the two off against each other and to see which of them is prepared to pay the higher price. The art market is essentially no more than a huge extension of this position, with thousands of art lovers of varying means competing for the possession of works by thousands of artists, both living and dead.

Many people despise the art market, or simply dislike the idea that money and art are in any way connected. All those who take pleasure in works of art should, however, be thankful that an art market of some sort has existed down the centuries. If there had not been art lovers from the earliest times, who were prepared to pay good money for what they wanted, artists would not have been able to afford to follow the promptings of their genius, and our great artistic heritage would never have come into existence. It is, of course, to the patrons and collectors who have taken a vivid interest in the art and artists of their times that we are most indebted. But others, who have enriched the knowledge and spread the love of works of art by bringing home foreign treasures, and have helped to create the museum collections and to promote the study of art in history through their own interest, also deserve much gratitude.

Today, with the increase in the number of museums, specially staged exhibitions, the easy availability of books with fine reproductions, and a growing art-historical industry, it is easy to forget this. It is possible to derive great pleasure and interest from art without spending a penny. With luck, you can even be paid for the interest you take. Art historians, restorers, auctioneers, dealers, agents, and even art journalists, all contribute to the smooth exchange of works of art between collector and collector, or collector and museum. And they are often highly paid for their services.

This is perhaps to over-emphasize the relationship between money and art. It costs money to eat, but many people give little thought to the economics of eating. It is extremely expensive to stage a play, but few theatregoers let their minds dwell on this aspect of the production. The exchange of money for goods and services, with all the complicated financial and economic structures that this involves, is the basic machinery by which twentieth-century life is propelled, and by which a good deal of the business of living has been organized for many centuries.

Many people prefer to ignore this machinery and concentrate on what it produces. In the field of art this is particularly easy to do, for the machinery hardly affects the inspiration or interest of the end-product. The fascination of the art market, however, lies in its reflection of the relationship between art and society. It is in a way a bridge between the intangible values of the human spirit and the human intellect and the material considerations that dominate everyday life, a link between immeasurable human aspirations and down-to-earth economics.

Many philosophers, historians, psychologists—and artists—have tried to define the nature of art. Why it is that some men have the power to create patterns which can stir others deeply? The mixture of pure visual satisfaction, of intellectual associations, and possibly of some vision or insight which can never be set down in words, are all components of the pleasure we draw from any individual work of art. They all contribute to its creation, though the relationship between the artist's creative inspiration and the reaction of each individual viewer is infinitely debatable. Marcel Duchamp went as far as to assert that a work of art is created to an equal extent by the artist and his public.

It is clear, however, that human beings have always derived some kind of intangible pleasure and inspiration from works of art and that this pleasure is generally considered of a higher order than most, superior to the pleasure derived from good food, good wine, or a good lover, a civilizing influence, of value to society in its own right. But, while the nature of the pleasure human beings derive from a work of art may not have changed substantially from the beginning of time, the role of art in society has changed fundamentally. Inevitably this role shapes the market in art and is reflected by it.

In the first place, art is a luxury. Artistic activity seldom flourishes in periods of war, plague, or material shortage. Together with other affairs of the spirit, it is set aside when the battle is for survival. On the other hand, art comes into its own in periods of peace and material prosperity, when people have time and opportunity to look for some higher satisfaction than that afforded by their everyday affairs.

Ancient Rome provides one of the earliest examples of prosperity and collecting fever going hand in hand. The spoils of the expanding Empire were at first brought home to decorate the temples and State institutions of Rome; but soon the noble Romans, fabulously wealthy as a result of their conquests and the revenues drawn from their extensive provinces, began to compete in filling their private palaces and villas with art treasures. Latin literature abounds with references to this passion for rare books and works of art. Collecting was at this time, of course, greatly simplified by the possibility of seizing the treasures you desired as a simple right of conquest—a pattern that has repeated itself throughout history, notably under the régimes of Napoleon and Hitler.

The Proconsul Verres has been immortalized in Cicero's *In Verrem*, an indictment of his spoliation of Sicily. A connoisseur and art lover of great stature, Verres stooped to any means to obtain the treasures he desired, including, besides purchase, blackmail and simple theft. Cicero sought an indemnity of

100,000,000 sesterces, or nearly £10 million (around $25 million) in today's money, for Verres's Sicilian thefts, according to the calculations of F. H. Taylor in his history of art collecting, *Taste of Angels*.

Mr Taylor also notes that 'a whole quarter of Rome in the vicinity of the Villa Publica was devoted to art dealers, book-sellers, and antiquarians – a quarter which was rife with the time-honoured practices of falsification and forgery, of "phony" restorations and rigged auction sales'. This darker side of the art market has always existed, especially in periods when the trade in works of art has been particularly flourishing. For when art collecting is fashionable, a large band of more or less gullible amateurs follows in the wake of the true connoisseurs.

But even this aspect of the art market, which of course flourishes again today, has its uses. It provides a form of protection for the true art market. Those who buy with love and knowledge are far less often caught out than those who buy for snobbish reasons. In a way, the pitfalls created by the criminal fringe of the art game provide an automatic protection against too many people getting involved for the wrong motives.

The art market of ancient Rome was, perhaps, a rather sterile affair. The fashion was for collecting great art works of the past, but this did not stimulate a parallel interest in and patronage of contemporary artists. It reflected a society based on great conquests and powerful administrative institutions. Collectors' interests lay among the artistic trophies of the great cultures they had themselves destroyed. Typical of this is the pride of place accorded to Corinthian bronzes, which were among the most avidly sought after and highly valued of all art treasures. Their rarity was assured by the devastating pillage of Corinth by the Consul Mummius in 146 BC.

The decay of the Roman Empire and the incursions of the bar-barians dimmed the lights of the art market, and it is with the Italian Renaissance that a flourishing trade revived in Europe. It is probably no coincidence that Tuscany in the late thirteenth and fourteenth centuries was the cradle both of modern capitalism and of the modern concept of a personal art. The Middle Ages had reduced the role of the artist to that of an anonymous crafts-man and decorator; with Cimabue and Giotto in Florence and Duccio in Siena artists began to be respected and admired for their personal and individual vision. This was also the period when the Tuscan bankers became the chief financiers of Europe.

Jean Gimpel in his polemic, *The Cult of Art*, carries this parallel a stage further. He points out that Giotto's death in 1336 was almost immediately followed by the first major crisis in European capitalism. In about 1340 the Bardi and Perruzzi banks were ruined by Edward III of England's refusal to repay loans amounting to 1,365,000 florins. This disaster completely undermined the Florentine economy and heralded a period of acute social unrest. This, in his view, explains the fact that Giotto's revolutionary artistic innovations were for the most part ignored by his followers, who concentrated on survival rather than experiment, and the great story of the flowering of Italian art is not again taken up until we come to Masaccio at the beginning of the fifteenth century.

This is, perhaps, to stretch the link between economics and artistic innovation too far. It was the start of the Medicis' rule in 1430 that restored peace and prosperity to Florence. But the Florentine merchants under the rule of the early Medici were the richest in Europe and it was in Florence that the Italian Renaissance began.

The fifteenth and early part of the sixteenth century saw a vastly important change in the role of the artist. He became the friend and companion of princes. He was bribed, blackmailed, and fought over by rival patrons desirous of obtaining the fruits of his genius, in marked contrast with the role of the humble artist-decorator of the Middle Ages. This attitude towards the artist, dating essentially from the Renaissance, though it remained of some importance in the intervening years, has today become the dominating factor. In buying a work by an individual artist, we feel that we are obtaining a portion of his genius, his vision.

It is no coincidence that the chief artistic centres of the Renaissance were Florence, Rome, and Venice–the richest cities of Italy, which were packed with prosperous patrons of the arts. In the smaller city-states it was generally only the ruling house whose wealth was sufficient to justify the luxury of collecting on a large scale.

In contrast to the art market of ancient Rome, that of the Renaissance supported a flourishing trade both in great works of the past and the work of contemporary artists, who in turn were fundamentally influenced by the revival of interest in the artistic achievements of antiquity. The role of the proto-dealers or agents in gathering great works of Classical times for the delectation of princes (and their own profit) should not be overlooked. It certainly contributed to the 're-birth' of art. This is perhaps an example of the most desirable mode of operation of the rich collector and the market in art which he generates. In seeking out the finest artistic achievements of the past, he is also providing the artists of his own time with a new inspiration, and helping to extend the cultural heritage for future generations.

In the sixteenth and seventeenth centuries, Flanders and Holland in the north began to rival Italy as centres of artistic innovation and production. The social context was, however, very different. The collecting fever of the Italian Renaissance was essentially limited to the rich and noble–including, of course, the princes of the Church. Fortune and power may have come to them from commercial grass roots, such as wool and banking in the case of the Medici, or Eastern trade in the case of the Venetian nobles, but patronage of the arts was still the prerogative of the few. In the north, in contrast, this period saw the rise of the middle-class collector.

The fortunes of the Netherlands, like those of Britain at a later stage, were based on trade and their dominance of sea traffic. Their merchant fleets gradually succeeded in ousting Venice from its key position as a trading gateway between Europe and the East. At the same time, Antwerp and Amsterdam became successively the great entrepôt centres of European trade, including, among other things, the trade in works of art. In the sixteenth century this was the basis of Antwerp's prosperity. The fabulous wealth of Spain, based on gold from the New World, served greatly to enrich the Hapsburg dominions and contributed largely to the city's commercial success. All the middle-class merchants took a handsome cut and began to spend lavishly on collecting paintings and works of art. Perhaps the most important element introduced into the art market at this period was speculation. The Antwerp bourse was at the time something like a European Wall Street, a centre of frenzied speculative activity. Then, as now, the gambling instinct, once encouraged, spread rapidly. Speculation on the fame of artists was a natural development, paralleled in seventeenth-century Holland by a wildly speculative market in tulip bulbs.

The prosperity of Antwerp and the southern Netherlands at the end of the sixteenth century passed in the seventeenth to the Protestant north. Art-market speculation caught the imagination of nearly all the citizens who could afford it. John Evelyn remarked, ''tis an ordinary thing to find a common farmer lay out two or 3,000 pounds in this Commodity'. The country was extremely prosperous and the production of paintings to meet this demand was prodigious. The large number of Dutch paintings still on the market today stands witness to this extraordinary era.

The prosperity of the art market in eighteenth-century France contrasts interestingly with its bourgeois heyday in the north during the previous century. Again, of course, this is a reflection of the essential difference of society and its values. The wealth which was lavished on the arts in eighteenth-century France was that of the nobles and the court, squeezed from the starving peasants in the decades which led up to the Revolution. The accent was on lavish elegance to suit a frivolous court. The artist lost some of the god-like stature he attained during the Renaissance. No longer the unique man of genius, he became again to some extent a mere decorator. His work was prized equally with that of the *ébéniste*, the goldsmith, or the maker of fine porcelain. While eighteenth-century France has determined international taste in expensive furnishings and *objets d'art*, up to the present day, its impact in the fields of painting, drawing, and sculpture has been more modest. This was reflected by the art market of the time. A commode inlaid with Sèvres plaques cost Madame du Barry the equivalent of roughly £40,000 (about $96,000) in 1785; Boucher or Fragonard would have been lucky to receive one-tenth of this sum for an important commission.

Coming closer to the present day, the role of Britain in the art market of the late eighteenth and nineteenth centuries is closely paralleled by that of America in the late nineteenth and twentieth centuries. The expansion of its trading empire, combined with the Industrial Revolution, gave Britain more than a century of power and tremendous prosperity.

Both Britain and America, at least at the start of their dominant periods, came closer to imitating ancient Rome in their approach to collecting than to imitating the Renaissance. The Grand Tour exacerbated the collecting fever of English noblemen in the eighteenth century, who returned to England loaded with treasures from foreign parts. There was tremendous enthusiasm for the works of Dutch and Italian artists in England at this period, and huge sums were spent on obtaining them, or on coaxing the artists to visit England. But among English artists it was only the portrait painters, with their clear-cut role in contributing to ostentation, if not to 'great art', who were paid commensurate prices.

In the nineteenth century English travellers continued to return from abroad laden with foreign treasures. In the field of painting Italy was a particularly rich source, though the products of seventeenth-century bourgeois Dutch taste had a natural attraction for British bourgeois collectors of the nineteenth. At the beginning of the century a flood of artistic spoils had arrived in England from Revolutionary France.

The Victorian era was, nevertheless, a Golden Age for contemporary British artists. Though they were relatively cut off from artistic developments on the Continent, an extremely active market developed in their work within Britain. Landscapes, genre paintings, and historical and religious pictures were tremendously sought after and a strong British school developed to meet the demand. At present, the art works of this prosperous age are not rated very highly. Compared to the periods in which the Renaissance bankers and the Dutch speculators were at their most active, the Victorian era constitutes one of the art market's failures.

American collecting only began to make a powerful impact in the market towards the end of the nineteenth century. The Metropolitan Museum and the Boston Museum of Fine Arts were both founded in 1870, and the new breed of American millionaires began to interest themselves in collecting. But, as in Britain, the early collectors, born of a new prosperity, limited their interest rather to foreign art treasures, and largely to those of the past. It must be said, however, that the interest of American collectors in the Impressionists was aroused long before the British woke up to their importance.

The extent to which American collecting has dominated the art market in the twentieth century need not be underlined. America, having become the richest country in the world, the art treasures of Europe have naturally flowed westward across the Atlantic. The activities of the English-born dealer, Joseph Duveen (later Lord Duveen), in the 1920s and 1930s form one of the great sagas of twentieth-century cultural history. The quantity and quality of the works he sold to American millionaires, coupled with the fabulous prices he charged, undoubtedly helped to establish there the fashion for collecting. Duveen, like most of the great collectors of the period, concentrated, however, on the treasures of the past.

It is only since the Second World War that American collectors have shifted their interest to the work of contemporary artists. And as with all American enthusiasms, the shift has been of momentous proportions. Financially, New York has become the most rewarding art centre for living artists and has attracted many painters from abroad. The financial breakthrough for any modern artist comes with the moment that the importance of his work is recognized by American connoisseurs.

But this is only one aspect of the sensational boom in the art market since the war. The Times-Sotheby Index shows that art prices have multiplied, generally, some ten or eleven times since the early 1950s, with values in the more fashionable fields coming closer to a multiplication of thirty or forty times. In 1958, Maurice Rheims estimated the volume of trade in the art world–in its broadest sense, including antiques and antiquities–at about £100 million a year, which passed 'through the hands of some five thousand dealers, a considerable number of agents and, of course, a great many clients'. Prices have at least doubled, if not tripled, since then; so has the variety of objects considered worthy of collection, and, probably, the number of dealers, agents, and clients. For the 1960s were a golden era for the art market. The trend had already started in the second half of the 1950s, and public interest in the sale and purchase of works of art continued to increase steadily as the 1960s advanced. The years 1967 and 1968 were outstanding. Hardly an auction sale went by without new price records being established for the work of individual artists. The Press and television threw themselves enthusiastically into recording the drama of the exchange of great art for great sums of money; articles on art as an investment proliferated; the art market itself gathered new momentum from this publicity and fed the Press with more and more amazing stories of price levels.

In 1961, one of the last important subject pictures by Rembrandt that is likely to come on the market, 'Aristotle contemplating the bust of Homer', was sold at Parke-Bernet in New York for the staggering sum of £821,428 ($2,300,000). By 1967 and 1968 two very fine early works by the prolific nineteenth-century artists Monet and Renoir were sold for £588,000 ($1,411,200) and £646,000 ($1,550,000) respectively.

But exceptional prices were only one factor in the art-market boom. Even more notable was the volume of trade; likewise, the tremendous number of people involved in its handling, and the great increase in the number of collectors. Everyone was wanting to get in on the act, down to the humblest housewife scouring her cupboards for undiscovered treasures. One of the more unsatisfactory aspects of the boom was the fact that relatively high prices were regularly asked for sheer junk.

The art market knows no frontiers; it is an international affair. Although America dominates the scene, there are many European collectors, among them collectors of particular importance in Germany and Italy. A newcomer to the scene is Japan; in the late 1960s Japanese collectors were beginning to have a powerful influence on the European art market and in 1969, for the first time, both Sotheby's and Christie's held sales in Tokyo.

But any market, however international, needs a market-place as a centre of operations, and since the war London has indisputably become the centre of the art market. Dealers' galleries have mushroomed and the turnover of the great London auction houses has rapidly expanded. Foreign dealers and collectors descend on London in force at the time of the major sales, and the London galleries flourish with this influx of buyers. No foreign dealer can afford to stay away from England, while the English dealers and auctioneers further extend their operations abroad year by year.

How it is that this happened during a period when, in general, British trade proved disastrously non-competitive abroad, is a fascinating and complicated story. The factors that have contributed to London's success are in part historical, in part financial and administrative, in part sociological, and of course partly personal.

The art market since the Second World War has naturally been created in the image of post-war society and by its attitude to art. The two most important aspects of this attitude can be roughly termed the religious and the financial. On one hand, there has been a growing feeling that art is a great good in its own right, a civilizing influence, a matter for deep study and deep appreciation verging on worship. On the other, there has been a widespread realization of the investment potential of art and its advantages in an inflationary period as a hedge against the dangers inherent in paper currencies.

The religious aspect is perhaps the more fascinating, as well as being fundamental to the long-term health of the art market, and is interwoven almost inextricably with the financial aspect. The twentieth century has proved a tough period for the idealist. The Christian Church has been seriously undermined and is dismissed by many as an anachronism. Few have managed to maintain their faith in Communism in view of developments in Soviet Russia and China. Charity has rather gone out of fashion, as its role has been steadily usurped by the State, and even the most up-to-date idealist, who devotes himself to the economic development of the third world, is not encouraged by seeing his work destroyed by political intrigue and corruption. The traditional values of society have been knocked one by one from their pedestals. Yet the belief in the value of art, which is out of the main line of fire, has survived. This makes patronage of the arts one of the few respectable forms of do-gooding that are left. It is, of course, in America that this is most obviously apparent; the scale of spending by museums is gigantic and is virtually financed only by private donations. Even in England, where museum directors complain bitterly of the meagreness of Treasury grants and of their inability to match American competitors in bidding for important items, private benefactors often step in with offers of outstanding generosity.

In America, where even small state museums often have a spending power of several million dollars a year, the financial side of patronage is mixed up with the idealistic. United States tax laws allow donations made to public museums, in cash or kind, to be set against the donor's current tax liabilities, up to a level equivalent to 30 per cent of his gross income in any one year. This in effect leaves one with a choice of paying tax or giving the equivalent amount to a museum–or buying pictures for the museum instead of paying tax. To anyone with an interest in art, this tends to be far more interesting and attractive than paying hard-earned wealth into the coffers of the central government.

As with any tax law, this one was at one time subject to frequent abuses though it has now been tightened up. A painting could be bought for £1,000 ($2,400), someone cajoled into valuing it at a much higher price, and that amount of tax deducted if the picture was given to a museum. In a case of this sort the donor could obviously show a substantial profit on his generosity. Until 1965, a collector could set the bequest of his paintings to a museum against tax and still keep them in his home until his death. But such manœuvres apart, this tax concession has resulted in untold treasures finding their way to America and has provided the underlying strength of the art market since the war. It has also spread the religion of art within America, for those who came to laugh–and dodge their taxes–have stayed to pray. Many people believe the tradition of art patronage in the United States is now so firmly established that if these generous tax concessions were repealed, there would be little or no reduction in the amount of money spent on works of art.

The fact that since the war so much American money has been spent in this way has undoubtedly favoured London as a centre for the art trade, for London forms a bridge between Europe and America. The reasons for this are as much psychological as practical. Americans, like the British themselves, are notoriously ignorant of foreign languages and feel more at home in London, where dealers and auctioneers speak English. Furthermore, the British are by tradition considered more straightforward in their business dealings than their continental neighbours. The American, therefore, feels safer with an English dealer and less likely to be sold a fake or grossly overcharged than he might be elsewhere in Europe. There are, of course, crooked dealers in London, just as there are scrupulously honest dealers in Paris, Geneva, or Rome; but by and large the English market is conducted on more straightforward lines than the market on the Continent.

On the purely practical side, the exchange of works of art in Britain involves less red tape than in any other country. In almost all other European countries, and even in New York, a sales tax must be paid on every transaction; its level varies from country to country and in some cases it is reclaimable on purchases from abroad. Italy still charges an absurdly high export duty on works of art. In France, all auctioneers are nominally civil servants and are beset by complicated legal restrictions on their activities.

All European countries now have regulations of some sort on the export of works of art of national importance. In Spain and Italy they are so strict as virtually to rule out the legal export of any fine painting; in France export can be stopped without any obligation by the State to purchase the work in question.

While paintings worth over £2,000 ($4,800) can be refused export licences in England, such a refusal is only imposed if an English museum is prepared to pay the declared export price. Thus London has great practical advantages as a trading centre for works of art within Europe, as well as its special advantages as a go-between in the transfer of European art treasures to the United States.

London's pre-eminence in the art market has been only gradually built up in the years since the war. While there was, of course, an active market in London in the pre-war years, with both Sotheby's and Christie's at work, as well as many dealers, it was only one of several important centres, including Paris, Berlin, and New York. Paris was perhaps the leader, especially in the field of Impressionist and modern painting.

The depression of the early 1930s, followed by the six war years, subdued art-market activity. Collectors' minds were on the whole concentrated on survival, and those with possessions hung on to them, if they could. Prices had slumped from their comparatively high levels in the 1920s, though there was a short-lived revival in the late 1930s eclipsed by the war, and prices did begin to recover about 1942–43. However, once the war was over, much of Europe lay in ruins. In particular, France and Germany had suffered far more than England.

In the late 1940s the market began to tick again. Sotheby's and Christie's still survived–although Christie's had been bombed –as did many of the pre-war dealing firms. Severe restrictions on currency virtually ruled out international trading, but this was a trouble shared by all the other European centres. It did not apply to America, but as most of the art treasures were in Europe –or already frozen from the market in American museums–this was not very relevant. It was still possible to sell works of art abroad, but one-way traffic is not a satisfactory basis for a healthy market. There was, indeed, a short-lived boom in English porcelain, especially Bow and Chelsea figures, in the late 1940s and early 1950s, based on the purchases of a few keen American collectors. But it is a curious fact that the average time-span of most collectors' active purchasing period usually seems to be about six years, and in this case the boom corresponded with this rule.

So few collectors were involved that the boom started with their first interest and finished some six years later.

London had some clear advantages from the start. England had not suffered so severely from the war, and the home market began to pick up more rapidly than it did elsewhere. Not only were the auctioneers and dealers still in existence, there were also collectors. And, above all, houses up and down the country were still filled with the spoils of the great collecting era of the eighteenth and nineteenth centuries. In the days of her glory and prosperity England had gathered treasures from all over the world. This was the work of private collectors and their treasures have not been handed on to museums on anything like the scale that has been common practice in America–and which was so much encouraged by Lord Duveen, in order to keep the treasures whose prices he had succeeded in inflating from returning to the market. The prosperous art market of the years between the wars had begun to deplete this store. But England was, and is still at the present time, by way of being the treasure house of Europe. It takes time to get rid of two centuries' acquisitions.

The first real sign that the art market was getting back on its feet again after the war came with the Cognacq sale in Paris in 1952. This was also the first pointer to the fashionable and expensive market in Impressionist and modern pictures that was to prove so important a feature of the post-war collecting era. The sale included a Cézanne still life, sold for £33,000 ($94,286), and a landscape, sold for £20,500 ($57,142); a lovely portrait by Renoir, 'Jeune fille au chapeau garni de fleurs des champs', at £23,000 ($64,285); and another fine Renoir 'Les deux sœurs', sold for £19,500 ($54,285). In the same sale a Degas pastel made £11,000 ($30,000). These were tremendous prices by pre-war standards and caused a wild flurry of excitement in the art market. Paris seemed set to take the lead in profiting by the art market's returning prosperity.

It was not until 1954 that things began to look up for London, when restrictions were removed on the amount of currency available for buying abroad. Purchases in soft currency were already allowed, but since 1939 no dealer had been able to use dollars to buy a work of art from a foreign owner. The new opportunities were quickly grasped, but it was only in 1956 that a major *coup* by Geoffrey Agnew in New York brought the expanding trade of the London market to the public's notice. In a sale of pictures belonging to the New York Public Library, he purchased two highly important paintings by Turner and one by Constable for a total of roughly £47,000 ($131,600). The Turners were among the most important examples of his work. 'A scene on the French coast' brought £20,000 ($56,000), and 'Staffa, Fingal's Cave', made £16,875 ($47,000). This second picture, a stormy, sunset scene of 1832, was the first painting by Turner ever to reach America. It had originally been bought from the artist himself in 1845 by a New York collector called James Lenox.

The drama of the new price levels commanded by Impressionist paintings was renewed in 1957, though this time London split its triumphs with Paris and New York. Sotheby's sold the Weinberg collection, which included Van Gogh's 'Usines à Clichy' at a price of £31,000 ($86,800); at Parke-Bernet in New York a more important collection belonging to Georges Lurcy brought the top price of £71,300 ($200,000) for Renoir's 'La Serre', and in Paris the Greek shipowner Stavros Niarchos carried off a Gauguin still life for £106,000 ($297,143). This was the first time in the history of the sale room that more than £100,000 ($280,000) had been bid for any painting at a public auction.

But it was in 1958 that Sotheby's brought off a *coup* which more than any other, contributed to establishing the supremacy of the London art market. This was the Goldschmidt sale of seven important Impressionist paintings, which brought the staggering total of £781,000 ($2,186,800). The top price was £220,000 ($616,000), paid for Cézanne's 'Garçon au Gilet Rouge', and the lowest £65,000 ($182,000) for a self-portrait by Manet. This was a far cry from the Cognacq sale. Never had so much publicity been accorded to a public auction; the art market had suddenly become news and the glare of publicity which from that time onwards has attended events in the sale room, certainly contributed significantly to the art-market boom of the 1960s.

Important sales have since followed each other fairly regularly and the results of each sale have duly made the headlines. In 1964, Sotheby's took over Parke-Bernet, the main auction firm in New York, and indeed in the United States, and its subsequent successes have thus been in a sense as indicative of the achievements of the London market as of New York itself.

But the success of London as a centre of the art trade has depended as much on the activities of London-based dealers as on the achievements of the two great auction houses, Sotheby's and Christie's. The number of established dealers has more than doubled since the pre-war years, and if the plethora of small or specialized operations is also taken into account, the increase is far greater. Almost every specialized field of collecting is catered for by dealers who often combine considerable erudition and connoisseurship with their market knowledge.

The most outstanding achievement in the dealing field since the war has undoubtedly been the establishment and rapid growth of the firm known as Marlborough Fine Art and the development, which they have done much to encourage, of a London-based trade in contemporary painting. This, however, cannot be claimed as an entirely British achievement, but rather as an achievement by men and women who have chosen England as their home. The foundations of the London market in contemporary painting were not, in fact, laid by the Marlborough, but by two foreign dealers who had settled in London after the war, Erica Brausen, of the Hanover Gallery, and Pierre Gimpel, of Gimpel Fils. They brought with them to London the concept of the artist-dealer relationship which Durand-Ruel originated as a way of handling the work of the Impressionists and which was afterwards adopted with much success by many other Parisian dealers. The idea is essentially that an artist contracts to sell his works only through the agency of one dealer, in return for which the artist receives an annual allowance, or simply a share of the higher prices for his work resulting from the dealer's promotional activities.

Erica Brausen was the first dealer to present Francis Bacon's work to the public, and Gimpel had Chadwick, Armitage, Davie, and Ben Nicholson in his stable. The Marlborough Fine Art, however, was later to take over all these artists, except Alan Davie, who remained with Gimpel Fils.

Marlborough Fine Art was founded by two Austrians, Frank Lloyd and Harry Fischer. In pre-war Vienna, Lloyd had run a chain of petrol stations and Fischer had been a bookseller. The fortunes of Marlborough Fine Art were at first based on the sale of paintings by old masters and Impressionists. It was only in the late 1950s that the firm began to take an interest in contemporary painters. Following the example of Erica Brausen and Pierre Gimpel, Marlborough Fine Art offered contracts to certain British artists on particularly favourable terms, relying on their own commercial acumen and contacts to make this strategy pay off.

And pay off it did. The number of artists on their list grew rapidly, and many others with already established names were tempted away from other dealers. The firm, which also has offices in New York and Rome, has a high proportion of important foreign artists on its list, but above all it has helped to create international recognition of the work of contemporary British artists, such as none before them has ever enjoyed.

The building up of Sotheby's fortunes by Peter Wilson and those of the Marlborough Fine Art by these two connoisseur-business-men from Vienna are the most outstanding personal contributions to London's special position in the international art market. Admittedly, Sotheby's was already a going concern when Peter

Wilson became its chairman in 1958, but he and his colleagues changed the image of the firm and built it up into by far the largest and most dynamic auctioneering complex in the fine-art market.

One other aspect of the post-war art market must be mentioned. This is the vast increase in the number of small-scale collectors. While the value of Impressionist paintings has multiplied from a few thousand pounds to thirty or forty thousand, the value of modest drawings or prints—or indeed of anything remotely artistic or antique—has multiplied from a few pounds, or even shillings, to tens or hundreds of pounds. The educated middle classes have taken up collecting on an unprecedented scale. This must largely be put down to the reverential aspect of the present-day attitude to art. This attitude is undoubtedly fostered by education and never before has education been so freely available to so many. This widespread respect for artistic genius and artistic achievement, combined with an appreciation of history—and of drawings, paintings and *objets d'art* which are a reflection of the life of earlier times—has brought into existence a huge new clientele for the more minor prizes of the art market.

CHAPTER 2

How the Art Market Works

The art market has always been international. The rapid communications which are so central a feature of life in the mid twentieth century have streamlined the administrative problems that this involves, such as getting the collector or dealer half-way round the world to a picture, or a picture half-way round the world to collector or dealer. One of the few factors in which geography remains a relatively important consideration is taste. The main market for English pictures is in England, for French furniture in France, for American painting in America, and so on. Even where national pride is not involved, taste is often dictated by a local fashion for a particular type of painting or antique.

Thus the prosperous art market of today exists to serve collectors in all quarters of the globe. The United States is, of course, a particularly important market, both on account of its great wealth and the degree to which the worship of art has been integrated into the structure of society. But an interest in collecting is growing both among private individuals and those responsible for national museums in high-income English-speaking countries, such as Canada and Australia. And the new financial prosperity of Japan has recently begun to affect traditional Japanese taste and the approach of the Japanese to art collecting. Collectors and dealers from Japan have begun to haunt the auction sales of London and take a growing interest in the art forms of the West, though these have little in common with their own cultural heritage. The flow of art treasures has for many centuries run from East to West; but fine Japanese works of art are now increasingly returning to Japan, and in addition Western pieces are finding their way there for the first time, though so far on a very limited scale.

In Europe there is a tradition of collecting which goes back for many centuries, and is still maintained not only by the rich, who can afford to compete in the international market for pieces of real importance, but by the less well-off, who haunt the antiquaries and junk shops in the hope of finding a bargain. Museums, too, by their purchases, affect the state of the art market. The idea of the museum is fundamental to the twentieth-century approach to art, as a place where the uninitiated can learn to indulge in the cultural pleasure of looking at works of art, where the initiated also can enjoy themselves, and where scholars can carry forward their researches. New museums are founded every year in various parts of the world, and old ones continue to build up their collections, the activities of both providing an important stimulus to the art market. In addition, there are now investors who are interested in buying works of art. It is often extremely difficult to make clear distinction between the collector and the investor; and the number of people who buy works of art solely as investments is limited. There is, however, an increasing number of people for whom the financial motive in building up a collection is at least as strong as the pleasure that derives from its possession. This again is a stimulus to the art market.

The function of any market is to match supply with demand. Collectors, investors, and museums throughout the world provide the demand for works of art, and the old collections of Europe, or such as are still in private hands, still form the main basis of supply—in particular for paintings, drawings, and prints by older masters. Although there have been keen collectors in America for roughly a century, many of their finest prizes, bought in Europe, have been given or bequeathed to museums, which means that they seldom return to the market. In the case of drawings and prints American interest is largely a recent development.

Impressionist and modern paintings return to the market from American collections more often than old masters. The families and friends of artists of the important European schools—who were the leaders of artistic developments up to the Second World War—are also an important source of supply. In Europe it often proved to be the professional classes—doctors, lawyers, academics, and the like—who had the foresight and understanding to collect the work of *avant-garde* artists before they were widely recognized and their paintings had become expensive; collections such as these also come back on the market. But by the late 1960s, the fashion for Impressionist paintings and those of the early school of Paris, had been in existence for roughly twenty years—with prices steadily rising—and a good proportion of the paintings sold at auction in these years represented judicious profit-taking on fairly recent purchases.

England stands in a rather special position as a source for the supply of works of art. The avid collectors during the country's prosperous years in the eighteenth and nineteenth centuries turned England into a treasure house. In most of continental

34

Europe, until quite recently, the structure of society was formed by a rich aristocracy, a small professional class, and a very much larger number of poor peasants. Only the aristocracy could afford to indulge their taste for paintings or works of art on any scale. In England, on the other hand, a large and comparatively affluent class of landed gentry had existed since the Middle Ages. Country gentlemen, as well as noblemen, could afford to decorate their homes with paintings and fine furnishings as such things became increasingly available. Thus the collecting class was far larger in England than elsewhere and remained so for a considerable period, during which its more ignorant heirs relegated many of their treasures to box-rooms and attics.

A market must necessarily have middlemen who busy themselves in matching supply with demand. In the art market this is the role of auctioneers and dealers, whose numbers have increased hugely with the prosperity of the market over the last twenty years.

The auctioneer's job is, on the face of it, the most straight-forward, since his aim is merely to sell as profitably as possible without taking unfair advantage of his clients; but a dealer must buy as well as sell. The first concern of the auctioneer lies in cataloguing, and this generally requires considerable specialized knowledge. It is vital to know what you are selling, and the reputation of the major auction houses rests to a large extent on their knowledge and expertise—to recognize an important painting when it comes in from an unlikely source, or the fake that comes from a highly reputable one. They should know each artist's work well enough to be able to confirm or deny an attribution and, most importantly, know where to go for further information or more specialized knowledge.

Besides this, the auctioneer usually has to agree a reserve price with his client below which the painting will not be sold. This is highly important, as it is the main guarantee that a picture will fetch its fair market price. The estimating of a reserve is often a delicate business. If the auctioneer over-estimates the value of a painting, he may scare away potential purchasers who would be pleased to buy it at a more reasonable price. Furthermore, once a painting has appeared at auction and been bought in, the bidding having failed to reach the level of the reserve, if it is put into another sale it is likely that the bidding will be even more timorous. Some feeling of *déjà vu* seems to affect the price; dealers appear to feel 'That picture again; well, nobody wanted it last time.' Thus if a reserve is set too high and the painting is bought in, its value can be materially damaged. In the case of an old master especially, this effect may take several years to wear off.

There are, of course, many other fine points to consider, the market being psychologically extremely sensitive. There is the problem, for example, of whether or not to illustrate a painting in the catalogue. As a broad generalization, prices of Impressionist and modern pictures seem to be favourably affected by the publication of an illustration, but the potential price of an old master painting may well be lowered. This must presumably reflect the different approach of dealers and collectors in the two fields. Purchasers of modern pictures appear to consider an illustration as a mark of the painting's importance, but the old master purchaser prefers to feel that he has made the discovery of its importance for himself. Or, more cynically, the value of an old master being far less easy to determine, a dealer might prefer such a picture not to be reproduced; he can then, with greater safety, ask for a higher price and the risk of his purchase price being discovered is substantially reduced.

A well-run auction house, staffed with good auctioneers and experts who know their subjects in scholarly detail, is a straightforward adjunct to a market fraught with complications. Even so, an auction house retains some aspects of the casino. It is fair game for a dealer to buy a picture at auction for well below the price at which he knows he can sell it, and this is every dealer's aim with his specialized clients and outlets. Even with the most careful cataloguing, mistakes may sometimes be made and sometimes unrecognized bargains may be picked up by the knowledgeable. On the other hand, the auctioneer may see a disgruntled dealer bidding against a private collector, who is himself hoping for such a bargain, until one or the other has paid far too much for a picture.

It is far more difficult to particularize about dealers than about auctioneers because each firm has its own *modus operandi*. Between their respective methods there are fundamental differences of approach. One dealer will depend on good contacts, both social and professional, and will rely on being the first to hear through such contacts that an important picture or collection is coming on to the market; or possibly count on being°able to influence the owner in favour of selling. This sort of approach is really only profitable when dealing with works of some importance. But the profits to be made on the purchase and resale—even at a modest profit margin—of one really important picture can be greater than the collective profit on several hundred lesser works. The type of dealer who adopts this sort of approach may scorn the public auctions.

There is also the contrasting approach of the dealer who will only buy at auction. The assumption here is that it is too difficult to agree privately on a price that will assure a reasonable profit margin – if you are to be fair to the owner; while public auctions, if assiduously attended, are sure to provide enough paintings at prices below their potential resale value, without any suggestion of cheating the owner. It is generally also considered fair to pick up bargains from *confrères* in the trade, if they have failed to appreciate the nature or value of the work – though this must, of course, depend on the relationship between the two dealers.

The sale of a work of art from one dealer to another is not merely accepted, it is common practice. There are, indeed, many dealers whose main business lies in sales to the trade. A picture may pass through the hands of five or six different traders on its way from one collector's wall to another. At the end of the line may be a dealer with a client who has commissioned him to search for a painting of a particular kind to fill a gap in his collection; the dealer may buy it from another who bought it in some other country, where the artist's work was not valued so highly as in his own; the man he bought it from may have got it cheaply at auction – where perhaps it had been sent by another dealer who had had it around for years and, failing to find a purchaser for it, decided to get rid of it. No dealer can be aware of what every collector in the world is looking for, and to him the value of a painting depends on the outlets available to him.

Methods of selling pictures also vary widely. Some dealers with a close relationship with their clients will seldom acquire a picture without a clear idea of who will be interested in buying it. Others depend on exhibitions of one artist's work or on a special genre of picture to interest the general public and attract purchasers. Or a dealer may specialize in a particular field and will rely on the fact that anyone interested in that field will come to him. A mixture of all these methods is perhaps most usual. And a close personal relationship, based on trust, with rich private collectors or museum curators is generally the best way to ensure big profits.

Many dealers try to avoid an outright purchase. They will look for paintings for their clients, check their authenticity, condition, and past history, and advise the client on what the price should be – in other words, they will work in an advisory capacity. This type of dealer will generally receive a commission on his client's purchases, perhaps 10 per cent of the painting's price. He may also get an introductory commission from the seller. Again, a dealer may act as an agent for the owner of a picture and sell it on his behalf, rather than buy it outright and sell it from his own stock. This is a very usual practice in Paris and other centres in continental Europe. London is exceptional in the number of dealers who make purchases on their own account and maintain a stock of paintings to interest the collectors who visit them. The amount of pictures which are available for sale in this way at any one time makes London a particularly attractive hunting ground for collectors.

The example of the picture which passes through a pipeline of dealers before it finally reaches a collector serves to underline the difficulties of establishing a 'right' price for any work of art. Valuations are, however, continually being demanded for tax and other purposes and can generally be made with some approximation to accuracy. The establishment of accepted price levels for works of art rests on the interplay between auctioneers and dealers. Public auctions are generally attended by a large band of interested dealers. When the bidding goes above a level which would assure them some profit on resale, they will usually drop out; when a picture appears to be going cheap, two or more of them will probably go after it and bid it up to a more normal price level. This gives a certain predictability to auction prices. Where the sale-room cataloguing is correct and the work is accepted at the auction room's estimation, its price can usually be predicted to within a bracket roughly equivalent to the dealer's margin. Whether it is bid close to the top of the bracket for immediate resale to a particular client, or secured at the bottom price for stock, is largely a matter of chance. The bracket is normally of the order of 20 to 40 per cent.

Not unnaturally, the greater the rarity of the painting, the more difficult it is to estimate its value. If a genre of painting, or the work of a single artist, is frequently seen in the sale room, the value of another example can be estimated on the basis of past prices. This method will not work in the case of a particularly rare artist, or of a painting which can be ranked as a masterpiece. In the case of a work of outstanding importance it tends to be the interest of private collectors or museums that determine the final price; it depends on who wants it, and how much the potential owner is prepared to pay. Determined competition between two private collectors can increase the value of a picture to two or three times above what it might normally be expected to fetch.

The extent to which 'right' prices can be determined thus varies considerably from one painting to another and from one field to another. The value of Impressionist and modern paintings, for instance, can be forecast with much greater accuracy than that of old masters. Impressionist paintings are seen at auction with some regularity and there is a large body of international dealers and collectors ready to support their prices. But the work of an old master may not be seen for ten or twenty years; which may mean either that an example of his work is highly desirable on account of its rarity, or that no collectors are interested in the genre because it is so seldom available. And there are many other considerations, such as condition, attribution, or provenance, which can drastically affect the price–more so in the case of old masters than in that of modern paintings.

There are, of course, a great many factors which go into determining the value of a picture. The two most obvious are its artistic merit, and the reputation of the artist. And these are, indeed, the main factors that affect prices in the more straight-forward market for works of the last hundred years–as long as their size and importance are considered as part of their artistic merit. A brilliant pencil drawing by Picasso, for example, would be considered much less important than a finished oil which reflects his genius to an equal extent. A tiny portrait by Renoir would be much less expensive than a large subject picture, even if both could be considered particularly successful.

For every artist there is a wide spectrum of price between that which can be expected for a modest work and the top level for a really fine and important painting. The concept of 'a Renoir' or 'a Picasso' simply is not relevant in art-market terms. A few colour notes on a small canvas by Renoir is likely to fetch around £3,000 ($7,200), but the most important work of his which has come on the market recently, his early Paris view, 'Le Pont des Arts', made £646,000 ($1,550,000) in 1968. The reputation of the artist does, however, determine roughly where this spectrum begins and ends. A modest watercolour, for instance, by the modern English sporting artist Alfred Munnings might be had for £40 ($96), but important oil-paintings by him have reached around £20,000 ($48,000). His work is not as expensive as that of Renoir, but the spectrum of his prices is as wide, if not wider.

The straight correlation between artistic merit and price is, however, complicated by the difference between what are some-times referred to as 'museum pictures' and 'private collectors' pictures'. A museum picture should be an important and success-ful example of the artist's work–unless this is so rare as to make anything by him acceptable. A private collector's picture need not necessarily be an important example, but it should be decora-tive and attractive. For example, a crucifixion, flagellation, or bloody and depressing scene of any kind, tends to put off the private collector who wants a picture to live with. If it is of major artistic importance, such considerations will carry no weight with a museum; but if it is not, it will be a hard painting to sell. Equally, very large paintings are usually acceptable to museums if they are of sufficient artistic merit, but are hard to sell to the private collector, whose wall space is generally limited. Thus, paintings which are not important enough to interest museums, yet not decorative enough to attract the private collector, can fall between two stools and fetch very modest prices.

This distinction points to another major element in the value of a picture, its art-historical importance. A preparatory drawing for a famous picture is generally more valuable than a preparatory drawing for a work whose final version is unknown. A painting is of particular interest if it has influenced others, or demonstrates an influence itself. When a painting is documented – particularly if the artist himself has written about it – its value is normally increased. It helps if a painting or drawing dates from a 'good' period in an artist's career; in other words, a period in which he is generally considered to have produced his greatest works. In the case of Rembrandt or Turner, for instance, this means their later years, when both in their different ways developed their greatest power and originality. Applied to Monet or Renoir, it means the late 1860s and 1870s, the years when the Impressionist movement was born and flowered; their later works are generally less highly regarded.

An even more significant feature in art-historical terms is the strength or weakness of an attribution. In dealing with modern paintings this is generally a clear-cut matter of distinguishing fakes from originals. The further the origins of a picture are hidden in the mists of time, the more important this consideration becomes. In the case of old pictures it is often complicated by the fact that successful artists usually maintained assistants in their studios. Arguments over the extent of an artist's involvement with a picture can continue for centuries. At any one time there is usually one particular scholar whose opinion is considered the most authoritative about the work of a particular artist, though sometimes several scholars may contend for this distinction. In expressing their opinions they may wield tremendous financial power. For instance, no definitive catalogue of Rembrandt's drawings existed until the 1950s, when Otto Benesch published the results of his long years of research. Around 1950 three drawings catalogued as 'School of Rembrandt' were sold at Christie's for about £100 ($280); another, attributed by Sotheby's to one of Rembrandt's contemporaries, fetched only £9 ($25). By the time Benesch's catalogue was published, its inclusion of these drawings had raised their value to something like £10,000–£15,000 ($28,000– $42,000) each.

The attribution of most old paintings is a far less certain matter than a visit to a museum or gallery would lead one to suppose. The neat gold labels inscribed with the name of the artist seldom reflect the many arguments which may have preceded the choice of his name, or the continuing discussion of its validity. There are many degrees of acceptability about an attribution. The soundest attribution is one that combines the opinion of scholars with contemporary documentation. This is hard to shake. A traditional attribution which has never seriously been questioned is perhaps the next best thing; followed by one on which most contemporary scholars are agreed and so on, down to the attribution for which at least one, more or less respectable, authority is prepared to vouch. Even a suggestion that the artist might have had a hand in the painting of a picture can be regarded as financially worthwhile.

The power that scholars wield in this way can have at least two unfortunate effects. The more honest may be so circumspect that they avoid publicly expressing their doubts about paintings on the market or in private hands which may pass or have passed, for years as definitely the work of the artist in question. The less honest may be prepared to exchange their confirmation of a painting's authenticity for a cash remuneration; there are many certificates of this sort in circulation, some signed by scholars of undoubted eminence. Often the wording is carefully devised to give the impression of authenticating the picture, but without its committing the expert to a definitive judgement.

Another surprisingly important price element is a picture's provenance. If it has at one time graced a well-known or particularly respected collection, its value is enhanced. If it comes directly from the hands of a collector whose taste and judgement is generally respected, this also is a major advantage; equally, if it comes from a dubious collection, this may substantially reduce its value. A painting which has been hawked round the trade seldom fetches a good price if it is subsequently put up for auction. Similarly, a picture which is known to have come from a dealer's stock seldom does well in a sale. In contrast, an important painting, if it has never been seen before—or perhaps not for many years—may well fetch an outstandingly high price.

The condition of a picture is of tremendous importance. It is also an extremely delicate subject, over which there may be considerable argument—to what extent, if at all, should it be tampered with? Most old paintings have suffered to some extent over the years through having been damaged, over-cleaned or over-restored. The less a painting has been touched, the greater its value at auction. The greatest damage is generally done by cleaning rather than by restoration. Pigment injudiciously removed can never be replaced, but an unfortunate restoration can usually be done away with by a good restorer. Relining can also be dangerous; when the lining is ironed on to the back of the canvas the impasto of the paint may be damaged. These are highly technical questions on which even the best dealer or auctioneer will often need to consult the opinion of an expert restorer, for such considerations may multiply or divide the value of a picture very substantially.

Rarity also contributes to the value of a painting, but this is a factor which can work either way. The scarcity of paintings of distinction by any of the great masters adds spectacularly to their value on the rare occasions when they do appear at auction. On the other hand, if good examples of a particular school or genre of painting are hard to come by, not many collectors will be interested in them. This may mean that occasionally a notable picture, although of great rarity, is not much sought after.

Rarity, or availability, may thus have an important influence on fashion – and fashion again on price. Fluctuations in fashion are hard to predict and, even with hindsight, hard to explain. But there is one prerequisite for the establishment of a fashion in any field of collecting – that there are enough interesting examples available to the market. This condition is met by the Impressionist and modern schools, which are greatly in demand today, and equally by the eighteenth-century Italian *vedutisti*, whose popularity has recently been climbing rapidly among the older schools of painting. The effect of fashion on price is not unnaturally to make works of a fashionable school more expensive than those of a less fashionable one. This is not generally reflected by the most important works, for masterpieces of any school or period are highly sought after. But if a school is fashionable, there will be many competitors even for run-of-the-mill or poor examples of that school. Fashion exerts its strongest effect on the value of minor works.

Besides the factors already mentioned which help to determine the value of a picture, its actual price is heavily dependent on who is selling it and who is buying it. A painting is likely to be worth a good deal more if it is sold by a dealer of world-wide fame than if it comes from the hands of someone unknown. Similarly, the interest of Mr Norton Simon or Mr Paul Mellon is likely to affect its value a good deal more than if interest is shown by Mr Smith or Mr Jones.

These are the sort of considerations which most closely affect the internal workings of the art market. Being an international market, it is also strongly affected by the legal, fiscal, and commercial policies of the countries in which it operates. And these apparently external factors can have a major influence on values. A Botticelli Madonna in Italy would be worth less than its market value in London or New York because of the restrictions on its export. Auction prices in Paris are normally at least 10 per cent lower than those in London because in France there is a sales tax. The situation varies considerably from country to country, but factors of this kind can be so important that it is certainly worth looking at their effect.

The United States provision for deduction of the value of donations to museums from current income tax liabilities has been of fundamental importance to the strength of the international art market since the war by providing American museums with tremendous spending power and by encouraging lavish spending on art by private collectors. It has also been a strong influence in spreading the idea of art patronage, and indeed the fashion for it, throughout America. It has in particular encouraged the fashion for collecting the more speculative schools of painting, among them twentieth-century pictures and—the most speculative of all—contemporary works. The lucky collector who buys a picture by an artist whose work then rises in popularity and value can deduct much more from his tax liability than he originally paid for the painting.

In England also there are similar factors which can affect the value of a work of art, though none of them are so important as the American tax provision. The capital gains tax introduced in 1965 affects all works of art sold for over £1,000 (then $2,800, now $2,400). This has involved auctioneers and dealers in an appalling difficulty—inventing theoretical, or to put it more accurately, justifiable 1965 prices—and has also given a strong fillip to the market in works worth less than £1,000.

There are also some special provisions concerning death duties. Any work of art of national importance can be exempted from death duties, national importance here being defined quite loosely. If the piece has sufficient distinction to have been acceptable as a gift by any English museum, major as well as minor, it can generally be exempted.

Until 1969, when exempted works of art were sold death duties were charged on the realized value at the rate calculated for the rest of the estate. In an extreme case this meant that on an estate composed entirely of exempted works of art no death duty was payable; a number of fortunes had been wholly or partially converted into works of art in the last weeks of the owner's life in order to avoid death duties in this way, causing a sharp rise in the value of important pieces. In 1969 a new provision was introduced. It became necessary to add the amount realized by the sale of works of art to the rest of the estate before the rate of death duty was calculated, if the pieces were sold within three years of the death of the previous owner, and affecting the position even after this three-year period.

When major works are sold to museums after the death of the previous owner, the museum is entitled to offer a 25 per cent rebate of duty on the picture's agreed value. The value of the work has, of course, to be agreed first with the museum, but as auctioneers and dealers can sometimes persuade the owner that the museum estimate is unrealistically low and justify their valuation, few works are in fact sold to museums under this arrangement.

The absence of any sales tax in England puts English auctioneers and dealers in a strong competitive position *vis-à-vis* other countries. English collectors, on the other hand, are harder hit by present tax provisions than those in most other countries. In France, for instance, there is no capital gains tax, which makes the operations of the collector-investor rather more profitable.

Another restriction on trading lies in the measures that have been adopted to prevent too many national treasures leaving the country. These restrictions, though less onerous in England than in most other European countries, mean that an export licence must be obtained for any work of art worth more than £2,000 ($4,800) which has been in the country for more than fifty years and is more than a hundred years old. The licences are granted by the Reviewing Committee on the Export of Works of Art, which has the power to withhold licences if any museum is interested in buying the work in question. However, its export can only be held up for three months, and if at the end of that time the museum has not found enough money – and it must pay the same price that has been offered from abroad – the export cannot be stopped. The probability that an export licence will be withheld sometimes discourages foreign bidders.

The art market in Italy provides an extreme case of legal, commercial, and fiscal restrictions shaping the operations of dealers and collectors. In the first place, all works of art of national interest are supposed to be listed. This list is kept by the local Soprintendenza delle Antichità e Belle Arti; each time that a painting on the list is bought or sold, the Soprintendenza have to be notified and have the right of forced purchase at the declared price, whether the sale is to a foreign or an Italian collector. Any work of art that is exported must, of course, have a licence. Furthermore, an export tax must be paid, which rises rapidly to a level of 30 per cent of the value of the work, and the Soprintendenza may, if they wish, refuse to grant such a licence, even though they have no intention of buying the work under their right of purchase. Since Italy became a signatory to the Treaty of Rome in 1958, the imposition of the export tax has been in contravention of the Treaty, and although a new law has been promised, no parliament has found enough time to pass it.

The export tax has meant that many works of art leave the country illegally. Once a picture has got on to the Soprintendenza's list, however, smuggling is too dangerous and the picture probably cannot be exported. This means that the main aim of both owners and dealers is to keep dark the existence of important paintings, and as a result, the Soprintendenza's lists are notably incomplete. But secrecy in the Italian art market goes further than this.

The avoidance of income tax is an accepted tradition in Italy and the Finance Ministry seizes on any outward and visible signs of wealth as a means of challenging tax returns. The purchase of an expensive painting is, of course, an obvious pointer – as is its sale. Few collectors wish to purchase a painting on the Soprintendenza's list whose sale is supposed to be notified, or to draw attention to their own collections. Such secrecy, though strongly against the interests of art history, may be an encouragement to the internal art market, which is certainly flourishing, since the purchase of paintings provides one of the safest ways for a rich man to spend his money without being pounced on by the Finance Ministry. Any work of art which gets on to the Soprintendenza's list almost automatically becomes worth only a small fraction of its value on the international market.

Spain also keeps a list of paintings of national importance, but the art market is not very active there.

France lies somewhere between Italy and England in its restrictions on the trade in works of art. It has already been mentioned that the sales tax puts Paris auctioneers at a disadvantage compared to those in London. In Italy there is also, of course, a sales tax. The national museums in France have a pre-emptive right at auction sales. This means that after any lot has been knocked down, the museum's representative may announce that he pre-empts the purchase and will pay a price equivalent to the last bid. The knowledge that this power may be used can, of course, discourage bidders. The auctioneer is also legally responsible in perpetuity for any fakes that he may unknowingly sell.

The factor which is, however, probably the greatest deterrent to France's participation in the international art market and a depressant of internal prices at the present time is the restriction of exports. Licences can be refused without any obligation on the State for it to purchase. If a painting has been refused a licence, its value is sharply reduced. Furthermore, the criteria on which paintings are judged are not clearly defined; there is a wide area within which it appears to be the luck of the draw as to whether a licence is granted or not. Owners are not unnaturally cautious about testing this, and dealers, of course, are unwilling to pay large sums without knowing whether they will be able to get their purchases out of the country.

These are some, though by no means all, of the considerations which affect the operation of the international art market. Its business is generally carried on under a veil of secrecy, and this is often taken to mean that there are dishonesties to cover up. The art trade is probably not more dishonest than any other. It is, however, more essentially based on human psychology than most—on its desires, doubts, fears, pride, and even ideals. This makes every participant's role an essentially personal one and cards are played close to the chest.

CHAPTER 3

Fashions in the Art
Market

Few people realize the extent to which their personal taste is
shaped by current fashions. Somehow the greater originality and
genius of one artist compared to that of another seems such an
absolute affair. For most people, however, to check their personal
appreciation against the financial rating accorded to different
artists by the art market reveals only minor disagreements.
And the art market is a faithful mirror of fashion. Its prices
reflect the general consensus of opinion at any particular point
in time.

The art market also provides a means of demonstrating the
fundamental changes in fashion that take place over time. Today,
Holman Hunt would not be referred to in the same breath as
Renoir—or at least only with a smile. But in 1874 Agnew's paid
Holman Hunt £11,000 (then about $53,460) for his painting 'The
Shadow of the Cross' together with full reproduction rights, while
Renoir's paintings were still virtually unsaleable. Even today a
distinguished painting by an artist with a strong international
reputation would be unlikely to bring him in as much as £11,000,
after his dealer had taken a cut; taking the fall in the value of
money into account, this must have been one of the highest fees
ever paid to a living artist. Of course, Holman Hunt, born in 1827,
was at this time at the height of his powers and success while
Renoir was fourteen years younger.

Most paintings of the Victorian era in England are only now
beginning to revert to the sort of prices that were paid for them
at the time, and even then only in terms of the much-debased
pound sterling, but the Impressionist school has climbed to a
place of particular distinction. More recently, the vogue for
English eighteenth-century portraits in the pre-war years has
been forgotten, with the help of the depression followed by the war.
In 1969 a Raeburn portrait of no outstanding interest was bought
in at Christie's at 7,000 gns ($17,640); in 1929 it had cost $75,000
or roughly £50,000 in terms of the purchasing power of 1969.
There has been a similar loss of interest in fine tapestries since the

beginning of the century, and eighteenth-century mezzotints have shared in the eclipse of the English portrait school.

These are well-known cases of the changes in general taste. But fashions are changing all the time; indeed, it is hard to keep up with them. Even more difficult to sift are the changes in comparative popularity of different fields of collecting. Here the Times-Sotheby Index of art prices has helped to highlight changes in collecting fashion since the war. The number of times prices in the six 'fine-art' fields discussed in later chapters have multiplied, on average, since the early 1950s varies from thirty-seven times for prices of old prints to only seven times for those of old master pictures. Further, the extent to which fine-art prices have risen is markedly greater than the rise in other collecting fields covered by the Index, which are not discussed in detail here. This can be seen from a summary table of the findings of the Index to 1969:

Price multiplications between 1951 and 1969

Fine Arts		*Other Collecting Fields*	
Old Master prints	37	Chinese ceramics	$24\frac{1}{2}$
Modern pictures	29	Antiquarian books	13
Old Master drawings	22	Modern books	9
Impressionists	18	English glass	9
English pictures	10	English silver	$8\frac{1}{2}$
Old Masters	7	French furniture	5
		English porcelain	4

One of the most notable features of collecting since the war has been the higher status accorded to artistic genius than to fine craftsmanship. No one seems to find it particularly surprising that a rough sketch by Picasso can be worth £2,000 ($4,800), but that a pair of simple Queen Anne candlesticks can cost £3,000–£4,000 ($7,200–$9,600) astonishes many people. Art appreciation has come to be used as a means of escaping from the crude materialistic values of everyday life; an escape to a higher plane where values are intangible, indefinable. The genius of an artist is the connecting link between the viewer and a higher order of things; his vision goes beyond the normal, everyday world. Thus collectors tend to be more interested in paintings, drawings, and engravings from which they can draw satisfaction from the vision and genius that an artist puts into his composition. The plane on which the craftsman operates is somehow considered a lower one. The fact that he may display just as much genius in his embellishment of a piece of furniture, porcelain, or silver as an artist

48

in his painting, is generally overlooked; or at least, if it is not overlooked, it does not alter an instinctive bias in favour of genius as crystallized on paper or canvas. This is undoubtedly what lies behind the more rapid increase in fine-art prices compared to prices in other collecting fields. This is in itself a fashion; there have been several periods in history when the decorative arts and the fine arts were considered on a par. Eighteenth-century France is the most obvious example.

A fashion in the general approach to art, such as this, is slow to crystallize in the universal consciousness and equally slow to be undermined. Fashions for individual artists and schools, on the other hand, can change with tremendous rapidity – or rather, they can come into fashion very fast, though their popularity is generally slower to fade. In 1968 Tiepolo's etchings came suddenly into vogue; in July two prints from his *Scherzi* series made £350 ($840) and £410 ($984) – the highest prices ever paid for any of these plates. In December two were sold for over £1,000 ($2,400) and a third for £700 ($1,680). In the same sale an impression of the artist's most famous print, 'The Adoration of the Magi', made £4,600 ($11,040); the last example of this rare print to come on the market had made £950 ($2,660) in 1964.

A similar sudden reassessment of the Surrealist school of painting was demonstrated in 1969. Up to the end of 1968, a Surrealist painting would have been most unlikely to fetch more than £4,000 ($9,600) or £5,000 ($12,000) at auction. At the end of that year a new auction record price was achieved at Christie's for a work by Salvador Dali, sold for £6,825 ($16,380); by March 1969 his 'Ossification matinale du Cyprès', an admittedly finer painting, left this price far behind when it was sold for £34,646 ($83,046). In July paintings by Max Ernst and René Magritte reached £18,000 ($43,200) and £19,000 ($45,000) respectively.

Fashions can be started in many ways, by an important exhibition, the publication of a new book, or simply a general need for a new collecting field. For instance, Italian eighteenth-century prints, especially those of Canaletto and Piranesi, rose markedly in popularity in the 1960s. For some reason Tiepolo had been slightly overlooked. This fact appears to have been suddenly appreciated independently by several collectors and dealers, with the result that his prints went sharply up in price.

Once a new interest in a particular artist or school has been sparked off, there tends to be a snowball effect, as an increasing number of dealers' and collectors' attention is drawn to the new fashion. Dealers in particular are able consciously to encourage the fashion by holding exhibitions or drawing clients' attention to the interest of the new field. Prices thus continue to rise until a saturation point is reached, when works become too expensive to encourage the interest of new collectors.

The death of a fashion is usually a much slower affair. The collecting fever may gradually have creamed off all the most important examples of the genre, leaving the market with only the less interesting. Or the interest of collectors may have shifted to pastures new. In either case, there are likely to be both dealers and collectors left a little behind the times to support the market – dealers in particular are slow to mark their stock down in price.

Some iconoclastic outside influence can, of course, upset this pattern. The depression followed by the Second World War brought a general collapse in prices and in collecting interest. Several fashions turned out to be long-term – possibly even per-manent – casualties, such as Renaissance furniture, for instance.

The period covered by the Times-Sotheby Index – roughly the two decades from 1950 to 1970 – has seen a major change in the nature of collecting, besides the emergence of many new collect-ing fashions. In 1950, the Western world was still pulling itself together after one of the most devastating wars in history. The following two decades witnessed the birth of the 'affluent society', which created a tremendous increase in average in-comes in the lower to middle stratas of society and a big extension in the numbers of the very rich. This, combined with the new religion of art, led to a massive increase in the number of art collectors, both among those who could afford to compete for the most expensive prizes and those keen to spend their small savings on minor works. The increases in spending power affected most importantly the top and the bottom of the market, in other words, the value of the most distinguished works and of the most modest.

To speak of 'the' art market is, of course, a gross simplification. The collectors who compete for a £50,000 ($120,000) Renoir are most unlikely to be the same as those in pursuit of a £50 ($120) watercolour. There are, in fact, a great number of essentially different though interlinked markets, which cater for the tastes and purses of widely varying collectors. A very rough and ready distinction can be made in terms of 1969 price levels.

Prices from £30,000 ($72,000) upwards can only be paid by museums, millionaire collectors, or the very rich. We have already seen how the American tax laws have provided museums with massive purchasing power; they have also encouraged an interest in collecting among rich Americans. The number of very wealthy people spread round the world is anyway increasing; thus the number of museums and private collectors prepared to pay prices in the £30,000 ($72,000) upwards bracket when works of major importance appear on the market is steadily increasing.

Thus a steadily increasing number of works of art must be found worth prices of this order.

The reputation of new artists must be built up to make them worthy. Since the last war, these artists have mainly been drawn from the Impressionist and modern schools, first from among the Impressionists themselves, then from their school-of-Paris followers. Other modern schools and artists are now beginning to follow in their wake. The result has been a tremendous multiplication in prices, as has been demonstrated by the Times-Sotheby Index; Impressionist paintings were shown to be eighteen times more valuable in 1969 than in the early 1950s, and modern pictures—the Index is based on the early school of Paris—had become twenty-nine times more expensive.

The reputation of a number of earlier artists has also been reassessed and found worthy by this class of collector in recent years, notably the great English sporting artist, George Stubbs, and the Italian eighteenth-century view painters Canaletto and Francesco Guardi.

Prices from £1,000 ($2,400) to £30,000 ($72,000) can be paid by museums or by the wealthy. Those who have newly acquired wealth usually prefer to ape the very rich and make for lesser prizes of the Impressionist and modern schools. Only a few turn their eyes to the older schools; while those with traditional wealth and tastes are a shrinking band. Thus, there has been no major increase in interest in old master pictures, prices for which usually fall in this bracket. The Times-Sotheby Index shows values on average only seven times higher in 1969 than in 1951 for this category.

Prices from £50 ($120) to £1,000 ($2,400) can be paid by the well-off—especially if they are able to encourage themselves with the feeling that their purchase is an investment. Their numbers have increased hugely and this has particularly affected prices for old prints, old master drawings, English watercolours, and Victorian paintings. Since prices in these fields in the early 1950s were generally extremely modest, there has been room for a massive multiplication. The average value of prints is shown to have multiplied thirty-seven times, of drawings twenty-two times, of watercolours thirteen times, and of Victorian paintings eight times. The rise in prices has, however, been reinforced by museum interest, particularly in the case of drawings.

Each of the six fine-art fields which are discussed in later chapters are subject to substantially different pressures and tend to display different patterns of collecting. The Impressionists and twentieth-century schools of painting are the pacemakers in the modern art market. The work of the Impressionists, their precursors, friends, and followers, and the work of most of the major twentieth-century artists, comes on the market in considerable quantities. The fact that works of good quality are quite often available—much more often than good works of the older schools—adds a particular interest to collecting. It is not surprising, therefore, that moneyed collectors should be particularly attracted by these fields.

The most outstanding feature of auctions of Impressionist and modern pictures is the sheer number of works that change hands at very high prices. The field is dominated by private collectors and there is a strong element of keeping-up-with-the-Joneses. Modern artists tend to have individual and easily recognizable styles; thus even a modest example of the work of Renoir, Picasso, Vlaminck, or Utrillo is likely to be recognized by visitors and can serve as a distinguished status symbol. It is quite normal for several thousand pounds to be paid for very moderate works.

The old master field provides a sharp contrast. Museum interest plays an extremely important part in the competition for the occasional paintings of outstanding quality that come on the market. The number of rich private collectors interested in old pictures is limited. And the motivation even of private collectors tends to be much more scholarly. There is a rich private taste for the decorative qualities of French and Italian eighteenth-century works, which is reflected by high price levels; but the market in old masters—especially of the prolific Dutch and Flemish schools tends to be among the more traditional and less wealthy collectors of Europe rather than in America. In particular, the early Italian and northern schools seem to appeal to a scholarly taste; prices of these paintings are supported by museum interest, but tend to be fairly modest.

When it comes to old master drawings and prints there is an even more definite split between the museum and private collector markets. There are very few rich private collectors in these fields and high prices tend to be paid only by museums. Scholarly criteria are definitely the most important in determining the value of either a drawing or a print, for it is mainly the art-historically minded, both amateurs and professionals, who are interested in these fields. It is generally only at the bottom end of the market that drawings or prints are sought after by collectors primarily for their decorative qualities.

English pictures present a rather special case. Here the most important criterion governing the value of a picture is not whether museums are interested, but whether American collectors are interested. Until quite recently, the work of English artists was appreciated very little outside Britain itself, and even now interest in the older schools of British painting is limited chiefly to collectors in England and America, and to a more modest extent those in other English-speaking countries – in other words, to those who share the British tradition.

When the market in the work of a particular artist or genre of painting is limited to English collectors, prices seldom go very high. However, once a spark of interest has been lit across the Atlantic, they may increase rapidly. A vogue in English sporting pictures in the 1960s was dominated by American collectors – indeed virtually invented by them. Quite high prices are still paid for works of the English portrait school – a hangover from its American heyday between the wars – while the boom in the markets for both English watercolours and Victorian paintings, which began with a fashion for collecting in England, has spread to America, though this fashion is still somewhat selective. Some artists are fashionable across the Atlantic and some are not, and this is markedly reflected by prices.

The Times-Sotheby Index shows the average value of English paintings as being some ten times higher in 1969 than it was in the early 1950s. This average, however, conceals a considerable disparity between the rapid increase in prices in fields where a new collecting fashion in England has been reinforced by American interest, and the more traditional fields where prices have not shown any major advance.

The multiplication in fine-art prices over these two decades, as measured by the Times-Sotheby Index, is particularly notable when compared with general economic indicators. In traditional fields of collecting where there has been no new fashionable interest to bolster prices, values tend to have multiplied between five and ten times between the early 1950s and 1969. In fields where a new collecting fashion has been at work they tend to have multiplied between twenty and forty times, depending to a considerable extent on how modest price levels were at the beginning of the period. The work of twentieth-century artists was, for instance, much cheaper than that of the Impressionists in 1950, while prints were much cheaper than drawings.

The Index is a measure of how prices have moved in terms of pounds sterling; although this was an inflationary period and included a sterling devaluation, the purchasing power of the pound in 1969 had been not quite halved since 1950. London stock-market prices had multiplied between three and a half and four times over the period covered by the Index, and the increase on Wall Street was only marginally higher. On the face of it, the fine-art market had a distinguished record from an investment point of view.

FASHIONS IN THE ART MARKET

There are, of course, many complications and disadvantages inherent in the fine-art market as an investment medium. The most obvious is that a painting pays no dividends; instead, it requires the extra cost of insurance premiums. It is an asset which cannot be easily or quickly realized, and furthermore, for a private person, rather than a dealer, to attempt to resell a picture too quickly after its purchase is generally dangerous. It is noticeable at auction that paintings which reappear on the market too soon tend to fetch less than their original purchase price; for older paintings it is necessary to wait at least four or five years, though paintings of the fashionable modern schools sometimes show a profit more quickly.

These difficulties and dangers have so far deterred those attracted by the idea of buying paintings purely for investment reasons, although much has been written and talked about this subject. On the other hand, collectors have become very conscious of the fact that their purchases are likely to appreciate in value. The feeling that the purchase of a painting that they particularly want may also prove to be a sound investment has loosened collectors' purse-strings and brought a great deal of money into the art market which would otherwise probably have been tied up in stocks and shares. This is a natural and sensible approach and has certainly been an important factor behind the recent rise in art-market prices.

This is only one of the specific reasons which can be found to explain the remarkable rate of appreciation of works of art measured by the Times-Sotheby Index. Over the twenty-year period which it covers a succession of special factors has been at work. In the first place, the Index is based on average prices in the three years 1950, 1951, and 1952, when the world was still recovering from the effects of a major world war; there had not yet been time for people to turn their minds to diversions such as art collecting, and prices in consequence were still in the main depressed.

The next ten years saw the birth of the religion of art, or, in less emotive terms, a tremendous upsurge of interest among the educated of Europe and America in art history and the art forms of both the past and the present. Over the same period, a new prosperous Europe emerged from the carnage of the 1940s, and America, already rich, maintained a steady rate of economic growth. The combination of a new universal interest in art and new wealth to indulge it brought new collectors into the market on an unprecedented scale. By 1960, collecting had become a more democratic and universal interest than at any other period of history, except possibly in Holland during the seventeenth cen-

54

tury. But Holland is a small country, and this time collecting fever had caught imaginations on an international scale.

In the 1960s this trend was reinforced, encouraged by the publication of quantities of glossy art books and an increasing taste for foreign travel. Travellers in the main have two alternatives, to lie in the sun and bake themselves, or to visit museums and 'do' the sights. Besides boosting the sales of sun-tan lotions, the new popularity of foreign travel has multiplied the attendances at museums many times over and thus helped to spread the religion of art.

In the second half of the 1960s, especially, the art market felt the impact of the idea that art is a good investment. This was particularly encouraged by widespread doubts about international currencies. Since the art market is international, any painting or important work of art could be expected to hold its value at least with the dollar, if not with the strongest of international currencies. The devaluation of sterling in 1967 served to underline this fact; auction prices rose sharply in sterling immediately after the devaluation announcement, and more than kept their parity with the dollar.

English collectors took this sharp rise in sterling prices as yet another sign that art was a good investment. Similarly, the 1969 devaluation of the French franc brought a spate of articles in France about the advantages of investing in art as prices again adjusted themselves to the dollar parity. On the other hand, the revaluation of the Deutschemark did not, as one might expect, have the reverse effect and discourage German collectors; rather, its impact was felt in greater German purchasing power abroad.

A number of specific factors can thus be pointed to in explanation of the remarkably rapid increase in art prices between 1950 and 1970. The question naturally arises as to whether new financial and sociological factors will emerge in the 1970s and 1980s to sustain this rate of growth.

One new development which was already beginning at the end of the 1960s could prove important. This was the creation of art investment trusts, a formally structured link between investment markets and the art market. This was no new idea; many individuals and groups had been trying to find a *modus operandi* for a trust of this sort for ten years and more. But in 1969 the first art investment trust received a quotation on an American stock exchange, and there were several more in the pipeline. If this idea proves successful in practice, it seems possible that investment money may flow into the art market on a very large scale. The annual turnover of the art market is hard to estimate, but it is unlikely that it is much more than £500 million ($960 million).

This is a mere drop in the ocean compared to the sums that change hands every year in the normal investment markets. Investment money would be likely to chase art prices rapidly higher. It could, of course, be dangerous; by chasing prices to artificial levels it could upset the art market as we know it today.

Another factor which has already strongly affected the art market, and is likely to continue to do so, is the steady extension of art-historical research. On the whole, collectors are not attracted to fields that are sparsely documented; they like to know what they are buying. As the frontiers of research are extended, more fields for collecting appear. So many art historians are now pursuing so many lines of research in Europe, America, and elsewhere that new fields are continually being opened up. The art-historical industry seems set to supply collectors well into the 1970s.

Another thought which may be relevant – or may be pure fantasy – is the effect that a united and prosperous Europe could have on the market in old master paintings. European collectors, much more than those in America, are interested in old pictures. This is natural in that they are a specifically European heritage. Were a United Europe eventually to emerge, with a large and prosperous economy comparable to that of America today, would the value of the work of older masters more closely match that of the newcomers, who are so popular and so expensive at the present time?

CHAPTER 4

Old Master Paintings

Any history of European painting tends to start with the artists working in Italy in the second half of the thirteenth century and the term 'old master painting', as used in the sale rooms today, includes the work of all the artists and schools which succeeded each other from that early period up to the end of the eighteenth century – even, at a stretch, into the nineteenth century. Thus the market in old master pictures is an extremely large subject. The availability of paintings varies greatly from period to period, and from artist to artist, and the nature of artists' approaches to painting, their motivation, and their style, has changed many times over the centuries. It is hard to generalize about the collecting interest in 'old masters' as such – the field is too wide.

Even so, a few general characteristics of the old picture market can be noted. To collect old paintings is not at present as fashionable as to collect the Impressionist and modern schools. This means that old paintings are generally cheaper. This applies particularly to works that are not of outstanding interest or quality. Museum competition and the interest of a few millionaire collectors may nevertheless mean that the occasional painting of major importance, when it comes on the market, reaches a very high price.

The supply of important paintings is strictly limited and most pictures that pass through the sale room are minor works, or by artists of minor importance in the history of art – if they are known at all with any certainty. The purchasers are in the main private collectors, who often have specialized knowledge and interests. Bidding for pictures with some pedigree and by a reasonably well-known artist usually finishes in the £5,000 ($12,000)–£30,000 ($72,000) range.

The nature of collecting in this field has altered radically over the last hundred years or so, with the establishment and expansion of public art galleries. The public's attitude towards art today is conditioned largely by the contents of the great museum collections of Europe and America. The museum idea began to flower late in the nineteenth century. Only a few public art galleries date from earlier times. The Louvre, for instance, was turned into a public collection at the time of the French Revolution, though it was notably added to by Napoleon's artistic spoils, and has since been much expanded and improved. The National Gallery in London started in 1823 with the Government's purchase of the collection of the banker, John Julius Angerstein. Most of Europe's public art galleries are based on collections of a similar kind, the Uffizi on that of the Grand Dukes of Tuscany, the Hermitage on the Romanovs' and the Prado on the Spanish Hapsburgs'. Political upheavals or the passing of a dynasty have led to such collections passing into public ownership.

Once a painting is owned by a museum it is virtually certain that it will never return to the market. Thus the development of museums has steadily reduced the opportunities of the private collector–and indeed of the new museum–to obtain important old pictures. The transformation of private into public collections in Europe in the nineteenth century substantially reduced the mobility of pictures. The build-up of the great American collections during the first half of the twentieth century has also radically reduced, in a comparatively short space of time, the number of fine pictures available. It was only in 1967 that the National Gallery in Washington celebrated its thirtieth birthday. To form a collection even remotely as fine is already inconceivable.

The fact that the work of artists such as Giotto, Leonardo, Jan van Eyck, or Vermeer is virtually never seen at auction does not mean that the present-day market is limited to the work of minor artists. Paintings by many of the greatest artists in the history of Western art do from time to time appear in the sale room. Rembrandt and Rubens are among those most often represented, but in recent years there have also been examples of the work of Botticelli, Titian, Veronese, Claude, Poussin, and El Greco. Naturally, the paintings that come up for sale are seldom of the quality of the artists' most famous works and opportunities for buying really fine pictures are better when it comes to the work of artists less well known. A great many artists belonging to the fashionable schools of the last hundred years or so are widely known and loved. The number of artists with whom the collecting or the appreciating public is familiar from the schools of the last hundred years far exceeds those who are remembered from earlier periods. The study and pursuit of the works of these lesser-known –though not necessarily less interesting–artists is one of the most rewarding approaches to collecting old pictures.

The increase in the number of museums and the expansion of others has markedly increased the scarcity value of very fine

Mr Norton Simon, the American collector paid £798,000 ($2,234,400) at Christie's in 1965 to secure Rembrandt's portrait of his son Titus.

paintings of all schools. Through a combination of public money and generous benefactors, museums' trustees can often lay their hands on very large sums when fine paintings become available. This not unnaturally leads to fierce competition between rival museums and between museums and the few private collectors who are rich enough to enter this field.

Paintings of sufficient importance to interest the major museums or to set millionaire collectors thinking in terms of six figures are, however, the exception rather than the rule. The real business of the sale room is based on lesser works. The prolific artists of the seventeenth-century Dutch schools are major contributors and the amount of work they produced leaves the present-day art market well supplied, though paintings of high quality are rare.

The early Italian schools are not so consistently represented and the attributions of those paintings that do come on the market are often doubtful and generally refer to lesser artists; furthermore, early Italian paintings in good condition are scarce. There is, however, a steady flow of minor panels and occasionally some fine works appear. The early northern schools are also rather patchily represented in the sale room, and on the whole by the works of minor artists.

From the sixteenth century the position changes. Apart from the works of Michelangelo, Raphael and the Venetian school, sixteenth- and seventeenth-century Italian paintings have been largely out of fashion since the early nineteenth century. Both 'Mannerism' and 'Baroque' were terms of disparagement until quite recently. This has resulted in paintings of both periods being relatively well represented at auction, and quite frequently by works of some quality. Italian paintings of this period, however, are greatly outnumbered by those of the Dutch and Flemish schools.

The leading eighteenth-century artists of France and Italy are also regularly represented at auction, though seldom by works of fine quality. Lush French works from the latter part of the century are quite often seen, and the occasional *fête galante* by Lancret or Pater still comes on the market; Watteau is one of the few artists of the period whose work now seems almost unobtainable. From Italy there is a steady flow of minor works–and a few of major importance–by Canaletto, Guardi, Tiepolo, Panini, and others. Again, pictures of the French and Italian schools do not reach the sale room as often as those of the seventeenth-century Dutch school.

Obviously, the nearer a school of painting comes to the present day, the less time there has been for its major works to have been removed from the market by museum purchases. Thus, none of the great schools of the past are as well represented in the sale room as the fashionable Impressionist and modern schools. There are also other considerations which, though they hardly affect the purchase of a recent painting, are of crucial importance in the assessment of an older work. The most obvious is that of condition. Over the centuries, a picture may have been damaged, restored, or overpainted, and it requires considerable expertise to determine how much of the original picture remains or is likely to be revealed underneath the surface by judicious cleaning. Attribution represents another problem. The old custom whereby a successful artist maintained a studio full of assistants leaves scope for endless argument over the extent to which the artist himself may have worked on a particular canvas or panel. In the case of the early schools the number of historically documented attributions is small.

Old paintings reappear from all parts of the world, though not by any means always from their country of origin. Through the centuries artists and their paintings have travelled incessantly.

For example, a number of the pictures which Andrew Mellon bought from the Hermitage for $19 million (£4,222,224) in the 1930s (a deal arranged with the Soviet Government to help bolster their foreign exchange reserves) had started out in the collection of the Dukes of Mantua. From there they had travelled to England with Charles I's block purchase of the collection early in the seventeenth century. After his execution and the dispersal of his paintings by the Commonwealth, they found their way into the Walpole collection, which in turn was bought by Catherine of Russia in the late eighteenth century. A hundred and thirty years later, revolution placed her great collection in the hands of the State.

This is only one example of the peripatetic life of works of art throughout the centuries. Many of them, irrespective of their origins, have long been on the move between the collections of Europe, and more recently of America, through being sold, exchanged, or seized as the spoils of war or revolution. Often they reappear from surprising sources, Germany, France, and England being among the best hunting grounds. Despite the massive scale of American purchases since collecting began to flourish there at the end of the nineteenth century, the donation or bequest of private collections to museums leaves the internal market sparsely supplied. Italy and Spain, both of which might be expected to be rich sources of treasures, exercise very stringent laws against the export of important works of art.

The paintings that come to auction today are drawn from many sources, for the market in works by the old masters is international. The most important and expensive–that is to say, those that reach six-figure prices–also meet with international competition. American and German museums and collectors are often among the strongest competitors, but both private and institutional purchasers from all parts of the world tend to be in the running. European collectors are generally more interested in the lesser prizes. Collectors from Germany, France, Italy, and England play a much more important role in this market than in the more dramatic competition for Impressionist and modern pictures.

The limited American interest since the war helps to explain the comparatively modest rise in prices for old pictures and their relatively low prices compared to those of the more fashionable schools of the nineteenth and twentieth centuries. Between 1951 and 1969 the Times-Sotheby Index showed that average prices had multiplied seven times; during the same period, the prices of Impressionist pictures were found to have multiplied eighteen times, and of twentieth-century paintings twenty-nine times. But, as in any period, there have been various shifts in fashion, with the popularity – and thus also the value – of some schools of painting growing more rapidly than others among collectors.

The Times-Sotheby Index indicates the broad outline of these shifts in taste. So far as the two earliest periods of Italian painting are concerned, that of the primitives – the works of thirteenth- and fourteenth-century artists – and of that described as the Early Renaissance – largely those of the fifteenth century – both show a substantial increase in average prices. Italian primitives rose seven times in value and Early Renaissance painters eight times. In these same fields, prices during the post-war period were severely depressed. In the 1920s the scholarship of Bernhard Berenson, combined with the marketing flair of Lord Duveen, concentrated collectors' interest on these schools. With the depression, followed by the war, American purchases dried up and prices for the modest works that were still available in the sale room fell back more sharply than for other schools. Thus the increase in values since the early 1950s is not as impressive as might at first sight appear; part of this increase simply reflects the return to a more equitable price relationship between the work of early Italian artists and that of other schools.

A gold-ground 'St Peter' by one of Giotto's pupils, Bernardo Daddi, sold for £10,000 ($24,000) in 1969.

Apart from the Venetian school, which maintained its popularity in the 1920s, the work of the Late Renaissance in Italy, or roughly the sixteenth century, was not in the main highly regarded before the war and has not been subject to any marked shift in popularity since then. The average value of such works as come up at auction has only multiplied four times since 1951. This is in sharp contrast with the value of paintings of the seventeenth century, which were also out of fashion in the pre-war era. Intensive art-historical study has been devoted to Italian painters of this period in recent years, with the result that many museums that lacked examples of their work have had to make good this omission and prices have multiplied rapidly – twelve times, according to the Times-Sotheby Index. Artists such as the Carracci, Guido Reni, Guercino, or Salvator Rosa, had been unfashionable since the mid-nineteenth century; their artistic merits have now been reassessed and there is strong competition for the finer works of such artists when they come up at auction.

Very few works of quality from the early northern schools have been seen at auction in recent years and the value of such modest examples as do come up for sale appears to have increased rather less than the value of their Italian counterparts. Both the early Italian and northern schools tend to be bought more for their scholarly interest than for their direct decorative appeal.

With the Dutch seventeenth century the position is reversed. The superbly decorative paintings of this period have been more or less unaffected by the whims of fashion over the centuries. They have always been bought as paintings to live with, and now that the fine works which decorated the homes of the great collectors of the past are mainly in institutional hands, purchasers have to make do with examples of lesser quality. Since the popularity of this school has never faltered, it is not surprising that average values have in general only multiplied some four or five times since the early 1950s.

The decorative qualities of eighteenth-century painting, on the other hand, have become increasingly fashionable. The work of the great French painters, Boucher, Fragonard, or Pater, is becoming scarce and average prices were seven times higher in 1967 than in 1951. The Romantic landscape painters of the same period, such as Joseph Vernet and Hubert Robert, have appreciated even faster, prices in 1967 being nine times higher than in 1951. And the Italian view painters of Venice and Rome, Canaletto, Guardi, and Panini, for example, have shared in the rise in popularity of a century noted for its lavish and Romantic taste. Prices of their work had multiplied, on average, seven times by 1967, and by 1969 almost nine times.

These are, of course, fairly crude comparisons. The quality of paintings available at auction today in comparison to the total *œuvres* of a period varies from school to school. The motives for buying an early Sienese altar-piece, a van Goyen seascape, a Tudor portrait, or a lavish *fête champêtre* by Pater, are essentially different. The interest that attaches to each artist, painting, and school of painting, derives from its place in the history of Western art and Western society, in the history of collecting, and in the visual qualities of the pictures. It is against this background that the present-day market in old paintings must be reviewed.

Collectors nowadays infinitely prefer to buy the work of a named artist. Even if he buys an anonymous work, the collector will often seek an authoritative attribution, for as a rule the twentieth-century collector's chief interest in a painting is in its reflection of the artistic genius and vision of its creator.

It was not until the second half of the thirteenth century in Italy that the individual personalities of artists emerged. Before this, artists were no more than artisans, who contributed to the decoration of churches and palaces; the name of the decorator was not important. With Cimabue in Florence and Duccio in Siena, however, the personal vision of the artist began to be appreciated and sought after. Giotto, a pupil of Cimabue, was the first painter to amass a substantial fortune based on his personal fame as an artist–and, incidentally, on his considerable ability as a money-lender.

At this period painting was used mainly as a propaganda medium for conveying religious messages to an ignorant and illiterate public and impressing them with the Church's mysterious grandeur. Detailed and precise rules were laid down for the way in which the artist should represent religious subjects, leaving little room for him to communicate his personal vision. This is why the Italian paintings that come on the market today, dating from the late thirteenth or early fourteenth century, are virtually all of a religious nature. To the untutored eye such pictures tend to look extremely alike, for even in the fourteenth century only small liberties were taken with the Church's rules on composition and the representation of sacred themes. However, there were many great and individual artists working in Italy at this time, particularly in Florence and Siena, and though their work is rare, as a rule the examples that come on the market are not expensive compared to the work of other schools.

The whole approach to collecting paintings of this period has been revolutionized by the researches of Bernhard Berenson. Up to the late nineteenth century, early Italian painting had never been popular among collectors. The rich and enthusiastic connoisseurs of the seventeenth and eighteenth centuries usually considered that 'art' started with Raphael. In the nineteenth century slightly more interest began to be taken in primitive painting, stimulated by the work of the Nazarenes in Germany, the Pre-Raphaelite movement in England, and the interest of the Prince Consort. Ruskin was also an important influence.

Berenson settled in Florence and devoted the rest of his life to the study of Italian painting. His scholarship encompassed the period from its thirteenth-century beginnings to the Late Renaissance, and his work in sorting, comparing, and cataloguing thousands of paintings provides the present-day scholar with a basis for the attribution of most of the early Italian works that come on the market.

In his dealings with the great Anglo-American art dealer Duveen, Berenson also directly affected the market. Duveen retained Berenson's services for the attribution and authentication of the pictures that he sold to American millionaires. The effect of this association between them was to make the collection of early Italian paintings an expensive and popular fashion in the 1920s. It also substantially reduced the availability of fine works of the period, since most of the important American purchases were eventually bequeathed to museums.

It was over a painting which Duveen believed to be by Giorgione that he and Berenson parted company. Berenson maintained that the picture was an early work by Titian, a prolific artist, despite the fact that Duveen had already sold it to Andrew Mellon as a Giorgione, whose works are very rare.

The market collapsed with a slump in 1929, and the outbreak of the Second World War helped to depress prices further. In the absence of the Berenson-Duveen partnership the market has never fully recovered and the lack of notable works for sale does not encourage collecting interest.

The fifteenth century in Italy was a period of unparalleled artistic innovation and activity in which the relation of art and the artist to society was revolutionized. Cosimo de' Medici (1389–1464) was the first Renaissance patron and collector among the rulers of the city-states. He was a close friend of Fra Angelico and Filippo Lippi and his example of intimate patronage was rapidly imitated throughout Italy – and soon spread further afield. The artist became the friend and intimate of princes. More important still, from the point of view of the modern collector, is the fact that out of this relationship was born the idea of secular art. Artists continued to work for the Church, but the connoisseur princes, dukes, popes, and cardinals of the Renaissance now began to decorate their palaces and to collect the paintings of the most distinguished artists of the day. The fashion which they started, of hanging paintings on their walls, created a demand for a new kind of art – not the altar-piece or fresco designed for a church or a chapel, but the picture as we know it today, a painting in a frame which can be moved from place to place and exchanged between collectors.

Most of the paintings of this period that come to the sale room today are still religious in nature, but occasionally a secular painting may also appear. The most important artists of the period, those of the great Florentine school, Masaccio, Filippo Lippi, Uccello, Ghirlandaio, and Botticelli, and of the Venetian school dominated by the Bellinis, and the northern artists working under the shadow of Mantegna, are only sparsely represented. But works attributed to the more minor artists of these schools come regularly on the market.

Many of the collections formed in this period have been broken up and dispersed. The collections of the Medici, however, are still in Florence and the Vatican collections assembled by Renaissance popes and prelates remain intact. Indeed, even from this early period many of the finest works went straight into such important collections and so have never come on the market.

The connoisseur-rulers of the small Italian city-states, the Medici in Florence, the Gonzaga in Mantua, the d'Este in Ferrara, paved the way for the great collector-monarchs of Europe. The Hapsburg collections, begun by Charles v in the sixteenth century,

A portrait panel attributed to
the French late fifteenth-
century artist known as The
Master of Moulins, sold for
£14,000 ($39,200) in 1965.

remain the glory of Vienna, Brussels, and Madrid. The French
royal collections were begun by Francis I at the end of the fifteenth
century though they were partly dispersed during the French
Revolution.

The development of the early northern schools followed a
different pattern from that of the south. In the small feudal
States an artist was generally attached to the court of a prince
or a noble as an all-purpose decorator, to design pageants, tapestries, and furniture, as well as to paint pictures although southern
artists did also apply themselves to these matters on occasion.
Before 1400 the painting of easel-pictures had hardly begun and

the earliest of them were naturally based on the traditions of manuscript illumination: that is they were miniatures.

In the north, as well as in Italy, the earliest paintings that have survived are mostly religious. Portrait paintings, however, developed in the north at a very early stage and some delightful examples still come to the sale room at reasonable prices. These portraits, too, reflect the traditions of the illuminator's art, it being a common practice to include in the miniatures that decorated a manuscript, a portrait of the patron who had commissioned it.

The first important school of painting grew up at the court of Philip the Good in Flanders in the middle of the fifteenth century with the van Eycks, Rogier van der Weyden, and others, and artists were also attached to most of the small German courts. In France they were centred mainly on Paris and Avignon, where the north had merged with the south at the exiled papal court in the fourteenth century.

The status of the artist remained that of a lowly artisan much longer in the north than in the south; less is known about the northern artists working in the fifteenth and early sixteenth centuries than about their contemporaries in the south. Contemporary documentation is also more scanty for the northern schools. The work of these schools was in general overlooked by the rich, noble collectors of the seventeenth and eighteenth centuries, as was the work of their southern counterparts.

The twentieth century has seen detailed and scientific art-historical research being pursued in every field. As Berenson set about bringing order to the Italian schools, Friedländer began to tackle those of the north. His work is still fundamental to present-day collecting and his attributions have always been regarded as authoritative. But he had no such relationship with any one dealer, as existed between Berenson and Duveen, and collectors' interest in the northern schools has never become a popular fashion.

The sixteenth and seventeenth centuries saw two complementary developments in collecting and patronage. It became the consuming interest of the great European monarchs. Their agents scoured Europe, particularly Italy, and their collections became symbolic of their glory; and in Rome the Vatican and the cardinals vied with each other in the splendour of their collections. At the same time, in the north, in Flanders, and in Holland, the bourgeois collector arose, together with the bourgeois genres of painting that appealed to him.

The tremendous achievements of Leonardo at the turn of the fifteenth century, of Raphael before his early death in 1520, and of

Michelangelo spanning a large part of the sixteenth century, naturally turned the eyes of all the new collecting monarchs towards Italy, though collecting by the princes of the Church was temporarily cooled by the Sack of Rome in 1527. Venice was at the height of its prosperity, based on its strategic position as a trading centre between Europe and the East. An outlet for this prosperity was found in patronage–to the great advantage of Titian–whom Charles v later appointed his Court Painter–Tintoretto, Veronese, and others. Thus Italian artists thrived and, not unnaturally, multiplied. Their work of this period remained in high favour and was much in demand by collectors throughout the seventeenth and eighteenth centuries. It contributed largely to the famous collections of Queen Christina of Sweden and Charles i of England. As the fashion for collecting spread more widely with the passing of time, Italy was more than ever looked on as the centre of the artistic world. Rubens and Velazquez came with reverence to learn from the Italian masters, and Claude and Poussin settled in Rome for good.

The Bolognese school, founded by the Carracci in the late eighteenth century, and their seventeenth-century pupils and followers, such as Guido Reni and Guercino, were hugely admired and their work was sought after. The Baroque painters of Rome, Naples, and Genoa were lauded not only in Italy, but throughout Europe.

However, in the nineteenth century most of these artists fell into eclipse. The enthusiasm of eighteenth-century collectors for 'old masters' gave way to a greater interest in contemporary painting. Only Leonardo, Raphael, and Michelangelo seemed to retain their magic, though their work seldom came on the market. To a lesser extent the Venetians, too, survived in public esteem.

Except for the interest of a small group of scholars, the position remains much the same today. All but a handful of very great names from the multitude of sixteenth- and seventeenth-century artists has been forgotten. The lesser Italian artists of the sixteenth century, including the powerful Florentine Mannerist school, whose influence spread throughout Europe, tend to be considered as having aped the great achievements of Raphael and Michelangelo without having had the genius to carry off such grand conceptions. Equally, until recent years the term 'Baroque' had been almost one of condemnation. Thus, the work of a large number of artists active in Italy during these two centuries, which was spread throughout Europe during the period of their popularity, now returns to the market from all quarters. It is still comparatively cheap, but increased knowledge is beginning to create a new market.

Since the Second World War the seventeenth century has fared decidedly better than the sixteenth. The Times-Sotheby Index shows prices for the work of this period multiplying twelve times between 1951 and 1969, as against a modest four-fold increase for works of the previous century. This is the result of a revival of scholarly interest. A reappraisal pioneered by the art historian, Denis Mahon, has awoken a new interest in many quarters, and a series of major exhibitions in Bologna in the 1960s helped to make this reappraisal more general. Most of the major museums, which built up their collections in the late nineteenth and early twentieth centuries, when these schools were out of fashion, are now filling this gap in their collections. Consequently, prices for seventeenth-century paintings have risen progressively, though so far this has mainly affected the more important works. Lesser works of both the sixteenth and seventeenth centuries remain comparatively inexpensive.

Turning north again, we come to the period when Flemish and Dutch painting came into its own. The Dukes of Burgundy had already emerged as understanding collectors and patrons of the arts in the period of Jan van Eyck and Philip the Good. The court continued to foster the development of an important native art and it was no bad thing for the artist when Flanders passed by marriage into the hands of the Hapsburgs around 1480. The dynasty had already proved themselves enthusiastic collectors and patrons of the arts. Flanders now shared in the tremendous prosperity of Spain and the Hapsburg dominions based on gold from the New World. Antwerp in the sixteenth century became an exceedingly prosperous trading centre and the rich burghers began to take a passionate interest in art.

This was the first time that the middle classes had played a major role in connoisseurship and collecting, with two results that are both highly relevant to collectors today. Rich burghers were buying pictures to hang in their houses, as well as entering into the excitement of a speculative art market, and consequently religious subjects began to lose their appeal as new genres of painting developed. At the same time, the demand for paintings was considerable and artists worked hard to match it. As a result, the art market in the 1960s was still well supplied with these pictures, though not generally with works of the highest quality.

Pieter Brueghel the Elder, working in the middle of the sixteenth century, was the first great artist to concentrate his energies on the new types of painting. The seeds of genre painting had from the earliest times been apparent in Flemish art, but it was the 'peasant Brueghel' who first achieved a great and fully merited success with paintings of everyday life. Landscape, too, had already begun to be seen as a pictorial subject in its own right with the work of Patenier and his followers, but Pieter Brueghel was the first to show that it was possible to produce great paintings in this genre. His innovations roughly mark the end of the period spanned by the 'early northern painters' in the Times-Sotheby Index.

Brueghel's work is now almost unobtainable, but that of his sons, Jan 'Velvet' Brueghel and Pieter the Younger is frequently on the market, as is that of their associates and followers, such as Joos de Momper, Jan van Kessel, and Abel Grimmer. 'Velvet' Brueghel's flower paintings are the earliest important works in this genre; his landscapes, which follow the tradition both of Patenier and his father, also still come on the market, as do works which combine landscape and allegorical or genre painting with Jan Brueghel's penchant for elaborate flower paintings, on which he often collaborated with other artists, and at one time with Rubens. Popular and prolific in his own time, Jan Brueghel had many imitators, with the result that there is still plenty of work of this type for sale.

Flemish paintings of the Brueghel school, dating from the late sixteenth and early seventeenth centuries, together with the work of Dutch artists of the later seventeenth century, form the main body of present-day trade in old master paintings. The prosperity of Holland, and particularly of Amsterdam, in the seventeenth century mirrored that of Antwerp a hundred years earlier. Similarly, it was based on trade, especially on bringing the treasures of the Orient to the European market. The northern Netherlands' long war with Spain, fought for religious tolerance and political independence, made religious subjects unacceptable, and the Dutch artists seized on the secular types of painting already popularized by the Brueghel family and their associates.

They concentrated mainly on still life and flower paintings, landscapes, marine pictures – naturally popular in a trading nation – of scenes of both low and high life, architectural and town views, and on portraits. Collecting became an absorbing passion up and down the social scale, and speculation, for which the public had already achieved a taste on the Amsterdam bourse and in the market in tulip bulbs, became also a dominating force in the picture market.

Paintings of this period have made an important contribution to nearly all the great collections of the past. This can be seen from a visit to any of the major European museums, which reflect, after all, the taste of a number of great individual collectors of former times. In England, Italy, Spain, France, Austria, or Germany – let alone Holland – splendid landscapes, genre paintings,

A seascape by Jan van de Cappelle, in excellent condition, brought £125,000 ($300,000) in 1969.

and still lifes by Dutch artists of this period are to be found. While major works of other schools might take pride of place in a picture gallery, these have always been paintings for the drawing-room or *salon* – pictures to be lived with, rather than lived up to.

Present-day visitors to museums may feast their eyes on fine examples of Cuyp's luminous landscapes, Hobbema's woodlands, or the Romantic landscapes of Wouvermans, peopled with cavaliers. They can be moved by the watery calm of Cappelle's seascapes, the charm of Steen's merry-making peasants, or the quiet everyday beauty distilled in Vermeer's interiors. And every major auction offers an opportunity for the purchase of works which reflect the same moods and the same painterly approach. The examples which now reach the sale room are seldom of the quality of museum pictures, but are still highly sought after in this spirit. Condition here is of overriding importance and on the occasions when a painting in good condition appears on the market, it can fetch a very high price.

In contrast to the simple Protestant aesthetic of the seventeenth century comes the frivolity and colour of the next hundred years. The most important artistic innovations of that century came from France and the small Venetian Republic, both struggling to

71

support political and social systems that were on the eve of their demise. These were the most fashionable schools of old master painting in the 1960s.

French taste in the eighteenth century was dominated by Madame de Pompadour. But Watteau, Pater, and Lancret, with their *fêtes galantes*, had already created a taste for beauteous frivolity before Boucher, Madame de Pompadour's court painter and close friend, launched a decorative extravaganza on a grander scale. It was a period of enthusiastic collecting in Paris. The Salon was an eighteenth-century invention and it aroused so wide an interest that many smaller rival exhibitions were held during the year. It was thus a rewarding period for the artist, who was required to be decorative above all, as well as light-hearted, and to keep his patron's mind off the ominous rumblings of revolution.

That pressures of a frivolous society could not obscure the vision and insight of great artists is, however, underlined by the work of Watteau and Chardin. Chardin remains one of the greatest of realist painters, while below the cheerful colours and capers of his harlequins, Watteau betrays his feeling for the real tragedy of their lot.

Venice in the eighteenth century was chiefly noted for its theatres, pageants, and gay, luxurious life. It attracted many visitors from foreign parts, young English noblemen on the Grand Tour, and others from the small German courts and neighbouring Austria. Rome, too, with its excavations and Classical remains, was a major attraction for visitors to Italy. The view painters of the period found a lucrative market among these visitors, anxious to carry home with them records of the romantic spots they had been to. In Venice, Canaletto and Guardi employed large numbers of assistants to help them produce these desirable views of Venice, and in Rome Panini painted similar views. The work of all three, though somewhat repetitive, is now tremendously popular.

The finer works of the French and Italian schools can easily reach the £30,000–£80,000 ($72,000–$192,000) price range, and even modest examples are hard to find for less than about £5,000 ($12,000) which are almost Impressionist price levels. The collecting fever of the eighteenth century, particularly in England and the small German principalities–not to speak of its effect on Catherine of Russia–served to disperse the work of the French and Italian schools throughout the collections of Europe, and it is from these collections that they return to the market today.

WHAT COSTS WHAT

Lord Duveen is supposed to have said, 'If I had the Sistine Chapel, I could sell it tomorrow half a dozen times over.' One wonders what price he would have put on it, for works of exceptional quality or importance are virtually beyond price. The actual sum paid when a very famous painting comes up for sale seems to be determined by some kind of universal consciousness of what is the maximum conceivable sum to pay for a picture.

At the end of the 1960s this sum may perhaps be taken as £5 million ($14,000,000), the price reputedly paid by the National Gallery in Washington for Leonardo's 'Portrait of Ginevra dei Benci', from the collection of the Prince of Liechtenstein. Most people, if asked to name the greatest artist of all time, would be likely to waver between Leonardo and Michelangelo. 'Ginevra' is an early work; her small delicately tinted face stands out against a dark background of juniper needles and her mood is reflected by the gentle dream-like landscape behind her. The sale of so important a picture–the nearest parallel in recent years to Duveen's hypothetical sale of the Sistine Chapel–is a very rare occurrence. But between 1957, when a still life by Gauguin was the first painting ever to make over £100,000 ($280,000) at auction, and July 1969 twenty-five paintings by old masters have been sold for between £100,000 ($240,000) and £1 million ($2,400,000) each, in spite of the

Leonardo's early portrait of Ginevra dei Benci, for which the National Gallery of Art, Washington, D.C. is said to have paid the Prince of Liechtenstein £5 million ($14 million).

Rembrandt's 'Aristotle contemplating the bust of Homer', for which the Metropolitan Museum of Art, New York, paid £821,400 ($2,300,000) in 1961.

fact that paintings of this quality tend to be handled by dealers rather than sold at auction.

To stimulate competition on this scale a painting must not only be by a famous artist, but of outstanding quality, though the extent to which each of these criteria affects the price varies considerably. Involved in prices of this range there is also an element of sheer chance–the chance that two or more people with sufficiently large resources want passionately to own the same picture.

In the case of one or two artists, such as Rembrandt, for example, special considerations arise. Rembrandt was a tremendously

74

prolific painter and is the only very great artist whose work appears fairly frequently in the sale room. Between 1960 and July 1969 eight of his paintings were sold for more than £100,000 ($240,000) each. The first, as it happened, was the most dramatic of them all and can be said to have set a price level for the others. 'Aristotle contemplating the bust of Homer' was painted for a Sicilian nobleman in 1653, three years before Rembrandt's bankruptcy, at a time when his popularity in Holland had already sharply declined. It is a painting of great power. Aristotle, in a wide-brimmed hat and dark robes, set off by a golden-yellow mantle, stands looking contemplatively at Homer's bust; behind him is a pile of books partially hidden by drapery. The picture's history is well documented. As a great painting by one of the greatest masters of Western art, its possession seemed equally essential to the Metropolitan Museum in New York and to the Cleveland Museum. The bidding ended at £821,400 ($2,300,000) and the painting went to the Metropolitan.

The next important work by Rembrandt to come on the market, the fine 'Portrait of the artist's son Titus', appeared at Christie's four years later, in 1965. It was bought by the millionaire collector, Norton Simon and cost him £798,000 ($2,234,000).

The fact that Rembrandt's work appears quite often at auction allows some scale of his values to be determined, this makes potential purchasers feel safer and encourages them to spend more liberally. Rembrandt's genius is manifold and can be read from a different aspect in each canvas. Values take account of this and vary very considerably between works produced at the height of his production and lesser works which also reflect the spectrum of his genius. A tiny Rembrandt portrait was sold in 1968 for £46,000 ($110,400).

Rembrandt's name plays an important part in determining the value of his work, though the quality of the picture will set it in the price scale somewhere between £40,000 ($96,000) and £1 million ($2,400,000). In the case of earlier masters, the great rarity of paintings of fine quality makes the artist's name a much less important consideration, as was shown by the sale of one Italian and two Flemish works in the 1960s.

Italian painting began to emerge from the anonymity of Byzantine decoration into a personalized genre in the middle of the thirteenth century. Cimabue and Giotto in Florence and Duccio in Siena, working about the year 1300, are the best-known very early masters. However, a crucifix by the Master of St Francis, an Umbrian artist whose name is not recorded, but who predated Cimabue, was sold at Sotheby's in 1965 for £100,000 ($280,000). A fine work in good condition from this early period is obviously

This tiny Rembrandt portrait, measuring only 8¾ by 6⅜ inches, was sold for £46,000 ($110,400) in 1968.

OLD MASTER
PAINTINGS

A crucifix by the thirteenth-century Master of St Francis, sold at Sotheby's in 1965 for £100,000 ($280,000) and now in the National Gallery, London.

a great rarity. It was bought by Agnew's, and immediately resold to the National Gallery in London at a small profit, although the Metropolitan, the underbidders at the sale, were by then prepared to pay much more for it.

The first important northern school of painting, which could compete with those of Italy, grew up in Flanders in the fifteenth century, headed by Jan van Eyck, Rogier van der Weyden, and others. Fine works of the fifteenth century are extremely rare and only two outstanding works of the early Flemish school were sold at auction in the 1960s. A large triptych, 'The Martyrdom of St Hippolytus', by an unknown master of this period was sold in France in 1962 for £103,000 ($293,700). The artist, close in style to Hugo van der Goes, had achieved a masterly effect of three-dimensional movement and the work was in perfect condition.

A late fifteenth-century Flemish triptych, 'The Martyrdom of St Hippolytus', which brought £103,000 ($293,700) in Paris in 1962. It is now in the Boston Museum of Fine Arts.

This postcard-sized 'St George and the dragon' by Rogier van der Weyden made £220,000 ($616,000) at Sotheby's in 1966. It is now in the National Gallery of Art, Washington, D.C.

This was a large and imposing work, in contrast with a jewel-like panel of St George and the dragon, which though only of postcard size, was sold at Sotheby's in 1966 for £220,000 ($616,000). In the sale-room catalogue it was attributed to Hubert van Eyck, but in the National Gallery in Washington, where it now hangs, it is described as being by Rogier van der Weyden, though the Master of Flémalle has also been suggested as the artist. Which of these great masters actually painted the picture is not of much importance. By itself it demonstrates the outstanding talent of its creator.

Minor examples and fragments of the Northern schools come on the market quite regularly, but they generally attract only modest competition from museums and important collectors.

As artistic innovation and achievement increased during the sixteenth and seventeenth centuries, collectors' interest and patronage gathered momentum and consequently there were far more artists at work. Fine Flemish paintings of the early sixteenth century are still great rarities; there are far more dating from the seventeenth century, and a great deal more is known about individual artists and their work during this period. This makes the name of the artist a much more important consideration and six-figure prices are generally paid only for notable works of the painters who stand high in public esteem. Rembrandt's genius is so universally appreciated that any reasonably accomplished work firmly attributed to his hand can be expected to top the £100,000 ($240,000) mark. The same may be said of Rubens, when he has not leant too heavily on the contribution of his assistants.

Occasionally, the same sort of price may be paid for a particularly fine work by an artist of somewhat lesser stature. It has already been noted that among the landscape and genre paintings that are typical of this period, the condition of the painting is of overriding importance in determining the price. In 1966 a wooded landscape by Hobbema made £125,000 ($350,000) at Sotheby's. Hobbema is one of the greatest artists of the naturalistic landscape school and his work is scarce. Nevertheless, this was an outstanding price, reflecting both the fine condition of the picture and its provenance; it had belonged for many years to the Dukes of Westminster.

Marine paintings of this period appear in the sale room as frequently as landscapes, yet in 1969 the same price was paid at Sotheby's for 'Vessels in a calm' by Jan van de Cappelle. Again, although the artist is one of the most distinguished of those who painted in this genre, and although his work is rare, so high a price would only have been paid for an outstanding example of his work in good condition. Such sums are generally reserved for

Rubens's 'Adoration of the
Magi' was bought for £275,000
($770,000) by Major Allnatt in
1959 and presented to King's
College, Cambridge.

Tiepolo's 'Allegory of Venus',
bought at Christie's for £409,500
($982,800) by the National
Gallery, London in 1969.

A small early panel by Raphael, 'St Jerome punishing the heretic Sabinianus', made £95,000 ($266,000) in 1963.

the occasional important work by a great artist. Rubens's 'Adoration of the Magi', one of the last full subject paintings by him that is likely to come on the market, made £275,000 ($770,000) in 1959. This does not seem expensive beside a major work by the eighteenth-century Venetian artist, Tiepolo, which fetched £409,500 (some $982,800) in 1969. At the time the Rubens was sold, however, no painting had ever fetched as much at auction. The maximum 'conceivable' sale-room price has changed since then.

Usually, in discussing these 'top' prices, the element of chance is not perhaps sufficiently emphasized. The Hobbema and the van de Cappelle were both fine pictures, but it came as a surprise that the bidding for them went up to six figures when other works that might have been expected to command the same sort of price failed to do so. For instance, a small early panel by Raphael, 'St Jerome punishing the heretic Sabinianus', reached only £95,000 ($266,000) when it was sold in 1963–this despite the fact that it was in fine condition and had (which is very unusual in the case of a picture of this period) contemporary documentation to support its attribution to Raphael. It was one of the very last works of this great artist which are ever likely to come on the market.

The price of an old painting is determined by many considerations. First, there is the attribution. Early paintings are seldom signed and the attribution is generally made on stylistic grounds; by the seventeenth century signatures had become more common, but frequently they are found to have been fraudulently added, or sometimes the artist has simply signed a studio work. In those rare cases where documentation exists as far back as the date when the painting was executed, this is of considerable importance in its effect on the picture's value; otherwise it must depend on the extent to which the work is accepted by leading scholars–among whom there are many shades and nuances of opinion. Some, less scrupulous than others, have always been prepared to authenticate a picture for a fee.

The condition of the picture is also of prime importance. The less it has been tampered with since it was painted, the better. The dirt of ages does not matter, but over-enthusiastic cleaning or repainting can be disastrous. The provenance, too, may be all important. If the painting comes directly from an old-established and reputable collection, it is bound to be highly prized. A picture which has been circulating in the trade for some time, or has been offered to many dealers, often suffers considerably at auction.

The significance of the painting in art-historical terms is also tremendously important. And last, but not least, comes that elusive criterion, the 'quality' of the picture. Every artist has had his successes and his failures which can be read both from the details and the overall composition. For the scholarly and museum market the quality of the painting of details is of overriding importance; to the private collector it is generally more important that the picture should be attractive in itself–and even scholars have been known to prefer this.

Generally speaking, the determining factors that maintain the market in old pictures can be divided into three: with the early schools, i.e., of the fifteenth and early sixteenth centuries in the north and the fourteenth to the seventeenth centuries in the south, it is mainly scholarly interest and art-historical criteria that determine price. Whereas Flemish painting of the later sixteenth century (the younger Brueghels and their like), and Dutch painting of the seventeenth century, is traditionally a private collectors' market. Pictures of this sort were mostly painted to decorate the homes of the well-to-do European aristocracy and middle class–and that is still their function today.

Thirdly, there are the eighteenth-century French and Italian schools, whose particular decorative appeal is fashionable today. The paintings of these schools appeal to many others besides traditional collectors; they provide a natural accompaniment to sumptuous furnishings.

Paintings of the fourteenth and fifteenth centuries, whether from Italy or the north, are generally to be seen in the form of minor panels, often in poor condition, or as fragments of larger works. Attributions are usually a matter of judgement, based on

Lorenzo Monaco's 'King David playing the psaltery', sold for £24,000 ($67,200) in 1962 – 'one of the most attractive paintings of the late Middle Ages', according to Bernhard Berenson.

the important systems of classification and comparison formulated in the pre-war years by Bernhard Berenson for the south and Max Friedländer for the north. On the whole, the south is the easier to deal with, contemporary sources providing far more abundant knowledge than is available in the north, where little is known about the lives of most of the artists. There is generally no clear proof of who painted which painting; an artist's *œuvre* is attributed on the basis of comparison and deduction. In some cases there are a few signed works with which others can be compared; in other cases, paintings are simply grouped together as probably the work of the same artist.

OLD MASTER
PAINTINGS

This triptych dated 1473, after which the artist who painted it, The Bruges Master of 1473, was named, fetched £26,000 ($72,800) in 1962.

This element of doubt about the origins of early northern paintings is probably one reason why they are generally cheaper than early Italian works. Another is that their appearance is usually colder and harder than that of southern works. But probably most important of all is the greater amount of art-historical research that has been devoted to the south as compared with the north.

It is extremely unusual for northern paintings of this period to fetch more than £20,000–£30,000 ($48,000–$72,000) at auction, and works of considerable importance can be bought within this price range. A comparison between two paintings sold in 1962 provides a good illustration of the relative cheapness of the northern school. A panel by Lorenzo Monaco, measuring $24\frac{1}{2} \times 14\frac{1}{2}$ inches, and now in the Metropolitan Museum, which shows 'King David playing the psaltery', was sold for £24,000 ($67,200). Lorenzo Monaco was perhaps the greatest Florentine interpreter of the International Gothic style and the painting, dated by Berenson around 1405–10, was described by him as 'one of the most attractive paintings of the late middle ages'.

In the same year, 'The triptych of Jan de Witte', by the Bruges Master of 1473, a superb painting from which this unknown artist takes his name, made £26,000 ($72,800) at auction. The three panels, each $28\frac{3}{4} \times 14\frac{1}{2}$ inches, show Jan de Witte and his second wife, Marie Hoose, with the Virgin and Child in the central panel. They are masterly examples of early genre painting, although they form part of a religious composition.

Apart from this triptych, the work of the Bruges Master is not well known. However, a year earlier (1961) a panel by Hans Memlinc, the greatest and best-documented artist working in Bruges in the late fifteenth century, was sold for £17,000 (then

84

A portrait panel by Hans
Memlinc, sold for £17,000
($47,600) in 1961.

A pair of massive panels by the fifteenth-century Venetian artist, Bartolomeo Montagna, made £12,000 ($33,600) in 1966 – two major works, marred by their poor condition.

$47,000). This fine example of the portrait genre, in which Memlinc excelled, had previously been exhibited in museums in Rotterdam and The Hague, and the price was by no means exorbitant for such an interesting work.

In the £10,000 ($24,000) class fall paintings which, though perhaps not quite good enough for major museums, are still of considerable art-historical interest. In 1969 a gold-ground panel of St Peter by Bernardo Daddi made £10,000 ($24,000). Daddi was a pupil of Giotto's and the St Peter has a three-dimensional sturdiness reminiscent of the master. In 1966 two massive panels, of fine quality and each measuring 112 × 54 inches, by the later

86

A portrait of a young prince by Joos van Cleve, knocked down for 12,000 guineas ($35,280) at Christie's in 1965, and again for the same price in 1969. On the second occasion its familiarity probably depressed the price.

northern Italian artist Bartolomeo Montagna, were bought in at £12,000 ($33,600) at auction and later sold to the Walker Art Gallery. These panels, depicting St Bartholomew and St Augustine, had been painted for the shutters of an organ in the Church of San Bartolomeo in Vicenza. They had an impeccable attribution, were of fine quality, though in poor condition, but in the sale room their unmanageable size told against them.

From the north, three fine paintings by artists whose prominence was demonstrated by Friedländer, sold for around £10,000 ($28,000). A charming portrait of a young prince, possibly Edward VI, by Joos van Cleve, made 12,000 guineas ($35,280) in 1965, and

'St Catherine disputing with the theologians' by The Master of Sainte-Gudule. This picture made 9,000 guineas ($26,460) in 1967.

'Landscape with the Flight into Egypt' by Herri Met de Bles, one of the earliest Flemish landscape painters. In 1965 it made 7,500 guineas ($22,050).

'St Jerome in a landscape' by Neri di Bicci sold for 3,800 guineas ($9,576) in 1969.

'A monk seated in a landscape' by Antonio Vivarini (*right*), a fragment of a larger panel, sold for 2,400 guineas ($7,056) in 1965.

exactly the same price when it returned to the sale room in 1969. An entertaining panel, now in the Louvre, showing St Catherine disputing with the theologians, by the Master of Sainte-Gudule, an artistic personality named from a painting of the façade of Sainte-Gudule in Brussels, made £9,450 ($26,460) in 1967. (It had passed through the sale room at £6,200 ($17,360) in 1961.) And in 1965 a 'Landscape with the flight into Egypt' by Herri Met de Bles made £7,875 ($22,050). This artist may have been the nephew of Joachim Patenier, the early Flemish artist generally credited with initiating pure landscape as a genre. Herri Met de Bles was strongly influenced by him and this particular painting, from the

'Scenes from the life of a saint', attributed to The Master of Sainte-Gudule, sold for £3,600 ($10,080) in 1966.

A 'Madonna and Child' (*right*) by the minor German artist known as The Master of Frankfurt, sold for 1,300 guineas ($3,376) in 1969.

Spencer-Churchill collection at Northwick Park, was considered one of his most typical and finest works.

It is still possible to find interesting panels in the £2,000 to £4,000 ($4,800–$9,600) range. A small 'St Jerome in a landscape' ($14 \times 8\frac{3}{4}$ ins) by Neri di Bicci, an amusing and decorative minor follower of Fra Angelico and Masaccio, made £3,990 ($9,576) in 1969, and a large section from a panel of St Francis by Antonio Vivarini, showing a monk seated in a landscape, made £2,520 ($7,056) in 1965; Vivarini was a reasonably important figure in the Veneto-Paduan school which nurtured Mantegna.

Two other substantial panels from the north were sold not long afterwards for prices in the same range. 'Scenes from the life of a saint' ($35\frac{3}{4} \times 19$ ins), attributed by Friedländer to the Master of Sainte-Gudule, fetched £3,600 ($10,080) in 1966, and in 1969 'The Madonna and Child adored by saints' ($21\frac{1}{2} \times 17\frac{1}{2}$ ins) by the German Master of Frankfurt, went for £1,365 ($3,376).

From about 1960 a major shift in the taste for northern works became apparent, namely a new enthusiasm for paintings related to the fantasies of Hieronymus Bosch. One minor painting, 'The

90

'The Last Judgement',
catalogued as from the
workshop of Hieronymus
Bosch, although it bears the
artist's signature. It was sold
for £6,000 in 1968. Any works in
the fantastic vein associated
with Bosch are becoming
rapidly more expensive.

temptation of St Anthony', illustrates this trend. It was sold at
Sotheby's in 1961 for £5,000 ($14,000) as the work of Herri Met de
Bles. It returned to Sotheby's in 1969, being attributed this time
to Jan Mandijn; the painting was sold on this occasion for £22,500
($54,000), more than four times as much as it had fetched some
eight years earlier.

Before leaving the subject of early Italian schools, a word must
be said about Botticelli. His 'Venus' and his 'Primavera', both in
the Uffizi, have made his name a household word even if his importance in art-historical terms, as an innovator, is not as great
as, say, Leonardo, Raphael, or Michelangelo. It is always hard
to determine the difference between a very fine work from Botticelli's studio and one by the hand of the master himself. The
difference is perhaps irrelevant in aesthetic terms, but it

OLD MASTER
PAINTINGS

'Christ as the man of sorrows',
thought to be a late work by
Botticelli, was sold for £10,000
($28,000) in 1963.

'The wedding feast of
Nastagio degli Onesti' (*below*),
a work from Botticelli's
studio, possibly with the help of
the Master, fetched 100,000
guineas ($294,000) in 1967.

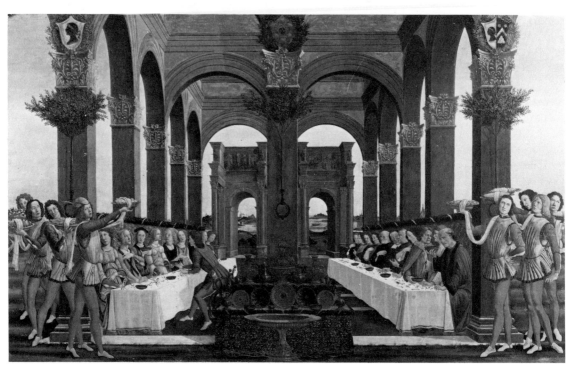

Salvator Rosa's 'The vision of Aeneas', from the Northwick Park collection, sold for 17,000 guineas ($49,980) in 1965.

substantially affects the price. Thus, two paintings of a quality to justify an attribution to Botticelli himself were sold in the 1960s. The difference in their prices reflects the premium that a really attractive painting commands in contrast to a difficult or depressing picture. A charming Botticelli portrait of a young lady, probably Simonetta Vespucci, was sold in 1967 for £95,000 ($228,000), while a late painting, 'Christ as the man of sorrows', from the period when Botticelli had fallen under the dismal influence of Savonarola, made only £10,000 ($28,000) in 1963.

On the other hand, a work traditionally accepted as being from his studio – from a design by him, but with little if any assistance from him – was sold in 1967 for £105,000 (about $294,000). This was a highly decorative work, 'The wedding feast of Nastagio degli Onesti', belonging to a set of four well-known panels, three of which are in the Prado. The price was paid for a sumptuous and extremely attractive Renaissance decoration, rather than for a work by Botticelli.

Italian paintings of the sixteenth and seventeenth centuries still belong mainly to the scholar's and the museum curator's market. The scholarly research devoted to the seventeenth

OLD MASTER PAINTINGS

Guercino's 'Christ and the woman of Samaria', from the Northwick Park collection, was bought for 15,000 guineas ($44,100).

century since the Second World War has escalated prices, especially for really notable paintings of the period; unlike those of earlier Italian schools, really important works of the sixteenth and seventeenth centuries do still come on the market, and while such important works are still available, minor works by leading artists of the period–and the occasional masterpiece by a lesser artist–can still be had for around £1,000–£2,000 ($2,400–$4,800).

The sale of the Ashburnham collection in 1953, and of the Spencer-Churchill pictures from Northwick Park in 1965, spanned the period of reassessment. Two superb works by Salvator Rosa made £3,300 ($9,240) and £2,800 ($7,840) respectively in 1953, but in 1965 another of his major works, 'The vision of Aeneas', was sold for £17,850 ($49,980). A fine Guercino made £1,900 ($5,320) in 1953, but in 1965 his 'Christ and the woman of Samaria' fetched £15,750 ($44,100). In contrast, major works of the sixteenth century are still generally cheap–excepting those by artists of the Venetian school, such as Titian, Tintoretto, and Veronese. A large and important 'Flight into Egypt' by Paris Bordone made £2,250 ($6,300) at the Spencer-Churchill sale, and from the Ferrarese school Battista Dossi's 'Adoration of the Magi' made £1,155 ($3,234).

Turning to the north again, we come to the prolific Dutch and Flemish schools of the sixteenth and seventeenth centuries. Paintings of these schools are bought mainly by private collectors to hang in their own homes; it is their decorative quality that is sought after, rather than their art-historical significance. Occasional works by Rubens or Rembrandt that come on the

94

market are, of course, another matter–as are the occasional masterpieces of the more ordinary, 'popular' genres–and here museum interest can force prices up to exceptional levels. But on the whole, the top price that a private collector seems to be willing to pay for a decorative painting appears to be about £30,000 ($72,000), and there are still plenty of paintings around the £1,000–£2,000 ($2,400–$4,800) mark or below it.

The popular enthusiasm for collecting which was centred on Antwerp during the late sixteenth century, and on Amsterdam in the seventeenth, caused huge quantities of paintings to be produced. An artist, often with the help of his studio, might repeat many a popular composition. To distinguish these works, which come genuinely from the workshop of the artist, from innumerable copies made at a later date is a challenge to the discerning

A tiny flower painting by Ambrosius Bosschaert, sold by Sotheby's in 1969 for £30,000 ($72,000).

OLD MASTER
PAINTINGS

A sombre still-life by Abraham Bosschaert, sold for 3,800 guineas ($9,576) in 1969.

collector. Both types of painting come on to the market regularly.

Still lifes – especially flower paintings – and landscapes are the most consistently popular genres today. In both cases the Brueghels and their associates in the southern Netherlands were the first to produce this type of picture in considerable numbers. In both cases they were enthusiastically followed by the Dutch in the next century. In the field of flower pictures and still lifes, the jewel-like precision of the earlier Brueghelesque painters, particularly Jan 'Velvet' Brueghel himself, tends to make for higher prices than the work of their Dutch counterparts. When it comes to landscapes, however, the greater freedom and truth to nature – as opposed to romantic contrivance – gives the Dutch landscapists a decided edge over the others in the matter of price.

Among still lifes, the flower paintings are usually the most decorative and consequently, as a rule, the most expensive. In 1969 two tiny flower pictures by Ambrosius Bosschaert, measuring roughly 9×7 inches and complete with the regulation dew-drops, butterflies, insects, etc., reached £30,000 ($72,000) and £32,000 ($76,800) respectively at auction. However, a third tiny Bosschaert, almost identical to the £30,000 ($72,000) picture, was sold three days later for only £11,500 ($27,600). The third picture was certainly a sale-room bargain, but equally £30,000 ($72,000) was quite a steep price for a type of painting that is not too difficult to come by. More often, good Dutch or Flemish flower pieces fetch between £5,000 ($12,000) and £10,000 ($24,000).

At the other end of the scale, the least popular type of still life

An attractive still-life panel by Jacob Fopsen van Es, which fetched £6,200 ($14,880) in 1969 – not as popular as a flower painting, but preferable to a *vanitas* composition.

is generally the *vanitas* composition, designed to symbolize the vanity of human life and usually including a skull, a guttering candle, and other similarly evocative features. As still life compositions are usually bought to decorate the home, it is understandable that works with this type of rather depressing message should be unpopular. Such a work came up for sale in 1969, a picture of fine quality, this time by Abraham Bosschaert, and was sold for £3,990 ($9,576).

Another common type of still life is that which depicts various kinds of food, fruit, bread, meat, wine, etc. Prices naturally vary with the quality of the painting and the attractiveness of the composition, but for this sort of picture they generally fall somewhere between that of the popular flower pieces and the less popular *vanitas* subjects.

The highest price recently paid for a landscape of the Brueghel school was £15,000 ($36,000), which was given in 1968 for an unsigned painting of outstanding quality attributed to 'Velvet' Brueghel. More often, attractive landscapes by either the elder

97

This landscape, attributed to
'Velvet' Brueghel on account
of its outstanding quality, was
bought for £15,000 ($36,000) in
Paris in 1968.

'A river landscape' by Joos de
Momper made £4,300 ($10,320)
in 1968.

or the younger Jan Brueghel, Joos de Momper, or other members
of this group, tend to make around £5,000 ($12,000). An attractive
'River landscape' attributed to de Momper, which fetched £4,300
($10,320) in 1968, is typical of the prices usually paid for this type
of painting.

Such a sum may be said to be roughly the price of the most

98

A modest painting attributed to van Goyen, 'A ruined farm' was sold for £3,333 ($7,999) in Amsterdam in 1969.

'A river landscape with a windmill' by Jan van Goyen reached £11,800 in 1968.

modest work attributed to van Goyen, and surely compares favourably with the painting 'Ruined farm', sold for £3,333 ($7,999) in 1969. Van Goyen was a prolific artist and a considerable number of his paintings still come up for auction every year. He was one of the leading exponents of the Haarlem landscape school

One of the finest van Goyen's seen at auction during 1969, 'A river landscape with a view of Overschie', fetched £23,000 ($56,400).

and the prices commanded by his works are very similar to those paid for the work of Solomon or Jacob van Ruysdael. With so many of his paintings coming on the market, the extent to which the attractiveness of the picture affects its price can easily be seen. In the late 1960s, for instance, his best work seemed to be worth something over £20,000 ($48,000) and his very minor works around £2,000 ($4,800).

The other major type of painting which comes up regularly for sale is that which catches a moment of everyday life – sometimes of low life, such as the peasant scenes painted by Teniers, the van Ostades, or Jan Steen, and sometimes of more genteel surroundings, such as the calm interiors of which Vermeer is the greatest exponent.

Modest pictures in this vein are not generally popular; they seldom fetch more than £10,000 ($24,000). 'The interior of an inn' by Adriaen van Ostade, sold for £3,675 ($8,820) in 1968, is fairly typical of the peasant genre, though in 1967 a 'Village wedding'

100

A modest peasant scene, 'The interior of an inn' by Adriaen van Ostade, sold for £3,675 ($8,820) in 1968.

'A village wedding' by Jan Steen, a relatively minor work by a great artist, sold for £24,000 ($67,200) in 1967.

With his father's paintings almost unobtainable, Pieter Brueghel the Younger's peasant scenes are becoming very expensive; 'A village festival' reached £25,200 ($60,480) in 1960.

by Jan Steen fetched as much as £24,000 (some $67,200)–a good price for a modest example of this important artist's work.

These Dutch peasant scenes were in part a development of the brilliant paintings of low life by Pieter Brueghel in the sixteenth century. His work is now virtually unobtainable. However, his son, Pieter the Younger, mass-produced paintings of peasant scenes based on his father's drawings. In contrast to the relative lack of interest in Dutch peasant scenes, Pieter the Younger's paintings shot up in price during the 1950s and 1960s. Around 1950 they were regularly sold for £2,000–£3,000 ($5,600–$8,400); yet by 1969 a 'Village festival' had made £25,200 ($60,480)–a remarkably high price in view of the number of paintings from his father's drawings that are in circulation.

Least popular of all among Dutch seventeenth-century paintings are portraits. Here works of real quality can be bought for £1,000 ($2,400) or less–especially if the portrait is of a man, though portraits of women, or children, if sympathetically treated, can fetch several thousands, as was shown at the Craven sale in 1968. Of two portraits by Gerrit van Honthorst, one of the first Earl of Craven made £1,600 ($3,840), while the other, of little Princess Françoise of Hohenzollern-Hechingen carrying a wreath of flowers, brought £4,800 ($11,520).

Finally, we come to the fashionable French and Italian schools of the eighteenth century. Here prices in the £20,000–£40,000

($48,000–$96,000) range are not exceptional. Outstanding paintings may fetch even more. And as for the Impressionist and modern schools, the prices of even minor works sometimes seem inordinately high in relation to the quality of the paintings.

The values of pictures of this period have climbed steeply since the war. This is particularly notable in the case of French works, such as those of Pater, Boucher, and Fragonard, which have been much sought after since the beginning of this century. The most expensive work of the French school at auction in the 1960s was Fragonard's 'La liseuse', sold in New York in 1961 for £312,500 ($875,000). The painting, now in the National Gallery, Washington, was painted in about 1776 and dated from the period when Fragonard had settled down with his wife, having given up producing the sumptuous decorations for the homes of courtesans with which he achieved his initial success. It was, indeed, an exceptional example of Fragonard's work, but no other picture of his has even approached this price. In 1969 a rather overblown early work, 'Le repos de Diane', failed to reach its reserve and was bought in at £27,300 ($65,520), while a charming oil-sketch, also

A portrait of William, first Earl of Craven, by Gerrit van Honthorst, sold for £1,600 ($3,840) in 1968; while in the same sale a charming child portrait by the same artist, Princess Françoise of Hohenzollern-Hechingen carrying a wreath of flowers, went for £4,800 ($11,520).

Fragonard's 'La liseuse', the
most important example of his
work to come on the market in
recent years, made £312,500
($875,000) in New York in 1961.

A small oil-sketch by
Fragonard, also called 'La
liseuse', which was sold for
£33,000 ($79,200) in 1969.

One of a pair of small charming
country scenes by Boucher
which together made £39,000
($93,600) in 1969.

Boucher's 'Le billet doux'
sold for £46,000
($110,400) in 1969.

'A regatta on the Grand Canal', a very fine example of Canaletto's Venetian scenes, sold for £100,000 ($280,000) in 1967.

called 'La liseuse', though a smaller and less important picture, was even more expensive at £33,000 ($79,200). However, in the same sale a large but rather coarse work by Boucher, 'Le billet doux', made £46,000 ($110,400); coming, as it did, from the collection of a Princess may have helped it to achieve this price. Two small and attractive oval country scenes by Boucher, seem quite cheap by comparison at £39,000 ($93,600) for the pair.

The Italian *vedutisti* are seen more often in the sale room, and as a rule are therefore possibly a little cheaper than French paintings of the type just mentioned. Two paintings by Canaletto have reached the £100,000 ($240,000) mark. In 1967 'A regatta on the Grand Canal', was sold for this sum, having been bought from the collection of the Duke of Buccleuch in 1953 for £12,000 ($36,600). This was a large and tremendously grand painting – Canaletto at his best – but even so, by 1969 prices of his work had increased still further, a smaller and less important work, 'The Prato della Valle, Padua', being sold for £105,000 ($252,000). The pleasure of seeing Canaletto's skill applied to something other

106

Canaletto's 'Prato della Valle, Padua', a change from his usual canal scenes, fetched £105,000 ($252,000) in 1969.

than his oft-repeated canal scenes undoubtedly added to the charm of the painting, but shortly afterwards two very conventional Venetian scenes made £68,000 ($163,200) and £86,000 ($206,400) respectively. Only a few years earlier they would each have cost £30,000 ($72,000) at the very most.

Guardi's major works surpass Canaletto's, but are much more rare. A large and important *capriccio* scene has fetched as much as £50,000 ($120,000) and even minor examples of his work fetch several thousands. Two tiny paintings, measuring only $3\frac{1}{4} \times 4\frac{3}{4}$ inches and not in the best of condition, came up for sale in 1968.

A superb Venetian view by Francesco Guardi brought £54,000 ($151,200) in 1965. This is still the highest price paid at auction for this artist's work, though less distinguished works have come close to matching it more recently.

A tiny Guardi capriccio, sold for £6,200 ($14,880) in 1968.

A very modest example of Francesco Guardi's work (*right*) which nevertheless was sold for £1,500 ($3,600) in 1968.

The more attractive of the two, a 'Landscape with a tower and a bridge', made £6,200 ($14,880), and the other, a picture of minimum importance 'Island in the Venetian lagoon', £1,500 ($3,600). Panini's romantic views of Rome fetch much the same prices as Guardi's work.

The boom in French and Italian eighteenth-century painting has affected the less important artists as well as the famous. French landscape painters, such as Hubert Robert and Claude Vernet, have shot up in price, perhaps even more rapidly than more important artists. Other *vedutisti*, such as Canaletto's nephew and pupil, Bernardo Bellotto, and the minor artist, Antonio Joli, have increased in value along with Canaletto and Guardi, though the rather different approach to landscape painting adopted by Zuccarelli and Marieschi is not generally quite so popular.

CHAPTER 5

Old Master Drawings

It is known that some drawings by Leonardo, Raphael, Michelangelo, Dürer, and most of the other very great artists of the past still remain in private hands. They are, of course, few in number, but in the last hundred years museums have concentrated mainly on buying important oil-paintings and consequently more important drawings than paintings have been left in circulation. It is still possible for a collector with lavish means to put together a collection of drawings that will include the work of the most renowned European artists.

The value of old drawings has increased very rapidly in recent years. The Times-Sotheby Index shows average values as having multiplied some twenty-two times between the early 1950s and 1969. The increase in prices proportionately outstrips even those of paintings by the Impressionist and modern schools. However, the factors that have led to this tremendous increase are very different from those that have affected the Impressionists' prices.

Drawings are of special interest to the art historian. They show, in a sense, the handwriting of the master and can give a real insight into his personal vision. Many drawings were made in preparation for a particular painting or piece of sculpture. They show the artist thinking out his composition, or working on a detail of the picture, a hand, a head, or perhaps a tree. Thus, such drawings may provide the art historian with indications of a new style or approach, or with grounds for new attributions, and may at the same time throw new light on ideas lying behind the artist's finished work.

Matters of this kind are extremely interesting to the new generation of American collectors and museum curators. Gone— or nearly gone—are the days when millionaire collectors measured the importance of a painting in terms of the price Duveen asked for it. The age of highly specialized research has taken the place of such arbitrary judgements, and drawings are the most splendid research material.

Museum purchases, in particular, drove prices very high in the late 1950s and 1960s, for behind every museum purchase is a museum curator making, in a sense, a personal collection, which, for the specialized collector is still a highly rewarding objective. With drawings of real interest and importance still on the market, a collection of considerable art-historical significance can be built up; which is precisely what several knowing connoisseur-curators have been doing for their respective museums. The funds available to museums in the United States have had an overwhelming effect on prices in what used to be a rather limited scholars' market.

At the same time, this new, very specialized approach to art history is not solely the preserve of the museum curator. A great many young scholars, both amateur and professional, are interested in buying for themselves whatever they can afford, and this has helped to push up the price of minor works, which might have fetched £10 ($28) to £20 ($56) in the early 1950s, to £200 ($480) or £300 ($720).

Further, it is not necessary to be a scholar in order to enjoy and appreciate old drawings. Many people buy them simply for their decorative appeal. Drawings are generally cheaper than paintings and, as the price of paintings continues to escalate, a number of collectors have turned their attention to drawings.

Although drawing as a means of expression goes back to the beginning of time, the earliest drawings that are now bought, sold, and collected date from the period when cheap paper began to be commercially produced in Europe. The secret of paper-making was first discovered in China in about 150 BC, but only reached Europe, through the Arab invaders of Spain and Sicily, in the twelfth century. The first European mills were established at Fabriano in Italy in 1276, and at Troyes in France in 1348. Paper began to become cheap and widely available in the fifteenth century and it is from this period that drawings first survive in any number.

It was natural for artists to make use of paper for their preparatory sketches, and it was particularly useful to studio assistants, enabling them to work from the artist's designs. At an early date artists began to prepare pattern books for the use of their assistants, who often started their training by copying their masters' drawings.

In the Renaissance the use of drawings increased, particularly in the preparation of important commissions. Three types of drawing were normally used – preparatory sketches of the overall composition, studies of the details, and finally a finished drawing or *modello*. The presentation of the *modello* and its acceptance by a patron was often written into the artist's contract for a picture.

110

For more than a century the artistic importance of drawings as something worthy of interest in their own right was little appreciated and they were left to lie around in the artist's studio. In the late sixteenth century a rescue operation was launched by various connoisseur-collectors. Giorgio Vasari, himself an artist, and author of the famous *Lives of the Painters*, was the first collector of real stature. His collection was partly brought together to illustrate the *Lives*, which contain numerous references to particular drawings. Each drawing was elaborately and distinctively mounted by Vasari himself, which aids their recognition today. The whole collection was sold in 1638 to some French dealers and later broken up and widely dispersed, though many of the better drawings ultimately found their way to the Louvre.

Collections have been formed, dispersed, and re-formed constantly over the centuries, and several collectors marked their drawings with some sort of stamp or inscription which, like Vasari's mounts, enable them to be identified. Today it is almost unthinkable that a drawing from Vasari's collection could be found for sale on the open market. But for a drawing to have come from a great collection can substantially improve its value.

The first major collectors in England were King Charles I, George Villiers, Duke of Buckingham, and Thomas Howard, second Earl of Arundel, all of whose collections were unfortunately dispersed. While Arundel was living in Holland, having fallen out of favour with the King, many of his drawings were engraved by Wencelas Hollar. Arundel, who was a patron of Hollar's, was a great connoisseur and any drawing identifiable from one of Hollar's engravings as having graced his own collection is particularly sought after today. It is, incidentally, because of Hollar's engravings that the superb album of Leonardo drawings in the Royal Collection at Windsor is known to have belonged to Arundel.

Many of Charles I's treasures were bought by Everard Jabach, a great French connoisseur, who got into financial difficulties in the 1670s and was forced to cede his collection to Louis XIV. The collection included 5,542 drawings, which formed the beginning of the royal Cabinet des Dessins and the nucleus of the collection in the Louvre.

The collecting of drawings was from the first something of a specialized taste. The fact that there were few collectors and many drawings were available helps to explain the size of the early collections, which often included several thousand drawings, as did Jabach's. In particular, artists if they could afford to do so, tended to collect drawings. This was in part a practical move, since in the days before photography the study of prints and

drawings by other artists was the main way of learning what was
going on elsewhere in the art world.

Collecting drawings and collecting prints have traditionally
gone hand in hand. Sir Peter Lely, presiding over the artistic
revival at the court of Charles II after the ravages of the Civil
War, brought together what was perhaps the most important
collection of drawings and prints formed in the seventeenth
century. The sale of his collection in 1688 is often said to have
inspired the more general interest in collecting drawings and
prints, which continued during the eighteenth and nineteenth
centuries and has persisted to the present day.

Among other noted collectors of drawings were Queen Christina
of Sweden, Rembrandt Pierre Crozat, agent to the Duc d'Orléans,
Pierre-Jean Mariette, a friend of Crozat's, Horace Walpole,
William Esdale, Jonkheer van Franckenstein, Sir Joshua Reynolds, and Sir Thomas Lawrence. Drawings which belonged to
their various collections still appear on the market from time to
time. In fact, many drawings may have belonged to more than one
of these connoisseurs. Queen Christina, who became, after her
abdication in 1654, the foremost among Roman collectors, pos-
sessed several thousand drawings, most of which, together with
her pictures, were bought in 1720 by the Duc d'Orléans, who gave
the drawings to Crozat as a reward for having obtained the
Queen's pictures for him. Crozat, a rich businessman, was a connoisseur and an early patron of Watteau. His collection of drawings is said to have numbered 19,000. It was Crozat's own wish that
the collection should pass *en bloc* to the Cabinet du Roi and it was
offered to the King at a modest price. The offer, however, was
refused – to the great advantage of present-day collectors, for in
1741 it was sold by auction.

The catalogue of the sale was prepared by Mariette, who made
extensive purchases at the sale and several drawings from this
collection later found their way into those of Reynolds and
Lawrence.

Mariette was an art historian of great knowledge and understanding and his writings may be said to have laid the groundwork
for modern scholarship. At various times he refused offers for his
collection from Maria Theresa of Austria, Catherine the Great,
the Elector of Saxony, and the Kings of England, Poland, and
Prussia. For a drawing to have belonged to Mariette adds more
distinction and value to it today than if it were to come from any
other collection. Indeed, drawings on his mounts are collected *per
se*, irrespective of their artistic quality or art-historical importance, in which he is unique among the great collectors.

A collection of drawings on the scale of Mariette's is seldom found today, though there are still five or six private collectors who have superb cabinets of drawings which they have built up during the last few decades and to which they are still adding. Outstanding among these collectors are Count Seilern in London and Fritz Lugt, and his Institut Néerlandais in Paris.

It is now something of a rarity for drawings of exceptional quality by famous artists to come on the market. When they do, the competition between the few important private collectors, and large museums like the Metropolitan and the Louvre, can force prices up to very high levels. As in the case of paintings, there seems to be some widely accepted norm of the maximum conceivable price that can be paid at auction, though this norm gradually changes with time. The way in which it has changed since the early 1950s can be traced through specific drawings. A study for Leonardo's painting, 'The Virgin and St Anne', now in the Louvre, was sold at Sotheby's in 1951 for only £8,000 ($22,400).

A study for Leonardo's painting, 'The Virgin and St Anne', in the Louvre was sold at Sotheby's for only £8,000 ($22,400) in 1951.

This price was matched by drawings of lesser artists in the mid-1950s as prices rose, and in 1958 a sheet of studies by Giovanni Bellini, father of the Venetian school, made £15,750 (around $44,100).

In 1961 a drawing of 'St Barbara' by Hugo van der Goes, the early Flemish artist, made £30,000 ($84,000); this price reflected both the artist's high reputation and the extreme rarity of any drawings dating from the fifteenth century. In 1964 this price was slightly exceeded when two drawings by Raphael—they had completely disappeared after being exhibited in London in 1856—came on to the market. One of them, a study for a painting of 'The Entombment', went for £27,000 ($75,600) and is now in the British Museum; the other, a preparatory design for a 'Madonna and Child with the infant St John', the painting of which is in Vienna, was bought by the Metropolitan for £32,000 ($89,600).

In 1969 the norm altered again, when one of the last two Dürer watercolours known still to be in private hands came up for sale.

In the same year, two Rembrandt drawings had each fetched over £30,000 ($72,000); but Rembrandt was a tremendously prolific graphic artist and his drawings are still available in some numbers, so neither of these two seemed as uniquely desirable as the tiny but perfect Dürer watercolour of a stag beetle, which went for £58,000 ($139,200). Thus, the 'maximum conceivable' auction price for drawings seems to have changed from around £8,000 ($22,400) in the early 1950s to around £60,000 ($144,000) in 1970, though it is possible that if the Leonardo of 1951 were to appear on the market again it would lift the ceiling even higher.

Dürer, Leonardo, Raphael, Bellini, and Hugo van der Goes are among the greatest artists in the history of Western art and these particular drawings were of outstanding quality and importance. Some of less importance by the same artists have been sold at lower prices, but most drawings that reach the sale room are by lesser artists and their market value is largely determined by their degree of art-historical importance.

As the practice of making drawings only began to flourish in the fifteenth century, drawings of this period are extremely rare—considerably rarer, in fact, than paintings of around the same period date. Almost any drawing made before 1500 is likely to fetch a high price on account of its rarity alone, and collectors will compete simply in order that the period may be represented in their collections. In 1969, a drawing of the 'Betrayal of Christ', believed to be by a minor German artist known as the Master of 1477, was sold for £2,000 ($4,800); as already mentioned, van der Goes's 'St Barbara', a really fine drawing, had made £30,000 ($84,000) as early as 1961. Prices were, of course, much lower around 1950;

114

'The Betrayal of Christ', attributed to a minor German artist, known as The Master of 1477. Its price – £2,000 ($4,800) in 1969 – reflected the great rarity of early drawings.

in 1949 a Pisanello, 'A nobleman carrying a falcon on his left wrist', made only £2,450 ($6,860), and a year before a 'Hooded lady' by van der Goes had made £2,200 ($8,866).

Drawing first began to be considered seriously as a discipline to be studied in its own right in Italy during the sixteenth century, when schools of drawing began to spring up. It is believed that Vasari established a school of drawing in Florence, and one of the outstanding characteristics of the Carracci Academy which was set up in Bologna in the 1580s, was the special emphasis given to life drawing.

It was in this period also that drawings began to be seriously

115

collected. With this encouragement, the number of drawings made in Italy in the sixteenth and seventeenth centuries was large and many are still in circulation. In fact, they are among the biggest contributors to most sales of old master drawings; this is in contrast with the old painting field for which it is the Dutch and Flemish schools that form the stuffing of most auctions. Drawings of these two schools, are sparsely represented in the sale room, compared to the Italians.

The value of sixteenth- and seventeenth-century Italian drawings multiplied at a staggering rate during the 1950s and 1960s. The Times-Sotheby Index shows the price of sixteenth-century drawings to have been, on average, thirty times higher in 1969 than in 1951, and those of the seventeenth century forty-four times higher.

This represents a fundamental change in the collector's approach to Italian drawings. The scholarly reappraisal of artistic developments in Italy in the seventeenth century, which has taken place over the last ten or fifteen years, has been mentioned in the context of old master paintings. Its effect on the prices of drawings has been even more marked, for two reasons: drawings of this period are available in much greater numbers than paintings; they were much cheaper than paintings at the beginning of the period and fine examples remain, in general, considerably cheaper today. In the early 1950s a preparatory sketch by Pietro da Cortona for a ceiling in the Palazzo Pitti was sold for £10 ($28); a drawing of two young women by Guercino for £20 ($56); and a group of wandering shepherds by Castiglione seemed on the expensive side at £52 (around $145). Each of these drawings would now probably fetch over £1,000 ($2,400).

By 1969, the most expensive seventeenth-century drawing that had been sold at auction was a brilliant sketch by Cortona, 'An allegory in honour of the House of Barberini', which went for £5,200 ($12,480) in 1968. The most expensive seventeenth-century painting that has come recently through the sale room is Gentileschi's 'Lot and his Daughters', sold at the Spencer-Churchill sale in 1965 for £39,990 ($111,972).

There is a sharp contrast between the increase in the value of sixteenth-century paintings and that of sixteenth-century drawings. The value of such paintings as have come on the market has done little more than keep pace with inflation, but drawings have increased in value almost to the same extent as those of the seventeenth century. This again probably reflects the much greater availability of fine drawings than paintings and thus the greater interest of the field for collectors. It is extremely rare for paintings by the great Italian masters of this period to appear in

Pietro da Cortona's 'Allegory in honour of the House of Barberini', sold for £5,200 ($12,480) in 1968, was the most expensive seventeenth-century Italian drawing to come up at auction in recent years.

the sale room, which discourages collectors' interest in such lesser works as come up for sale. On the other hand, many important drawings of the period have been seen at auction, Leonardo, Raphael, and Michelangelo, have all been represented, as have Veronese, Correggio, and Fra Bartolommeo. Drawings by Parmigianino and the Carracci are quite regularly on the market.

The tremendous new interest in sixteenth- and seventeenth-century Italian drawings stems mostly from the enthusiasm shown by American museums and scholars, though it was sparked off by British scholarship. Two people who have played an important role both in buying drawings and preaching the gospel to others, are Mr Jacob Bean, Director of the Drawings Department of the Metropolitan Museum, and Miss Felice Stampfle, who is in charge of the collection of drawings in the Pierpont Morgan Library in New York. Both have built up the collections of which they are in charge and have brought very substantial buying power into the market. Through the organization of exhibitions in New York, and the publication of a scholarly magazine, *Master Drawings*, they have aroused in many people something of their own enthusiastic interest in old drawings.

The prolific Dutch and Flemish artists of the sixteenth and

117

seventeenth centuries were much more commercially minded than the Italians. A successful composition, once devised, was constantly repeated with variations so slight that hardly any preparatory drawings were required; for which reason relatively few preparatory drawings survive; there are, however, many finished sketches which were made with the idea of immediate sale. The landscapes, for example, of Jan Brueghel, Allaert Evedingern, van Goyen, and Pieter Molyn are usually finished drawings and as such have a ready market today as decorative pictures, but are less sought after by the art historian. They do not provide such an interesting base for iconographic studies as Italian drawings, nor do they give evidence of the artist's preparatory thoughts about the building up of a major composition. This is reflected by the Times-Sotheby Index, which shows Dutch and Flemish landscapes as only twelve times more expensive in 1969 than in 1951, although at the start of this period their prices were also extremely modest.

Rembrandt, Rubens, and Van Dyck were given to making preparatory drawings for their major compositions, but the importance of their work has been recognized for so long that their drawings seldom come up for sale, and when they do, their prices reflect these artists' exceptional stature. Rubens's interest in copying prints and drawings by other masters occasionally makes it possible to buy his work comparatively cheaply. These copies are not as sought after as his other drawings. A drawing of 'The Triumph of Mordecai', after an etching by Lucas van Leyden, made £1,000 ($2,400) in 1968, whereas three years earlier two drawings reflecting his own inspiration made £5,000 ($14,000) and £8,000 ($22,400) respectively.

The influence of scholarship on values has been well illustrated over the last two decades by some of the prices paid for drawings by Rembrandt. A definitive catalogue of his drawings prepared by Otto Benesch, was published between 1950 and 1960. Before its appearance the attributions of some drawings were uncertain. Three drawings sold at Christie's in 1950 and catalogued as 'Rembrandt'—implying that they were school drawings—fetched around £100 ($280); they have now been accepted in the canon and, if sold again, would probably be worth at the least £15,000 ($36,000) each. A similar drawing, believed at the time to be by one of Rembrandt's contemporaries, was sold at Sotheby's for £9 (around $25) in 1950. The value of his drawings has certainly risen steeply, but not to the extent that these prices would imply. As early as 1948, when prices were still depressed following the war, a portrait of Hendrickje Stoffels made £3,000 ($8,400), and in 1949 a sheet of studies was sold for £4,200 ($11,760). By 1969, however, three Rembrandt drawings had fetched over £30,000 ($72,000) each.

With the eighteenth century the focus of interest shifts towards drawings as highly finished works of art in their own right. The use of watercolour and gouache becomes increasingly common to add charm and colour to drawings. In France, the influence of the Académie meant that French artists took a far greater interest in drawing than did their Dutch predecessors. As a result, one sees in the sale room not only highly finished drawings by French artists, but also many studies.

The French school of the eighteenth century has been extremely fashionable throughout the twentieth century and drawings by artists belonging to the school have long been sought after, and are consequently expensive. In the 1930s, finished drawings by Boucher and Fragonard had already fetched between £2,000 ($9,720) and £3,000 ($14,580) each, and a sheet of studies by Watteau—whose drawings still come on the market, although his paintings have almost disappeared from it—had fetched nearly £6,000 ($29,160).

The fact that French drawings were already very expensive in the early 1950s helps to explain the comparatively modest increase in their price since then. The Times-Sotheby Index shows their values as multiplying, on average, some seven times. The drawings of this school are bought more than others for their sheer decorative appeal, the gouaches of Moreau l'Aîné, for instance, or the brilliant ink and wash drawings of Moreau le Jeune. There is, however, considerable art-historical interest in studies and sketches by Watteau, Lancret, Boucher, and Fragonard.

Interest in Venetian artists of the eighteenth century is also centred on highly decorative finished drawings. Fine drawings by Canaletto and Guardi are rare, and would be potentially the

A highly finished drawing of 'Tobias and the angel' by Marco Ricci, sold for £688 ($1,651) in 1968.

most expensive if they were to appear on the market. A superb Guardi drawing of a papal reception was sold for £4,400 ($12,320) in 1951, though his rough ink sketches can still be had for much less than this. The genre scenes of Giovanni Domenico Tiepolo are also finished decorative pieces and can fetch several thousand pounds. At the cheaper end of the price spectrum come Marco Ricci's gouache landscapes and Giacomo Guardi's views of Venice.

The tradition of earlier Italian schools of drawing is carried on with Giovanni Battista Tiepolo, in whose paintings is seen the last fine flowering of the Baroque. He was a brilliant and prolific draughtsman and his drawings appeal both to the art historian and to the decorator-collector.

There has been a major increase in the popularity of Venetian drawings since the early 1950s, with prices multiplying some fifteen times. The better drawings were already expensive at the beginning of this period – much more expensive, in fact, than those of the sixteenth and seventeenth centuries, which fetch high prices today. However, the fashionable popularity of the eighteenth-century Venetian schools has substantially increased compared to other schools during this period. This is shown by the rapid increase in the price of paintings and engravings as well as drawings of the eighteenth century.

WHAT COSTS WHAT

Drawings offer opportunities to collectors both rich and not so rich. The less you spend, the more care is needed to sort out drawings of interest from those that are worthless – and they may cost you anything between £50 ($120) and £60,000 ($144,000).

A tiny pen and ink drawing, 'Madonna and Child with a cat', by Leonardo fetched £19,000 ($53,200) in 1963 – a minute memento of his genius.

Opportunities of buying works by the most famous masters are more or less limited to the purchaser with a good deal of money to spend. Two drawings by Leonardo came to the sale rooms in the 1960s. Both were tiny sketches and their prices, calculated in pounds sterling per square inch, were extremely high. Both appeared during the 1962–63 season; at Christie's a caricature head of an old man in pen and brown ink, measuring only $4\frac{1}{4} \times 3\frac{1}{4}$ inches, made £14,700 ($41,160), and at Sotheby's an even smaller drawing, 'Madonna and Child with a cat' ($3\frac{1}{4} \times 2\frac{3}{4}$ ins), made £19,000 ($53,200).

Although the very name of Leonardo acts as magic, these tiny drawings were not of great importance; certainly they were less important than two Raphael drawings sold at Sotheby's in the following year – and justifiably less expensive. Both the Raphael drawings were of great art-historical interest. 'The Entombment' was a study for a painting, now lost, commissioned by Atalanta

A preparatory study for Raphael's painting, 'Madonna and Child with the infant St John', in the Kunsthistorisches Museum in Vienna–one of four known studies for this painting, which was bought by the Metropolitan Museum of Art, New York for £32,000 ($89,600) in 1964.

Baglioni in Perugia. Several other studies for this painting exist –in the British Museum, the Ashmolean at Oxford, the Uffizi, and the Louvre. This drawing had a special importance as belonging to a sequence from which the process of Raphael's preliminary thoughts about the painting can be deduced. This drawing was refused an export licence after it had been bought by the Metropolitan for £27,000 ($75,600) and is now in the British Museum, which already had earlier and later drawings in the same series.

The second drawing, 'The Madonna and Child with the infant St John', was also a preparatory study for a painting, now in the Kunsthistorisches Museum in Vienna. The drawing was one of four known preparatory studies and was bought by the Metropolitan Museum for £32,000 ($89,600). On the reverse of both

One of the last of Dürer's
watercolours left in private
hands, this precisely painted
stag-beetle was bought for
£58,000 ($139,200) in 1969.

drawings were other studies not immediately traceable to any
known composition, thus providing extra interest by offering an
opportunity for further study and detective work. These two drawings, if they had come up for sale in 1969, could hardly have
fetched less than the £58,000 ($139,200) paid in that year for Dürer's
stag-beetle. The most important drawings by the greatest artists
of the past seem now to have reached a price level of around
£50,000–£60,000 ($120,000–$144,000).

Not all artists are equally interested in graphic work, nor
equally successful. A reputation based on an artist's work in oils
is immediately reflected in the value of his drawings, for the art-
historical interest of his drawings is not necessarily lessened by
his prowess with a pen being less than that with a brush. On the
other hand, admiration for an artist's brilliant technique as a
draughtsman will not necessarily be reflected in an equal

A late drawing by Rembrandt, 'The mocking of Christ', sold for £35,000 ($84,000) in 1969.

appreciation in the value of his paintings. Rembrandt is one of the greatest graphic artists of all time, as well as being one of the greatest painters. His interest in drawing and etching, closely related techniques, is shown by the amount of his graphic work which still comes on the market. The availability of his drawings means that they are generally cheaper than the very rare drawings of Leonardo, Raphael, or Dürer. Even so, in 1969 two very fine Rembrandt drawings were sold at auction for £35,000 ($84,000) and £31,000 ($75,600) respectively. The more expensive drawing, 'The mocking of Christ', dated from the last years of Rembrandt's life. The structural simplicity of his grouping speaks of the originality and greatness of his achievements in these last years. The second drawing, 'King Solomon and the Queen of Sheba', dates from an earlier period and its Baroque conception is more obviously decorative. In a scholar's market it proved the less expensive of the two. Minor sketches by Rembrandt could not be expected to match these two drawings in price; it would be surprising, however, if any work by his hand fetched less than £10,000–£20,000 ($24,000–$48,000) today.

One example should perhaps be given of an artist whose graphic work is more appreciated than his oils. Ingres's oil-paintings seldom come on the market, but his drawings are seen in the sale room from time to time. He was far more prolific as a draughtsman than as a painter and it is his drawings that are particularly admired. Several of his portrait drawings have come up for auction during the last few years and have fetched prices

One side of a sheet of studies by
Veronese, with exploratory
thoughts about a composition,
'The death of Adonis'; the
sheet was sold for £9,800
($23,520) in 1969.

ranging from £6,000 ($14,400) to £11,000 ($26,400). While demonstrating his extraordinary powers as a draughtsman, they were
not among the finest of his drawings.

This is the type of price range that can be expected for rare
fifteenth-century drawings by noted artists, or for the very finest
works of certain later schools. A sheet of studies by Veronese, for
instance, has fetched as much as £9,800 ($23,520).

As has already been mentioned, Italian drawings of the sixteenth and seventeenth centuries are essentially a scholars'
market, where considerable spending power is usually available,
and the best drawings tend to fetch prices in the range of £3,000–

124

A study of a young man's head in red chalk heightened with white, by Annibale Carracci, sold for £3,300 ($7,680) in 1969.

£10,000 ($7,200–$24,000). Drawings by Veronese, Tintoretto, and Parmigianino all fell within this price range during 1968 and 1969. Out of five drawings by Veronese, sold during the year, the highest price paid was £9,800 ($23,520) and the lowest £1,900 ($4,560). One look at the most expensive of these, a large sheet of paper with studies of 'The death of Adonis' on both sides, mixed up among figures, notes, and doodles, serves to underline that it was scholarly criteria that determined the price of the drawing. In the brilliant flowing line of the studies, the master's handwriting is certainly there to be read, but so is much else. In contrast, a tiny pen sketch of 'St George and the Dragon', measuring roughly $9 \times 5\frac{1}{2}$ inches, made £4,000 ($9,600), largely because of its decorative quality. A chalk drawing of a seated female figure, which made £1,900 ($4,560), was not particularly indicative of Veronese's genius; its price was largely a reflection of the greatness of his name.

Also in this sort of price range can be quoted a fine drawing by

OLD MASTER
DRAWINGS

Parmigianino, 'The Death of Dido', sold for £5,600 ($13,440); another related drawing exists, but this one was particularly prized, as it came from the Arundel collection. However, in the same sale a finely executed study of a lion, also by Parmigianino, failed to make its reserve price and was bought in at £2,000 ($4,800). A powerful chalk study by Tintoretto of the head of Michelangelo's statue of Giuliana de' Medici, once in Sir Joshua Reynolds's collection, made £3,300 ($7,680) in 1968, and a year later the same price was paid for a red chalk study of the head of a young man by Annibale Carracci.

Parmigianino and the Carracci are perhaps the most important artists whose drawings appear often enough in the sale room to

The drawings of the Genoese artist, Castiglione, are sought after almost more than his paintings; this drawing of 'A Roman sacrifice' is half-way towards a painting and is in brown, blue, green, and red oil-paint on buff paper. It fetched £2,800 ($7,840) in 1967.

Even this rough pen and ink sketch by Castiglione of 'The finding of Cyrus' brought £1,000 ($2,400) in 1968.

be used in calculating the Times-Sotheby Index. Veronese and Tintoretto are not included. The best drawings of the former fetch several thousand pounds, as do those of Pietro da Cortona and Castiglione from the seventeenth century.

Cortona was virtually the founding father of the Roman Baroque, and one exceptionally important drawing 'An allegory in honour of the House of Barberini', fetched as much as £5,200 ($12,480) in 1968; more modest drawings by him fetch considerably less. Castiglione, on the other hand, is rather exceptional. He stands out as a draughtsman among his contemporaries even more than he does as a painter. Many of his drawings are oil-sketches on paper – a sort of half-way house between a drawing and a painting. A particularly fine example, 'A Roman sacrifice', painted on buff paper in blue, drown, green and red oil-paint, heightened with white, made almost £3,000 ($8,400) in 1967. Even his pen and ink sketches are expensive; 'The finding of Cyrus', sold in 1968, went for £1,000 ($2,400).

Drawings by sixteenth-century artists, such as Federico Zuzzaro and Luca Cambiaso, both reasonably important Mannerist painters, and Guercino or Stefano della Bella from the

Guercino

An attractive landscape drawing by Agostino Carracci (*above*); unfortunately a small piece was missing. It made £450 ($1,080) in 1968.

A drawing by Guercino of great art-historical interest – a study for 'The Madonna and Child with the patron saints of Modena', now in the Louvre. It had been in Pierre Crozat's collection and fetched £1,750 ($4,200) in 1968.

seventeenth century, are as a rule rather cheaper. The best examples of their work can fetch over £1,000 ($2,400), though their lesser drawings tend to fetch around £200–£800 ($480–$1,920). Drawings by Carlo Maratta, the last great artist of the Roman High Baroque, also tend to fall in this price range, as do those of Agostino Carracci. Fine anonymous drawings and work by minor artists of the same period may well fetch prices in the region of £50–£200 ($120–$480).

The prices of Dutch and Flemish landscape drawings recorded in the Times-Sotheby Index fell mainly into the £200–£1,000 ($480–$2,400) price range during 1968 and 1969. Drawings by van Goyen and Pieter Molyn, two of the greatest exponents of the Haarlem landscape school, fetched over £1,000 ($2,400) each, but only by a narrow margin, and their normal prices are around the £500 ($1,200) mark.

The price difference generally reflects the difference in completeness and finish of the drawing. This can be seen by comparing Pieter Molyn's 'Winter landscape', sold for £1,450 ($4,060) in 1966, with the much more sketchy 'Coastal landscape', which fetched

A highly finished and
successful 'Winter landscape'
by Pieter Molyn, sold for
£1,450 ($4,060) in 1966.

This 'Coastal landscape' by the
same artist cost £630 ($1,512) in
1969.

130

This black chalk drawing of 'Cottages by a roadside' by Jan van Goyen fetched £1,100 ($2,640) in 1969. This was a larger and more finished drawing than his 'Figures on a dyke', which made £220 ($528) in the same sale.

A fine drawing by Willem van de Velde the Younger; 'A Dutch merchantman and a flagship at anchor' made £504 ($1,209) in 1968.

£630 ($1,512) in 1969. The point is reinforced by the prices paid for two van Goyen drawings included in the same sale, 'Cottages by a roadside', a large and fairly complete sketch, which went for £1,100 ($2,640), and a small drawing 'Figures on a dyke', sold for £220 ($528).

The earlier landscapes of Jan Brueghel and Abraham Bloemart are more rare, but have not yet reached the £1,000 ($2,400) mark at auction. The seascapes of the two van de Veldes tend to vary

'La soirée de Saint-Cloud' in pen, ink, and brown wash heightened with white, a lovely finished drawing by Moreau le Jeune which fetched £2,250 ($6,300) in 1963.

This fine 'Study of a water-nymph' by François Boucher made £2,800 ($7,840) as long ago as 1964.

132

Less distinguished were a drawing of 'Two *putti*', sold for £893 ($2,143) in 1969, and a rough sketch of a group of women, again by Boucher, which made only £399 ($958) in 1968.

in price from several hundred pounds to around £100 ($240); again, the more finished drawings command the higher prices.

Moving on to the eighteenth century, we come to the most 'fashionable' period of all; scholarly interest here overlaps with the taste of private collectors in search of decorative drawings, and fine drawings by Fragonard, Boucher, Hubert Robert, Gabriel de Saint-Aubin, or Moreau le Jeune might fetch £2,000–£3,000 ($4,800–$7,200), though prices around the £1,000 ($2,400) mark are more usual. Drawings by all these artists still come on the market regularly enough for rarity not to play too strong a part in determining prices; these depend rather on the quality and charm of the work itself. This can be clearly shown in the case of Boucher. The finest and most expensive of his drawings to come on the market in recent years was a 'Head of a young woman', sold for £5,500 ($15,400) in 1967. Drawn in black, red, and white chalks touched with grey wash, this gentle and lovely creature could equally well have graced the wall of a private collector or been a significant addition to a museum collection. But 'Two *putti*' in red chalk, sold for £893 ($2,143) in 1969, was much less interesting, and a black chalk 'Group of women', sold in 1968 for £399 ($958), has little of Boucher's characteristic flowing grace.

Watteau is, of course, something of an exception. His drawings are rare and even his minor sketches are very expensive. In 1969 a 'Study of a young lady'–in fact, more a study of drapery–was bid up to £1,400 ($3,360), although it failed to reach its reserve

133

OLD MASTER
DRAWINGS

This 'Winter landscape' by
Jacques-Guillaume van
Blarenberghe sold for £120
($288) in 1968.

G. B. Tiepolo's 'The Holy
Family' in ink and wash made
£3,100 in 1965.

'Hebe', an ink and wash sketch by Giovanni Domenico Tiepolo, a less sought-after type of drawing, was sold for £315 ($882) in 1966.

A fine example of Giovanni Domenico Tiepolo's genre scenes, 'A minuet in a ballroom', bought for £5,600 ($15,680) in 1965.

price. This was definitely a scholar's drawing. In contrast, the finished drawings of Moreau le Jeune and Moreau l'Aîné are expensive because of their decorative quality. An outstanding example is Moreau le Jeune's 'Soirée de Saint-Cloud', sold for £2,250 ($6,300) as early as 1963.

Very minor drawings by Fragonard or Hubert Robert can fetch around £200–£300 ($480–$720), and there are several minor artists of the period whose graceful drawings and gouaches can be had for around this price, for instance, Blarenberghe or Pillement. Drawings by artists such as these are charming and relatively inexpensive decorations.

Finally, we come to Venetian drawings of the eighteenth century. Here again scholarly interest competes with decorative appeal, and fine drawings can fetch several thousand pounds. The two Tiepolos are the most important contributors to the sale room, both in terms of quality and quantity. G. B. Tiepolo was probably the most outstanding artist of the Venetian revival, and this is reflected by the high prices paid for his studies and preparatory sketches–valuable material for study. So far, the highest price at auction for one of his drawings is £3,800 ($10,640), paid in 1965, for a pen and ink drawing of 'The Annunciation', but many of his other drawings have come close to this price. In contrast, the highly finished genre scenes of his son, G. D. Tiepolo, have fetched even higher prices on account of their decorative quality. 'A minuet in a ballroom', made £5,600 ($15,680) in 1965; but his less

A rare pen and ink view of 'The Grand Canal' by Canaletto, sold for £2,400 ($6,720) in 1963.

Giacomo Guardi's ink and wash views of Venice are often in the sale room; these two made £250 ($600) in 1969.

finished sketches are, rightly, by no means as expensive as those of his father, as for instance his 'Hebe' in brown ink and wash, which was sold for £315 ($882) in 1966.

Finished drawings by Canaletto and Guardi rank with those of the two Tiepolos in price, but are far more rare. A fine drawing of the 'Grand Canal' by Canaletto made £2,400 ($6,720) in 1963.

Marco Ricci and Giacomo Guardi provide the bulk of the cheaper drawings of the period. They are generally highly finished, drawn in gouache or ink and wash, and designed to be hung as pictures. Good examples of their work fetch around £500 ($1,200) and minor drawings can be had for £100–£200 ($240–$480).

CHAPTER 6

Old Master Prints

Since the war, the prices of old master prints have risen more steeply than those of any other field covered by the Times-Sotheby Index; on average prices multiplied thirty-seven times between 1951 and 1969. As much as £32,000 ($66,800) has been paid for a single print—admittedly, it was for the only known impression. But in spite of all this, old prints are one of the few remaining fields where collecting need not be expensive; it is still quite normal to find interesting prints at under £100 ($240) and many of high quality and considerable art-historical significance fetch less than £500 ($1,200) at auction. It remains a field where 'investment' buying has hardly gained a foothold.

To understand this apparently contradictory situation, the nature of a 'print' must be understood. A large number of techniques have been developed over the centuries for the multiple reproduction of pictures. With the exception of photography, all these techniques, from the first European woodcuts, made in about 1400, to lithography, which came into its own in the nineteenth century, are generally known as 'prints'.

A vital difference between a print and a photograph is the extent to which the artist himself has been involved in its production. An etched plate by Rembrandt could be printed many times, but it was his hand that used the etching needle; the composition was conceived and executed to take advantage of the effects that could be achieved by this medium, just as a painting is intended to use the visual possibilities of oil-paint on canvas. A Rembrandt etching is thus a work of art in its own right, to which the artist has applied his own imagination and skill. That the result need not be unique, as it is in the case of a painting or a drawing, is a reflection of the medium in which he was working.

The first European prints date from the beginning of the fifteenth century. As with drawings of the same period, the manufacture of paper in Europe was a vital factor. The number of fifteenth-century prints which come on the market today is extremely limited and they are, therefore, much sought after and consequently have become expensive.

From the early sixteenth century, engravings, woodcuts, and etchings began to be made after the work of noted artists, sometimes after their drawings and sometimes after important paintings. These forms of reproduction flourished until the dawn of photography and have continued since. Over the centuries several gifted artist-craftsmen have turned their hands to the copying of works by others, and such productions, if they are of fine quality, can fetch high prices.

Prints may be sought after either as original works of art by great artists, or because of their rarity, but above all they are valued for their technical and aesthetic qualities. Prints tend to attract a rather specialized and scholarly interest closely linked

A very rare Florentine engraving of 'A bear hunt', dating from around 1470, was sold in 1965 for £1,900 ($5,230); it had been sold at Sotheby's for £21 ($102) in 1824.

to the vital role of the print-maker in the development of Western art.

The rapid rise in the value of old prints has been largely due to new museums building up print collections, especially museums in America. In the main, it is the trustees of museums who are prepared to pay prices of £5,000 ($12,000) and upwards which are now quite frequently recorded for good impressions of old prints, and it is their ability to find large capital sums which can drive important and rare impressions up to very high prices, such as the £32,000 ($89,600) paid at Sotheby's in 1966 for the only known impression of 'The women's bath' by the fifteenth-century German artist known as the 'Master P.M.'; or the £30,000 ($84,000) paid in London in 1966 for an impression of Rembrandt's 'The three crosses'. This print, in its third and finished state, was dated 1653; a few years later Rembrandt completely reworked the plate.

There must be several million old prints in circulation, and fashion plays a considerable part in determining which are sought

The only known complete impression of 'The women's bath' by the early German engraver known as The Master P.M. It dates from the late fifteenth century and was sold for £32,000 ($89,600) in 1966.

140

'La danse sous les arbres', an etching by Claude Lorrain; a fine third-state impression was sold for £240 ($567) in 1969.

after at any given time – setting apart the work of the very great graphic artists such as Dürer or Rembrandt. Any collector who is determined not to be affected by fashion can put together a cabinet of prints of considerable interest and importance for a modest outlay. As F. L. Wilder has said, 'The subject is so vast that few collectors will have time to do more than specialize in one branch or period, and it is, in fact, the specialist who stands most chance of recognizing something that may pass unnoticed by others.'

The main factors which contribute to the value of a print are the fame of the artist print-maker, the technical quality of the print itself, its rarity, and the fineness of the impression. It is in the nature of a print that many copies of it can be made, but usually it is only the earliest impressions, taken before the plate begins to wear, that reveal the artist's true intent. The first few pulls, therefore, are usually the most valuable. However, in some cases the artist may have made improvements to the plate after the first trial impressions, in which case the second or third state may be the most highly prized.

Only a few of the great artists of the past tried their hands at print-making, and even fewer devoted sufficient time and effort to it to leave a large body of successful work. There are, however, a few artists whose distinction stems primarily from their graphic work rather than from their paintings. Important drawings and paintings by old masters are now almost unobtainable and present-day collectors must content themselves with the work of followers or less distinguished artists; but in the case of prints, the greater the success of an artist print-maker in his own day, the more

141

copies were made of his work, and thus the more easily are they obtainable today.

It is much easier to buy an etching by Rembrandt than by his less distinguished forerunner, Hercules Seghers, and there are far more engravings in circulation by Claude than by his fellow Lorrainer, Jacques Bellange. It is almost true to say that the greater the print, the easier it is to buy a copy of it, though there are exceptions and early pulls in good condition would in either case be both rare and expensive.

The difficulties of finding one's way among the different states and impressions of well-known prints, not to speak of the many copies, some made honestly, some fraudulently, virtually restricts purchasers in the print market either to the museum or to the specialized amateur. There are, however, huge numbers of prints which do not interest the specialists, because they are late impressions or the work of unfashionable artists or schools, and as there is no wider public poised to snap up bargains, such prints can cost next to nothing.

Until the late nineteenth century, prints, whether woodcuts, engravings, etchings, or lithographs, were the principal medium of communicating artistic ideas. The decadent Italianization of the Antwerp Mannerist artists of the sixteenth century is attributed to the impact of Italian prints in the north. Similarly, Dürer's prints had great influence in the south and he himself complained to the Venetian Senate about the flagrant copies of his work produced by Marcantonio Raimondi. At the time of Rembrandt's bankruptcy in 1656 there were sixty folios of prints and drawings in his collection illustrative of the Italian, German, and Netherlands schools; he is said to have bought all the engravings of paintings of the Venetian school that were obtainable.

In Rembrandt's lifetime his work became widely known through his etchings. The Italian artist Guercino wrote in 1660: 'I have seen various of his works in prints which have come into our region. They are very beautiful in execution, engraved with good taste, and done in a fine manner, so that one can assume that his work in colour is likewise of complete exquisiteness and perfection. I sincerely esteem him as a great artist.'

In addition to the circulation of original prints by great artists there was for centuries a vigorous trade in prints made after famous pictures or drawings. The very high prices paid in London in the eighteenth and early nineteenth centuries for paintings inaccurately attributed to Correggio can be explained by the fact that the rare works of this highly esteemed artist were known in England almost solely from engravings. Connoisseurs, and artists themselves, collected prints after the works of the masters

142

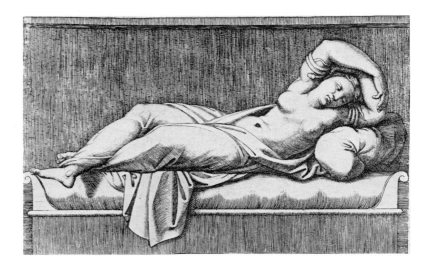

'Cleopatra', an engraving by Marcantonio Raimondi, after Raphael; a very good impression was sold for £90 ($213) in 1969.

in the same spirit as the art historian today builds up a library of photographs.

Marcantonio Raimondi has been widely regarded as the inaugurator of interpretive prints – copies of works by the great masters. His first prints were copies of Dürer's works. He then made engravings of paintings by Raphael and other great artists of the day. His lead was quickly followed and engravings of drawings and paintings by noted artists were made in great quantities for almost 400 years.

Present-day collectors are more selective in their appreciation of these interpretive prints than they are of original graphic compositions. Although photography has in the main destroyed their commercial value, there are still a few prints whose technical quality is such that they are sought after and expensive. The engravings published by Hieronymus Cock after drawings by Hieronymus Bosch and Pieter Brueghel the Elder are greatly coveted; the chiaroscuro woodcuts made in the sixteenth century by Ugo da Carpi, Andrea Andreani, and Coriolano of the work of the great Italian artists of the time are still greatly admired; and the engravings and etchings of Watteau's complete *œuvre*, commissioned by Julienne, are among the most expensive and sought after of French eighteenth-century prints.

In contrast, the work of Marcantonio has almost completely fallen out of favour. In the nineteenth century, with the upsurge of interest in the Italian Renaissance, they enjoyed a brief period of great popularity which came to an end with the advent of photography. The extent to which his engravings have lost their appeal was shown at a sale at Sotheby's in 1965 of an important Victorian collection of prints formed by Barwick Baker. 'A grotesque letter E', by the German Gothic Master E.S., purchased in

143

A tiny *niello* print (shown, *above*, actual size) made in Italy in the late fifteenth century; the picture is engraved on a silver plate and the method is closely allied to the goldsmith's craft. This 'Head of a boy in a *calotte*', measuring only 1¾ by ¾ inches, was sold for £2,542 ($6,100) in 1969.

1834 for £2 12s 6d (around $12), made £1,000 ($2,800), and Rembrandt's 'Three trees', purchased for 6 gns (around $30) in 1831, made £3,000 ($8,400); but Marcantonio's 'Massacre of the Innocents', bought by Baker for 15 gns, the most that he paid for any print in his collection, was sold for £15 ($42) in 1965.

The print sales of London, Paris, New York, and Switzerland which are the main centres today, consist largely of prints by well-known artists rather than of copies of their work. The real money-makers for the auction rooms are the prints of Rembrandt, Dürer, Canaletto, Tiepolo, and Piranesi, for their work is still available in some quantity, though it is expensive. This, however, gives an artificial idea of the achievements of print-makers over the centuries. The first European prints were woodcuts, which began to be made in about 1400 and took the form of playing-cards and coloured prints depicting religious themes issued by monasteries. Of most of these very early prints, only a single copy now exists and they are virtually unobtainable. Line-engraving on a metal block was developed in about 1430, probably as an extension of the goldsmith's craft. There is some doubt about where these techniques were developed, whether in Italy or north of the Alps. Wherever they originated, they spread rapidly both north and south during the fifteenth century, though any prints of this period are now exceedingly rare.

The names of most of the early northern engravers have been forgotten and they are now known only by initials inscribed on their plates, or the date or subject of a famous print, the Master E.S., the Master of the year 1446, or the Master of the Gardens of Love, for instance. Martin Schongauer is the first of these northern engravers to be known by name, and is also one of the first great artists to apply himself to print-making. In recent years an impression of his print 'The censer' was sold for £9,450 ($22,680). A brilliantly decorated letter M by the Master E.S., of which only six impressions are known to exist, went for £13,000 ($36,400), and the only known complete impression of 'The Women's Bath' by the Master P.M. for £32,000 ($89,600). Even minor engravings or woodcuts by entirely unknown artists of this period sell for several hundred pounds.

In the south few of the great Renaissance artists turned their hands to print-making, although Michelangelo is said to have been so fascinated by Schongauer's prints that he copied them in oils. Pollaiulo made one superb print, 'The battle of naked men', which is virtually unobtainable, and seven plates are attributed to Mantegna. These have been so admired and copied over the years that when they do appear in the sale room they are usually falling to pieces. Even in this state they can still fetch between £50

'The Virgin and Child' by
Mantegna. A good impression
of the second state made £3,050
($7,292) in 1969.

($120) and £300 ($720) and fine impressions are worth several
thousands. Two other distinguished Italian engravers of this
period are Jacopo de' Barbari and Giulio Campagnola, a follower
of Giorgione. The prints of both these artist-engravers are rare
and good impressions are worth several thousands.

Print-making had got well under way in the sixteenth century
and prints of this period survive in sufficient numbers for fashion
and scholarly selection to make some of them virtually priceless,
while others are quite inexpensive. Dürer, working at the end of
the fifteenth and the beginning of the sixteenth centuries, dominates the scene, but there were active schools of engraving in
Italy, France, and the Netherlands in addition to Germany.
Furthermore the technique of etching, which leaves an artist far
more freedom of artistic expression than the woodcut or engraving, appears to have been invented shortly after 1500.

145

Dürer's achievements in the expressive use of line as exemplified in his woodcuts and engravings—and three of the earliest-known etchings on iron—have influenced painters, draughtsmen, and engravers throughout the centuries. Dürer was a great admirer of Schongauer and of the Italians, such as Mantegna and Jacopo de' Barbari, and brought together the intricate and fearsome decorative style of the north with the grace and beauty of the south. All his prints are now highly sought after, more especially among his woodcuts the sets known as 'The Apocalypse', 'The Large Passion', 'The life of the Virgin', and 'The Little Passion', and among his engravings those known as his 'Master Prints'; these are 'The Knight, Death and the Devil', 'St Jerome', and 'Melancolia'.

Dürer's blocks have been printed and reprinted many times and there is a wide disparity between the value of fine early impressions and later reprints. A number of his prints were copied and faked during his own lifetime, a process that has continued for several centuries, so great care needs to be taken in purchasing his work.

The influence of Dürer, which spread throughout Europe, was felt especially in Germany and the Netherlands. The German artists Cranach and Altdorfer, 'the father of German landscape', both made a considerable number of prints which clearly show the influence of Dürer, though their work is important in its own right. Both also experimented with coloured prints, each necessitating the use of several different woodblocks; Cranach is sometimes credited with the invention of chiaroscuro woodcuts, in which three or more blocks were used to imitate the effects of a painting. One block was used for printing the coloured ground, one the black outline, and one for highlights in white or gold.

Altdorfer also belongs with the 'German Little Masters', a group of early sixteenth-century painter-engravers known in this way because of the tiny proportions of many of their engravings and woodcuts. Many of them are in the Dürer-esque vein; indeed three of the Little Masters, Hans Sebald Beham, Barthel Beham, and George Pencz were pupils of his.

Lucas van Leyden in the Netherlands was one of the most important northern artists of the early sixteenth century, but his woodcuts and engravings have brought him an almost greater fame than his paintings. He was strongly influenced by Dürer and his output was large. There are still many examples on the market but good impressions of his work are rare. Many of his engravings date from his last years, when he was an invalid, and his touch was so light that only the first pulls printed satisfactorily.

Late impressions of the work of most of these artists who

followed in Dürer's footsteps can still be picked up for £5 ($12) or £10 ($24), but a fine early impression may fetch several hundreds or even thousands of pounds.

It was not until the sixteenth century that the possibilities of print publishing as a lucrative enterprise began to be realized. The fashion spread from Rome, where a publisher called Il Baviero had the first major success by publishing Marcantonio Raimondi's prints after Raphael. The most famous of these publishers was Hieronymus Cock in the Netherlands, whose prints after Italian masters were highly successful. He is best known today as the publisher of prints after Hieronymus Bosch and Pieter Brueghel the Elder. These prints, which can still be bought fairly easily, suffered, until the early 1950s, from the general unpopularity of prints engraved 'after' the work of a noted artist and were not generally worth more than a few pounds. In the late 1950s and 1960s, however, they suddenly became popular; particularly fine plates after both artists have fetched thousands at auction and more modest examples regularly sell for around £300–£400 ($720–$960).

The fantasies of Bosch and Pieter Brueghel the Younger have always exerted a peculiar fascination, but today this fascination seems to have expanded into the dimensions of a widespread fashion. Any painting with diableries reminiscent of Bosch's masterpieces now fetches a very high price, while Pieter Brueghel the Younger's repetitive paintings made from his father's drawings are also climbing steeply in value.

Pieter Brueghel the Elder may himself have worked for Hieronymus Cock in his early days, but only one etching survives that can be firmly attributed to his hand. It is 'The Rabbit-Shooters', and is very rare, and of course extremely valuable. In 1964 a good impression of it made £10,500 ($29,400).

In France the only highly considered engraver of this period was Jean Duvet, a goldsmith and *orfèvre du Roi* under both Francis I and Henry II. He was known for many years as 'Le maître à la Licorne' because of his set of six engravings, 'The Hunting of the Unicorn', in which Henry II and Diane de Poitiers were depicted. Duvet probably had little or no contact with the school of Fontainebleau artists, which included Il Rosso, Primaticcio, and Niccolo dell' Abate, who were imported from Italy by Francis I and Henry II. A studio of engravers and printers was established at Fontainebleau, and engravings and etchings made after the paintings of the Fontainebleau school are just beginning to make money.

Apart from Raimondi, the most important print-maker of the sixteenth century in Italy, other Italian artists worked on their own compositions; among them were Federico Baroccio, whose etchings are highly valued today, and Parmigianino who made a few excellent and very influential etchings. The Carracci's work in this medium is generally considered of poor quality and can still be bought for a few pounds. There was also a group of artists which included Ugo da Carpi, and Andrea Andreani, who made chiaroscuro woodcuts after the work of the great painters of the period. The effects achieved with these woodcuts, with coloured washes and white highlights added, are greatly admired by some specialists and consequently can be expensive.

With the seventeenth century the centre of interest moves to the Netherlands and the great achievements of Rembrandt. He started as a conventional etcher, making brilliant portrait plates of his mother and father and their family circle, but soon began to experiment, working extensively in drypoint–scratching directly on the copper–on an etched basis. He brought a freedom and artistry to the medium which was in its way revolutionary and has hardly been equalled ever since. He etched more than 300 subjects, which have been printed and reprinted down to the present day. It is a tribute to his genius that even modern reprints, which are no more than a pale shadow of the early impressions, still find buyers at £50 ($120) or £100 ($240) a time, while fine early prints regularly fetch several thousands–'The three crosses', in fact, has fetched as much as £30,000 ($84,000). Rembrandt has been held in such esteem for so long that it is not surprising that over the centuries deceptive copies have been made of nearly all his etchings.

There are several different types of Rembrandt etchings. Scenes from the Old and the New Testaments, portraits, landscapes, and a miscellany of other subjects. The combination of deep religious feeling and great artistic skill that he poured into some of his scenes from the life of Christ place them among his greatest achievements–etchings such as 'The three crosses' and 'Christ healing the sick', which is commonly known as the 'Hundred-guilder print', this being the price it was supposed to have fetched in his own lifetime. The portraits of himself, his family, and his friends are not just portraits; they are brilliant linear explorations of character.

Rembrandt was, of course, only one among the Dutch artists of his day who turned their hands to print-making. He is believed to have learnt to etch in the studio of Jan Lievens, who also made some fine etchings, which can fetch several hundred pounds today. The experimental techniques used by Seghers must have been an inspiration to Rembrandt, but Seghers's prints are so rare as to be virtually unobtainable. Esaias van de Velde and Jan

'Christ healing the sick' or the 'Hundred-guilder print', one of Rembrandt's most famous etchings; a very fine second-state impression cost £26,000 ($62,400) in 1966, though poor late impressions, when the block was wearing out, can be found for less than £100 ($240).

van de Velde II made interesting prints. Adriaen van Ostade and Van Dyck both made fine etchings. Van Dyck's series of portraits are held by some to be the finest portrait etchings of all time and good impressions can fetch several thousands of pounds. Jacob van Ruysdael, and other artists of the Haarlem landscape school, also made some fine landscape etchings.

By the seventeenth century, of course, print-making was a flourishing trade and there were keen collectors throughout Europe. Rembrandt's achievement lends overwhelming importance to the Dutch school, but there were also active schools in France and Italy. In France, the school of Nancy was the most distinguished. Of the work of its members, that of Jacques Bellange is the most rare and highly sought after today. The voluminous output of Callot includes some brilliant plates which are generally quite inexpensive, and Claude Lorrain's etchings are by no means as dear as their artistic quality might lead one to expect. They were so greatly admired in his own day that very large numbers of them were published. To some extent familiarity had bred contempt; the easy availability of modest late impressions has perhaps made the fine early impressions seem less desirable.

Today, they seldom fetch more than £500 ($1,200) at auction.

Callot worked extensively in Florence and the name of the Florentine etcher, Stefano della Bella, is often linked with his. Both worked on a very small scale, both were exceedingly gifted draughtsmen, and both were prolific–and in both cases their prints are cheap today–they can still be found for a few pounds. On the whole, Italian seventeenth-century prints are not much sought after today. Salvator Rosa, Castiglione, and Ribera (who worked largely in Italy) all left some fine graphic work, which is not expensive.

The eye of fashion has so far concentrated on the eighteenth- rather than on the seventeenth-century Italians. In fact, with the eighteenth century the centre of interest shifts from the Nether- lands to Italy, and especially to Venice. The romantic landscape etchings of Canaletto, Bellotto, and Marco Ricci in Venice, and the architectural views and fantasies of Piranesi in Rome, became very popular in the 1960s, as was shown by the Times-Sotheby Index. Canaletto's etchings doubled their value between 1951 and 1960 and, between 1960 and 1969 they multiplied in value fifteen times. Piranesi's work is shown to have risen in value to the same extent–thirty-three times since 1951, compared to thirty times in the case of Canaletto. This is particularly remarkable in view of the fact that complete sets of his *Carceri* or *Vedute di Roma* are seen at auction rather than individual plates. It is the rise in the price of single plates, from £3 ($7) to £300 ($720), combined with a more modest appreciation in the value of sets of the *Vedute*, that lies behind Canaletto's extraordinary statistical record.

The Tiepolos, father and son, have more recently followed in Canaletto's footsteps. Only the brilliant etched plates of G. B. Tiepolo have so far reached the £1,000 ($2,400) mark, though his 'master print', 'The Adoration of the Magi' has made as much as £4,600 ($11,040). Etchings by his sons, Giovanni Domenico and Lorenzo, are, however, sharing in the new popularity of their father's work and rising steeply in price.

This is in sharp contrast with the fortunes of French eighteenth- century prints. French *estampes galantes* after the work of Wat- teau, Boucher, Moreau le Jeune, and others, were tremendously popular before the Second World War. This popularity they shared with English eighteenth-century mezzotints after the work of the great portrait painters, such as Gainsborough, Reynolds, and Romney. Their popularity must to some extent have reflected the activity of Lord Duveen, who was busy selling portraits of Eng- lish aristocrats to American millionaires at what seem today highly inflated prices. The popularity of English eighteenth- century artists went hand in hand with that of Fragonard,

L'ENSEIGNE

'L'enseigne', a plate from *L'Oeuvre d'Antoine Watteau*, published by Monsieur de Julienne; a complete set was sold for £5,500 ($13,200) in 1968.

Boucher, and other artists of the French school.

The collapse since the war of the markets created by Duveen has been one of the most notable features of the art market. English mezzotints now only excite interest if they are very fine examples, but French engravings seem to have fallen from favour more gradually. Interest has slipped steadily from year to year. The only survivors appear to have been the large and tremendously decorative prints after Watteau which are known as the 'Recueil Julienne'. Julienne, a friend and patron of Watteau's, decided to honour his artistic achievements by having engravings or etchings made of all his paintings. The *Oeuvre Gravé*, published in two folio volumes in 1735, contained 270 plates. Only 100 copies were printed. A complete set was sold for £5,500 ($13,200) in 1968, and individual plates from sets that have been broken up are also extremely expensive.

With the turn of the eighteenth century we come to another of the great artist print-makers, Goya. Most of his work was done in a combination of etching with aquatint and, like Rembrandt and Dürer, with an experimental approach to the medium he managed to achieve entirely original effects. But his prints, unlike those of his two great forerunners, were a failure in his own day.

151

He made four important sets of etchings, but only the *Caprichos*, and *Tauromaquia* were printed in his lifetime. The *Desastres de la Guerra* and *Proverbios* were first issued in the 1860s. A particularly distinguished set of the *Tauromaquia* from Victor Hugo's collection made £250 ($750) in 1949; in 1968 another first edition made £8,100 ($19,440). On the whole, single plates from the early editions do not come up at auction, apart from an occasional and much-prized artist's proof. The Times-Sotheby Index shows prices multiplying almost twenty times between 1951 and 1969.

Goya's work can be reasonably taken as the dividing line between 'old prints' and 'modern prints'. At the end of the nineteenth century and the beginning of the twentieth, a major interest in this type of work developed among artists, and today limited editions of prints by famous artists are major money-makers for both the publisher and the artist. The 347 etchings produced by Picasso between March and September 1968 can be estimated to have earned the artist and his publisher roughly £3 million ($7 million) apiece. The market in modern prints is, however, fundamentally different from that in the work of older masters.

There are and always have been print collectors *per se*. In continental Europe particularly this has tended to be a rather dry, specialist study. The aim of such a collector is to obtain as many different states as possible of a particular print, sometimes on as many different types of paper as possible. For such collectors the interest of a print lies not so much in its artistic effect as in its rarity and the number of different states in which it was printed before the artist stopped working on the plate. In the late eighteenth and early nineteenth centuries, this became such a fetish that artists deliberately produced as many states as possible. It has been suggested that Rembrandt also reworked his plates in order to cater for this taste.

Collectors of this type have virtually disappeared. Their numbers are anyway too limited to have much effect on the market. The collecting interest which lies behind present-day print values is predominantly that of museums in the higher price ranges. Lower down the scale prints are bought as the tools of the art historian—in cases where the print has had a demonstrable influence on artistic development—as connoisseurs' items—though collectors of lavish means are the exception rather than the rule—and to hang on the wall—where the print is of a reasonable size and sufficiently decorative. The work of Canaletto or Piranesi, for instance, can make a handsome decoration.

WHAT COSTS WHAT

The value of a print is largely determined by how soon after the block was made a particular impression was printed. The effect that the artist or engraver desired to achieve is only fully illustrated by the early pulls. The matter is complicated by the fact that every print that comes on the market has a different history of artistic creation, of printing, and of distribution. Consequently, there is a special scale of values between the best and worst examples of each individual print.

The Times-Sotheby Index of auction prices for old prints was based on the work of five artists who are particularly admired today – Dürer, Rembrandt, Canaletto, Piranesi, and Goya; on the engravings after Pieter Brueghel the Elder's drawings, which have sprung recently into considerable prominence; and on German Gothic prints of the fifteenth century, whose rarity and historical importance has long appealed to the print collector. This choice gave a wide conspectus of print-making in different countries and at different periods.

A careful look at some of the prints by these artists which have been sold at auction should give a clearer idea of the complicated factors that contribute to the value of a print.

Impression and state are much less important in determining the value of fifteenth-century prints than for late work, because so few of them have anyway survived. The example *par excellence* of this is 'The women's bath' by the Master P.M. The impression

'The letter M', a fine impression of the engraving by the fifteenth-century Master E.S.; it fetched £13,000 ($36,400) in 1966.

sold at Sotheby's for £32,000 ($89,600) in 1966 is the only more or less complete example that is known; only one other fragment – a single figure – appears to exist. The Master P.M. is thought to have worked in the region of Cologne and the Lower Rhine in about 1490; only five of his plates are known. His greatest innovation was in the portrayal of the nude, which was highly unusual at that time. Thus, the price for this print was determined by its quality, its extreme rarity, and its art-historical significance.

The decorated letter M by the Master E.S., sold in the same year for £13,000 ($36,400), was one of six recorded impressions, and also one of the finest. The Master E.S. is considered the most important of the anonymous northern engravers of this period; he is known to have been working between 1450 and 1467, probably in the neighbourhood of Lake Constance, and impressions from 317 of his plates have survived. Rarity was thus of less significance in determining the price of this print. Important factors were the name of the Master, and the extreme ingenuity of the composition, with its finishing flourishes compounded of birds, three dogs, and a fox.

Martin Schongauer, thought to have been a pupil or follower of the Master E.S. and a contemporary of the Master P.M., was the first print-maker whose name has come down to us. Also a noted

Martin Schongauer's well-known engraving, 'The censer' (*left*); a good impression fetched £9,450 ($22,680) in 1969.

(*Right*) the same artist's 'Christ taken captive', a plate from a Passion series. A fine impression made £800 ($2,240) in 1965.

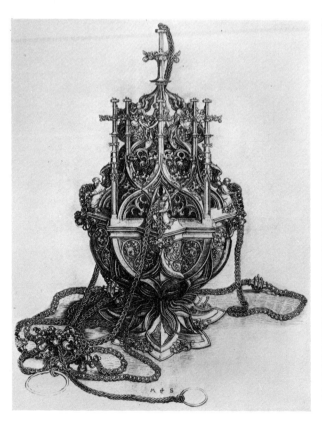

artist, he achieved considerable fame with his prints even in his own day. This meant that far larger editions of them were printed, so that many of them have survived. Hence, the quality of the impression is an important consideration in his work. A very fine impression of his well-known print, 'The censer' made £9,450 ($22,680) in 1969. A good impression of 'Christ taken captive', a less important print forming part of a Passion series, made only £800 ($2,240) in 1965. The relative availability of his prints makes them less expensive, in spite of his great importance as an artist and engraver.

At the other end of the spectrum, a number of anonymous woodcuts from Germany and the Netherlands, dating from around 1490, made prices ranging from £95 ($228) to £440 ($1,056) at Sotheby's in 1969. These were crude, primitive coloured woodcuts of religious subjects by artists or craftsmen whom art historians are unable to identify.

With Dürer the quality of the impression of a print begins to be of first importance. Joseph Meder, before the war, spent years

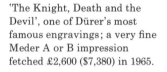

'The Knight, Death and the Devil', one of Dürer's most famous engravings; a very fine Meder A or B impression fetched £2,600 ($7,380) in 1965.

Dürer's 'Five soldiers and a
Turk on horseback', a less
highly prized engraving; a
good Meder A impression was
sold for £620 ($1,488) in 1968.

A plate from Dürer's *Large
Passion* (*right*); the set of
twelve plates, including the
title with the text of 1511, was
sold for £4,200 ($10,080) in
1969.

studying his prints and classified many fine differences between
early and late impressions. This classification was largely based
on watermarks in the paper; scratches that appeared on the
plate from time to time and other signs of deterioration were also
taken into account.

In 1965, an example of his famous engraving 'The Knight,
Death and the Devil' came up for sale and made £2,600 ($7,280).
This was thought to be a very fine Meder A or B impression; in
other words, one of the earliest-known examples of the print. Five
or six later impressions of this engraving have appeared in the
sale room since then at prices ranging from £920 ($2,576) to
£1,900 ($5,320).

Dürer's less famous engravings are, of course, not so expensive.
A Meder A, or very early, impression of 'Five soldiers and a Turk
on horseback', admittedly not in very good condition, made £620
($1,488) in 1968. This dates from a period when Europe was at
war with the Turks, and Dürer's Turk looks very depressed and
may have been a prisoner.

156

Of Dürer's woodcuts, the three large sets are the ones most sought after, 'The Apocalypse', 'The life of the Virgin' and 'The Large Passion'. Dürer called them his 'Large Books'. A set of 'The Large Passion', with the text with which it was published in 1511, was sold in 1969 for £4,200 ($10,080). Accurate identification of this set of prints involves many complications. Pre-publication proofs without the letterpress on the back are the earliest and most prized versions of the single plates. Then comes the published edition of 1511, with the letterpress on the back; then reprints, still with the letterpress, which can be identified either by the watermarks or cracks in the wood. Then come the later reprints of single plates, often without the letterpress, which may be confused with the very early pulls. Many of the blocks still exist and many reproductions were made in the late eighteenth century.

There are twelve plates in the 1511 edition of 'The Large Passion', which may cost anything between £300 ($720) and £400 ($960) apiece. Early pulls without the text could be worth well over £1,000 ($2,400) each, but late reprints might be worth no more than £40–£50 ($96–$120). The range of values is very wide, and the ability to tell early from late impressions certainly pays off.

With engravings of Pieter Brueghel the Elder's drawings, published by Hieronymus Cock, the quality of the impression is again the main determinant of price. Most engravings were printed in only one state, though occasionally there were small variations, such as the omission of the publisher's or the engraver's name, in earlier states. A superb impression of the very fine

'Euntes in Emmaus', an etching after Pieter Brueghel the Elder. A superb early impression was sold for £2,200 ($6,160) in 1964.

EVNTES IN EMAVS

'Luxury', an engraving by Pieter van der Heyden after Pieter Brueghel the Elder. The inscription can be translated as 'Lechery stinks, it is full of uncleanness, it breaks the powers and weakens the limbs.' A good impression was sold for £320 ($896) in 1964; by 1969 it it would have proved a good deal more expensive.

landscape engraving, 'Euntes in Emmaus' made as much as £2,200 ($6,160) in 1964; yet in the same year a good, though not outstanding, impression of his 'Luxury'—a wild phantasy reminiscent of Bosch—made only £320 ($896).

Rembrandt is perhaps the greatest name in the history of print-making, and it is not surprising that some of the highest prices ever recorded for prints at auction have been paid for etchings. To learn to find your way among the various states of the individual prints, let alone the many reprints and copies, is a life's work. Indeed, some collectors devote themselves entirely to his work. The Nowell-Usticke collection, sold by Parke-Bernet in New York in three separate sessions during 1967, 1968, and 1969, was one of the most distinguished of these collections to be formed in America.

'The three crosses', sold for £30,000 ($84,000) in 1966, remains the most expensive example of a Rembrandt etching ever sold at auction. The print is extremely rare because Rembrandt later reworked the plate to represent a later stage of the Crucifixion— 'when the veil of the temple was rent'—darkening and closing in the right-hand side of the composition.

The impression sold in 1966 was also rich in drypoint, a technique much favoured by Rembrandt. It consisted of raising a burr on the surface of the copper by using a special needle. Extra ink was held in the curls of copper, with the result that the plate printed with an extra layer of rich velvety tone. The drawback of this technique, from the collector's point of view, is that the rough

158

edges raised by this process soon wore down and only the first pulls convey the full effect desired by the artist.

With other etchings, such as the 'Hundred-guilder print', 'Christ healing the sick', of which a great many copies exist, the drypoint effect can be all important. Three states of this print are generally identifiable. A very fine second-state impression made as much as £26,000 ($72,800) in 1966. Less fine impressions can also make several thousands of pounds, though sometimes they are down in the hundreds. And very poor impressions can even be bought for £30 ($72) or so.

This is one of Rembrandt's most famous etchings, and fine impressions of it are particularly sought after. His less famous etchings are naturally not so expensive. A very good clear impression of his 'Landscape with a cottage and large tree', for instance, an attractive though not exceptional work, which may

'The three crosses' by Rembrandt. A very fine and rare third-state impression was sold for £30,000 ($84,000) in 1966.

One of Rembrandt's many landscape etchings, 'Landscape with a cottage and large tree'; a very good impression made £1,400 ($3,360) in 1968.

have been etched directly from nature, made £1,400 ($3,360) in 1968.

Rembrandt's etchings have always been sought after by print collectors, and a tremendous expansion in the number of collectors and in museum interest has forced prices to rise rapidly in the last ten years or so. In contrast, Canaletto's etchings used perhaps to be underrated. Before the war, a first-state impression

of one of his large views could be had for about £10 (about $48); today, a single plate has been known to top the £1,000 ($2,400) mark. In 1957 a complete set of the thirty-one plates of his *Vedute* was sold for £700 ($3,402); in 1968, another set cost £13,000 ($31,200). Good first-state impressions of 'Le porte del Dolo' and 'A village on the Brenta', sold for £230 ($644) and £290 ($812) respectively in 1965 and 1964, seem by 1969 standards under-priced by a factor of two or three.

Similarly, Piranesi's etchings have recently become extremely popular. The first edition of his *Carceri d'Invenzione*, wild and brilliant architectural phantasies, said to have been worked while he was in a high fever, made as much as £11,500 ($27,600); in 1969 the second edition reached £6,500 ($15,600). The finest individual plates can be worth £500 ($1,200) or so, but late impressions can be had for much less.

The *Vedute di Roma*, a set of seventy plates, has not so far made more than about £2,000 ($4,800) at auction. These views of Rome, with their fern- and weed-encrusted ruins, are delightfully romantic, but they lack the artistic fire and intensity of the *Carceri* plates. Most of the plates of both sets are still in existence

In 1965 a good first-state impression of Canaletto's 'Le porte del Dolo', (*left*) fetched £230, while in 1964 'A village in the Brenta' (*below*), again in its first state, had made £290 ($812); similar plates had fetched around £1,000 ($2,400) by 1969.

161

A plate from Piranesi's *Carceri d'Invenzione* (*left*); the first edition of the set of sixteen plates has made as much as £11,500 ($27,600), and the second edition has reached £6,500 ($15,600).

A plate from Piranesi's *Vedute di Roma* (*above*); these picturesque etchings are not as sought after as the *Carceri*. A good Roman edition of the seventy plates fetched £1,500 ($3,600) in 1968.

and they have been continually reprinted since Piranesi's day. Naturally, the early impressions are the most valuable.

Goya is something of a special case. His brilliant and original graphic work achieved so little success during his own lifetime that the two important sets, the *Proverbios* and the *Desastres de la Guerra* were not published until the mid-nineteenth century.

A plate from Goya's *La Tauromaquia*; the set of thirty-three etchings with aquatint in the first edition of 1816 made £8,100 ($19,440) in 1968.

163

OLD MASTER PRINTS

Late impressions of all four sets are generally considered as respectable 'editions' rather than reprints. All the same, the early editions are particularly sought after; the first edition of the *Caprichos* has made as much as £10,500 ($25,000), and of the *Tauromaquia* £8,100 ($19,440). The sets that were printed later cannot match these prices. The third edition of the *Caprichos* has been sold for one-tenth of the price of the first. Again, late impressions of individual plates can be had for £40 ($96) or so.

Rarity, however, carries the day. One powerful Goya plate known as 'The giant', for which he used an entirely original technique between aquatint and mezzotint, has made £20,000 ($56,000) at auction. Only six impressions of it are known.

Goya's 'Giant'. Only six impressions are known of this plate, for which Goya used a new experimental technique to tremendous effect; a single impression was sold in 1964 for £20,000 ($56,000).

CHAPTER 7

English Pictures of the Eighteenth & Nineteenth Centuries

England is an island and over the centuries the English Channel has proved a formidable artistic barrier. British artists have, of course, drawn on the artistic experience and achievements of continental Europe, but the schools of painting that have flourished in England have in general been only very loosely linked to European movements. In return, continental Europe has taken only a perfunctory interest in artistic developments in Britain. The Impressionists were great admirers of Constable, whose work had been exhibited at the Paris Salon, but this was the exception rather than the rule.

As a result, European collectors have never paid much attention to English pictures and there is little market for them on the Continent today. The main source of supply remains the country-houses of England, and the most enthusiastic collectors today, as in earlier times, are Englishmen. However, since the beginning of this century, American collectors have been interested in English pictures, especially eighteenth-century portraits, and financially this American interest is an extremely important factor in the market. Interest is also growing in Canada and other 'high-income' English-speaking countries, where there is a natural affinity with the 'Englishness' of English painting.

Only one school, however, has achieved an international financial standing comparable to that of the great European masters of the past, namely the eighteenth-century portrait school, which includes painters such as Gainsborough, Reynolds, Romney, and their like. Their pictures were immensely popular with American collectors before the war and enormous prices were paid for some of their more important works. After their period of glamour, however, they now share with the old masters the characteristics of an expensive traditional market. They are bought largely by rich private collectors rather than by museums, and are still popular in America. Steadily but undramatically

ENGLISH PICTURES
OF THE EIGHTEENTH
& NINETEENTH
CENTURIES

their prices increase. English marine paintings also belong to this type of market. They have never hit the headlines, as have the works of portrait painters, and are generally cheaper than their Dutch counterparts. They appeal mainly to the more traditional collector with a good deal of money to spend.

English sporting pictures, on the other hand, while also belonging mainly to a private collectors' market, have definitely come into fashion since the war. Their rise in popularity, though considerably more modest, is rather similar to that of Impressionist and modern pictures. The interest of a few American collectors has increased prices dramatically, and Stubbs, the undoubted master of the school, has achieved standing as a 'great master' in his own right. Even his most minor pictures are extremely expensive. He is an excellent example of an artist who has been 'up-graded' into the highly desirable or 'museum' class.

The market in Victorian paintings and in English watercolours is different again. Here the very large increase in the number of small collectors has had an overriding effect on prices. And this explosion has in the main taken place within England itself. Victorian painting, having been dismissed as sickly sentiment–or even more simply as 'Victorian'–since the rise to fashion of the Impressionists at the beginning of the twentieth century, there was virtually no market in Victorian pictures immediately after the war. However, the enthusiasm of young collectors has brought these paintings back into fashion, though in general they are still not expensive. The same thing has happened to watercolours, which are now widely collected in England. Traditionally, watercolour was looked on as a far less important medium than oil and until recent times there was only a small number of specialist collectors interested in the English achievements in this medium in the eighteenth and nineteenth centuries. Now important watercolours by Cozens, Cotman, Girtin, or Bonington are very hard to come by.

American collectors are beginning to take an interest in both Victorian paintings and Victorian watercolours and this is an important factor behind the occasional very high auction price. In particular, the anglophile American millionaire Paul Mellon and his Foundation for British Art have had an important effect in promoting the study of British painters and raising prices. Once an artist has found favour with Mr Mellon and his advisers, his work is likely to become rapidly more expensive. Mr and Mrs Mellon's collection now undoubtedly contains the best representation of English nineteenth-century artists to be found anywhere in the world. And even in Europe there are a few collectors of Victorian painting, particularly in Switzerland and Italy.

Thus the genres of English painting considered here do not make up one homogeneous market. The portrait school belongs to an expensive traditional market similar to that of the old masters; sporting pictures are enjoying a new and expensive vogue parallel to that which exists for modern European painting, though on a more modest scale; watercolours and Victorian paintings provide opportunities for the new band of minor collectors whose enthusiasm usually exceeds their purchasing power, with competition from America for the more important pictures.

The study of the market in English pictures must inevitably be limited more or less to the eighteenth and nineteenth centuries. Very little work by artists born and bred in England survives from an earlier date. This may be partly the result of the wholesale destruction of pictures in the time of the Commonwealth, but more importantly it reflects the lack of any generalized interest in painting in England until a fairly late date. The reign of Charles I saw the first great connoisseur-collectors in England, the King himself, the Duke of Buckingham, and the Earl of Arundel being notable among them. But in both Tudor and Stuart times there was a tendency to import art and artists from abroad – though there were already British-born portrait painters in the sixteenth century. There was always a greater demand for portraits than for 'subject' pictures among the prosaic British. However, against competition from such men as Holbein, Rubens, Van Dyck, and Sir Peter Lely it was hard for the British artist to make a living.

A good many early portraits still come on the market and this little-documented school is still comparatively cheap. Fine portraits by Kneller, Lely, or Eworth – from earlier times – seem at present to be decidedly undervalued. However, the scholarship of Dr Roy Strong, Director of the National Portrait Gallery, and of Mr Oliver Millar, Deputy Keeper of the Queen's pictures, in this field was beginning to change the position in 1969. English portraitists whose names have long been forgotten were being rediscovered and paintings long attributed to foreigners such as Gheerhaerts were being reclaimed as home-grown products of the British school. A reappraisal of early English artists seemed to be getting under way.

However, British art has traditionally been considered to start with the eighteenth century – perhaps with Hogarth, the first English artist of any stature. He illustrates a peculiar and continuing characteristic of art in Britain – the propensity for great figures to emerge unconnected with trends, schools, or disciples – lonely and individual masters. He can be grouped with Turner,

167

Constable, Blake, Stubbs, and Gainsborough as the 'great masters' of British eighteenth- and nineteenth-century art. Gainsborough, and to a lesser extent Stubbs, are the only ones who fall into natural grouping with other artists of their time.

Hogarth fought a lonely battle both against the smart portrait painters of his day and the predilection of English connoisseurs for collecting dark, time-stained old masters from foreign countries. He achieved a certain popularity mainly through the engravings of his brilliant genre scenes, such as 'The Rake's Progress'. He despised the contemporary habit of keeping a studio full of assistants and, partly on this account, his output was not very great and consequently his work very rarely comes up for sale. But this scarcity does not make for huge prices. A genuine, though unattractive work was sold during the 1960s for less than £1,000 ($2,800). There are no 'Hogarth collectors' to compete in the sale room, because his work is too rare to collect *per se*. Good examples, of course, fetch better prices, as did his 'Portrait of Daniel Locke', sold for £52,500 ($147,000) in 1965 and should a major work come on the market its price would undoubtedly run into six figures.

The earliest of the schools of English painting we have considered in detail are the marine artists. While Hogarth succeeded in creating some demand for his genre scenes, few Englishmen in the eighteenth century could be persuaded to buy a landscape, if it was by one of their countrymen. Claude, Zuccarelli (who was an RA), or the Dutch school were acceptable, but the home industry was beneath consideration. Despite this, the English marine painters managed to find a modest market by keeping close to the admired Dutch school, introduced to England by the van de Veldes, father and son. Much of the work of Charles Brooking, one of the earliest of these artists, has only recently been distinguished from that of the van de Veldes, and partly as a result has risen steeply in price. Dominic Serres and Peter Monamy slightly anglicized the genre by introducing a note of pomp and circumstance, great naval battles, the flagship of a famous admiral, etc. Their work can also make high prices.

The English marine school remains much cheaper than its Dutch counterpart. But now, as then, the Englishman's love of the sea gives the school a certain popularity and standing in Britain. The works of later exponents, such as Thomas Luny and William Anderson, regularly fetched less than £100 ($280) in the early 1950s, while Brooking, Serres, and Monamy made modest three-figure prices. It is not surprising that from these levels they have appreciated more rapidly than the Dutch school. Prices in 1969 were some eight and a half times higher than in 1951.

The post-war period was punctuated in 1964 by what has become known as the 'Brooking boom'. One London gallery, in setting up an exhibition of marine paintings, needed a few really fine examples to round off its collection. The price of Brooking's seascapes mounted until two particularly fine pictures fetched £14,500 ($40,600) and £15,500 ($43,400) respectively. In 1953 a picture almost identical to the first of these had been sold as one of a pair which together made £400 ($1,120). No seascape, even by the elder van de Velde, the father of the genre, had fetched more than £15,000 ($42,000) at auction since the war. Prices then fell back, but the boom undoubtedly helped to establish the English marine painters. Four-figure prices which had previously been extremely unusual, have recently been paid for all the more important English marine artists.

The lack of interest attached by eighteenth-century connoisseurs to English landscape painting was not even overcome by Gainsborough's superb work in this genre. His house was still stacked with unsold landscapes at the time of his death in 1788. He did, however, achieve contemporary fame as a portrait painter; for however much his contemporaries might have admired foreign artists, it was necessary for portraits to be painted *in situ*. From this simple fact the great British portrait school of the eighteenth and early nineteenth centuries derived not only a stimulus, but also massive financial rewards.

This was the only field which offered the possibility of big money to an ambitious artist. Reynolds amassed a huge fortune in this way; by present-day standards he was probably a millionaire by the time he died. But although the demand for portraits brought fat rewards, it imposed a considerable strain on the artist's productive capacity. It was a common practice to employ assistants to work on a portrait from a preliminary sketch. Reynolds always insisted on painting the face himself and had a knack of adding finishing touches to his assistants' work which brought the whole canvas alive.

The combination of a strong demand and the practice of using many assistants resulted in a copious output, and works of the great artists of the day, Gainsborough, Reynolds, Romney, Raeburn, Hoppner, Lawrence, are still frequently on the market. After falling into eclipse in Victorian times, their work began to recover popularity towards the end of the nineteenth century.

In the 1860s the interest of American collectors began and increased steadily, reaching dizzy heights in the 1920s. This must be largely ascribed to the activities of Joseph Duveen, one of the greatest art dealers of all time. He was an ebullient character, with a real and immense enthusiasm for the pictures he was selling. One secret of his success was charging very high prices, and his millionaire clients were often convinced by their sheer cost that Duveen's pictures were worth their attention. Duveen dealt in many schools of painting, but during the period of his greatest success, English eighteenth-century portraits were the market leaders. One collector, Henry E. Huntington, built up what is perhaps the finest collection of eighteenth-century portraits anywhere in the world. It is now in the Huntington Library in San Marino, California. The following prices give some idea of the cost involved in doing so:

	Price at the time	Approximate equivalent today
Gainsborough–'The Blue Boy'	£148,000 ($719,280)	£600,000 ($1,440,000)
Gainsborough–'The Cottage Door'	£73,500 ($357,210)	£320,000 ($768,000)
Reynolds–'The Tragic Muse'	£73,500 ($357,210)	£320,000 ($768,000)
Romney–'The Misses Beckford'	c. £70,000 ($340,200)	£280,000 ($672,000)
Lawrence–'Pinkie'	c. £90,000 ($437,400)	£360,000 ($864,000)

The recession in America, followed by the war, pricked the bubble of this market and prices have not returned to these levels. They are not, in fact, ever likely to do so, for in their enthusiasm, the pre-war collectors removed much of the finest work by English artists from the market, to which it is now lost for good, for many American collections have been bequeathed to public galleries or turned en bloc into such institutions. One 'great' work did, however, come to the sale room in 1960. This was Gainsborough's 'Mr and Mrs Andrews', today considered by many to be his masterpiece, although it belongs to his early Suffolk period, when his approach was very different to the later feathery and romantic style which was popular in the 1920s. At £130,000 ($364,000) it was cheap by comparison with the prices that were paid for his work before the war.

Since the 1950s, there has been a steady flow of portraits through the sale room. Although they have been of varying quality, generally below that of the 1920s, they have remained among the most consistently expensive of British pictures and are still popular among American collectors. Between the early 1950s and 1969 they multiplied in value on average seven times.

Portrait painting was undoubtedly the most profitable genre for artists of the late eighteenth and early nineteenth centuries, but there was a modest yet comfortable living to be made out of sporting pictures, a kind of equine portraiture, whose exponents were closely linked to the print market. It was in the sporting print engraved from a picture that the real money lay.

Stubbs was among the earliest and certainly the greatest of these artists. His illustrated treatise, *The Anatomy of the Horse*, based on long hours spent dissecting their carcasses, brought him considerable fame in the middle of the eighteenth century and remained for many years the basic reference book on this subject. He combined an exceptionally sensitive treatment of horses and other animals with a fine feeling for landscape.

Several families specialized in this genre of painting, which appealed to the Englishman's love of both field sports and racing. Among them were the Alken, Ferneley, Herring, and Sartorius families. There is usually only one outstanding artist in each family, though he was not always the father of the line; Robert Pollard, for instance, was a minor sporting artist, whose son James achieved much greater fame with his pictures of coaching, racing, and steeplechasing.

The real cult of sporting pictures has developed only in recent

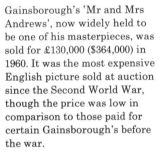

Gainsborough's 'Mr and Mrs Andrews', now widely held to be one of his masterpieces, was sold for £130,000 ($364,000) in 1960. It was the most expensive English picture sold at auction since the Second World War, though the price was low in comparison to those paid for certain Gainsborough's before the war.

ENGLISH PICTURES OF THE EIGHTEENTH & NINETEENTH CENTURIES

years. They did not share in the pre-war boom in English pictures, but only swung into fashion in the 1950s and 1960s. It is difficult to say whether the reassessment of Stubbs's work, which has brought him the standing of a great master, has also brought the school as a whole into fashion, or whether the fashion for sporting pictures has encouraged the reassessment of Stubbs's work. Probably both trends have been at work.

One of the finest of Stubbs's racing pictures, 'Gimcrack' fetched £12,600 ($35,280) in 1951 a low figure by present standards although it seemed sensationally high at the time; another painting of exceptional quality, 'Goldfinder with mare and foal', made £75,600 ($211,680) in 1966. But by 1968 this picture seemed a bargain when £37,000 ($88,800) was paid for a 'Huntsman in a Long Green Coat', better paintings having been sold for between £14,000 ($39,200) and £17,000 ($47,600) only two years earlier. Stubbs was not a particularly prolific artist and the comparative rarity of his work has caused it to increase rapidly in value. By 1969 it was virtually impossible to find a painting by him, even

Stubbs's 'Goldfinder with mare and foal', sold for £75,600 ($211,680) in 1966. By 1969, the new popularity of sporting pictures made this seem a bargain.

over-cleaned and in poor condition, for less than £6,000–£7,000 ($14,400–$16,800).

At the same time, the prices paid for the work of Ben Marshall, John Ferneley senior, John F. Herring, Henry Alken, and James Pollard have risen steeply. By 1968 all these artists had come close to touching the £20,000 ($48,000) mark in the sale room, and one exceptional Marshall had made £58,000 ($139,200) though minor works by him could still be found for around £1,000 ($2,400). On average, the prices paid for sporting pictures at auction multiplied eleven and a half times between the early 1950s and 1969.

The prices that were being paid for, say, Henry Alken and James Pollard by 1969 were remarkable in that much of the working life of both of them belongs essentially to the Victorian Age and their work has a decidedly Victorian flavour. Any popular genre of painting has a built-in tendency towards self-perpetuation, and sporting pictures are no exception. Stubbs was a true exponent of the eighteenth-century spirit; Ben Marshall bridged the centuries, though his work is closer to the eighteenth century in feeling. Ferneley, Herring, Alken, and Pollard continued the genre into the Victorian Age, with their work reflecting a change in aesthetic fashion. Munnings continued the tradition in this century. Today, sporting pictures tend to be collected as a genre and the prices commanded by the later artists are remarkable by the price levels of nineteenth-century painting as a whole, for despite the new popularity of Victorian artists, the eighteenth century still has a much higher standing in the sale room.

The English school of watercolour landscapes also effectively bridges the centuries, though its roots are firmly in earlier times. Although Gainsborough found it extremely hard to sell his landscapes, today they are almost as highly prized as his portraits. Richard Wilson, the 'father of English landscape'. died deeply embittered, having seen the work of Vernet and Zuccarelli, companions of his during his years in Rome, achieve popularity among English collectors. who could hardly be persuaded to buy even his Claudian classical landscapes.

The distinction between oil-painting and watercolour is here extremely important. There is still a feeling that watercolour is a less important medium than oils, although in modern painting a greater freedom in the choice of medium has been achieved than ever before. In the eighteenth century, watercolours were not thought of as being in the same class as 'pictures', i.e. oil-paintings, which explains the existence of a flourishing watercolour school concurrently with a total lack of interest in more ambitious oil landscapes by English artists.

The painting of topographical views in watercolour could be a reasonably remunerative trade. They were often engraved and published in folios or as book illustrations. From much earlier times, itinerant artists had travelled about the country making a modest living from country gentlemen by painting views of their homes, to which were added views of the cathedrals, churches, and country towns of England. Views of foreign countries, particularly Italy, were also in demand for engravings.

This was the basis of the watercolour school, though there were also amateurs without commercial ambitions whose love of the countryside found a simple expression in paint. Turner in his early days made a living in this way. At one time, he travelled the country with Girtin, making drawings that were later engraved. Among other notable early exponents of the watercolour school were Sandby, Alexander Cozens, his son John Robert, Francis Towne, and of course, Rowlandson. In his caricatures of English social life Rowlandson owes a debt to his great forerunner Hogarth. His landscapes are generally full of a bustling country life, untypical of other exponents of this school.

Turner was by no means alone in carrying the watercolour tradition into the nineteenth century, though his achievement in this medium was so important and individual. John Sell Cotman, John Varley, Peter de Wint, and David Cox all worked largely in the nineteenth century, and Samuel Palmer painted a number of superb pictures in this medium in his visionary Shoreham period around 1830. There were also many other distinguished artists who painted landscapes in watercolour throughout the century; Edward Lear's views of Italy and the Middle East are particularly notable.

Watercolour landscapes, though not generally thought of as 'pictures', have always found a market. Before the days of photography, a watercolour would serve as a record of a dearly loved home, or an exciting visit in England or abroad, as would an engraving from an original watercolour. Watercolours have been collected by a small number of devoted connoisseurs throughout this century, but it is only since the second half of the 1950s that they have really begun to come into their own, financially speaking.

The very large increase in the number of small collectors, combined with a general reassessment of the artistic importance of the English watercolour school, has brought the watercolour a degree of popularity and attention hitherto unknown. In the early 1950s it was only the most exceptional pictures, or those with some particular social or historical interest, that fetched over £100 ($280), as for example John Robert Cozens's 'View of Sir William Hamilton's villa at Paltici', which was extremely expensive at

Sandby's 'The North Terrace at Windsor Castle' cost £8,925 ($24,990) in 1965 – the highest price ever paid for a work by this artist at auction.

£720 ($2,016) in 1950. By 1968 another picture dating from Cozens's travels in Italy, 'A grotto in the campagna', was sold for £4,200 ($10,080).

In the early 1950s, attractive watercolours by Varley, Cotman, or Cox could be picked up for £5 ($14), or if you were particularly lucky for 30s. ($4.20). Even modest watercolours are now likely to cost £30 ($72) to £60 ($144), while particularly fine works by Sandby, Palmer, Rowlandson, or Cozens could cost several thousands. Prices for the school as a whole were found to have multiplied thirteen times between 1951 and 1969. In some cases the rise has been far steeper than this. Important in this connection has been the incursion of American buyers into the market. The multitude of small English collectors can seldom raise themselves above the £200–£300 ($480–$720) mark. But there are now healthy collectors interested in fine examples of the genre who help bid prices up into the thousands. The case of Edward Lear provides a dramatic example; in the 1950s his finest views fetched £20–£40 ($56–$112). In 1968 a 'View from above the village of Ascension, Corfu' was sold for £1,600 ($3,840).

This spectacular price increase is also a symptom of the general reassessment of Victorian painting. After half a century of almost total eclipse, Victorian artists began to come back into fashion in the 1950s and 1960s. Enough time had elapsed to counteract the charge of sentimentality and niggling realism with which they had been condemned when the Impressionist and abstract schools became the focus of artistic interest. Their technical qualities as artists are now increasingly appreciated, while the Victorian

175

**ENGLISH PICTURES
OF THE EIGHTEENTH
& NINETEENTH
CENTURIES**

content of their pictures is seen as a fascinating reflection of the social and domestic history of the times.

It was the Age of the Industrial Revolution and artists were required, both in their paintings and in the popular prints that were made from them, to help the general public forget the ghastly reality of the First Machine Age. Sweet sentiment, pastoral idylls, the drama of history or of the Bible story, the strangeness of foreign climes, were popular themes and helped to keep the mind off conditions in the factory and the grinding poverty of new industrial towns. Indeed, Agnew's, the well-known picture dealers, started life in Manchester.

The dark and generally heavy styles of mid-Victorian interior decoration helped to encourage artists to use bright colours. This was particularly important, since bourgeois patronage boomed in the nineteenth century. 'Subject' pictures were in strong demand; it was a highly rewarding period for the artist, who no longer needed to concentrate on portraits to amass a fortune. At the same time, cheap methods of reproduction were discovered which gave rise to a mass market in prints. The copyright in a picture became of great financial importance to an artist; the value of the reproduction rights could massively inflate the price paid to the artist for a picture. Holman Hunt's 'Finding of Christ in the Temple' was bought from the artist for £5,775 ($28,067) by the dealer Gambart, who made £4,000 ($19,440) out of 1s. (25c.) exhibition fees, £5,000 ($24,300) out of sales of engravings of the picture, and finally sold the original painting for £1,500 (around $7,290). The corollary of this was that the artist's interest lay in pictures that would appeal to a wide public through the medium of an engraving, often of poor quality. The accent lay on the message. Millais's 'Cherry Ripe' sold 600,000 copies.

The return to popularity of Victorian painting was led by the Pre-Raphaelites. Their coherence as a movement, the colour they brought, as people, to the Victorian scene, and possibly the rediscovery by decorators of William Morris wallpapers and chintzes – William Morris was a friend and sympathizer although not, of course, a member of the group – all helped to revive interest in the Pre-Raphaelites ahead of other Victorian artists.

The Pre-Raphaelite Brotherhood, founded in 1848, had among its members Rossetti, Holman Hunt, Millais, and Ford Madox Brown. Closely associated with them was Burne-Jones. The Brotherhood's name reflects these artists' veneration of early Italian painters, particularly Benozzo Gozzoli, and their wish to return to pure art as practised by these masters. The movement flowered in the decade 1850–60, overlapping with the beginning of Impressionism and sharing one basic aim, 'truth to nature'.

Holman Hunt's 'Lady of Shalott', sold for £9,975 ($27,930) in 1961.

Unlike the Impressionists, the Pre-Raphaelites interpreted this as meaning precise realism.

In the early 1950s, it was extremely unusual for Pre-Raphaelite pictures to fetch as much as £100 ($280); often they were considered unsaleable. Holman Hunt's 'Valentine rescuing Sylvia' became a landmark when it fetched 240 gns ($706) at Christie's in 1950. However, by 1961 his 'Lady of Shalott' (admittedly a finer picture) reached a record price for Hunt of £9,975 ($27,930).

The recent revival of interest in–and controversy over–the relationship between Ruskin, Millais, and Ruskin's wife Effie, whom Millais subsequently married, has given a special interest to all three players in this drama. In 1965, Millais's 'Portrait of John Ruskin' was sold for £25,200 ($70,560), the highest price that

'Peace concluded: 1856' by Sir
John Millais, sold for £11,500
($27,600) in 1968. Effie, who was
married to Ruskin and later to
Millais himself, was the model
for the wife in the painting.

any picture by a Pre-Raphaelite artist had fetched by 1968. In that
year his charming family scene, 'Peace concluded, 1856', in which
Effie is portrayed as the mother of the family rejoicing over the
news of the ending of the Crimean War, made £11,500 ($27,600).

The Pre-Raphaelite Brotherhood lasted only four years. Millais
abandoned it for popular success – which meant at the time
sentimental paintings suitable for mass reproduction – and the
Royal Academy. Rossetti gravitated towards the William Morris
circle and its anti-Industrial Revolution enthusiasm for arts and
crafts. Holman Hunt alone stuck to his interpretation of 'truth
to nature', but the whole school was edged out of fashion by the
artistic revolution fomented by Impressionism.

The rediscovery of the Pre-Raphaelites has roughly brought
their prices back to what they were in their own day. Important
works by them now fetch several thousand pounds, and their
minor paintings or good drawings can fetch several hundreds. On

One of Frith's set of four pictures entitled 'The road to ruin'; the set was sold for £6,300 ($30,618) in 1878, £1,575 ($7,655) in 1886, £460 ($2,235) in 1919, and £7,200 ($20,160) in 1962.

average, their prices multiplied four times between 1951 and 1960, and another three times between 1960 and 1969. In the 1960s, other Victorian artists also climbed back to popularity. A rather mixed bag were grouped together in the Times-Sotheby Index in order to assess the movement in prices. Average prices were found to have doubled between 1951 and 1960, and between 1960 and 1969 to have multiplied four and a half times.

The finest example of the decline, fall, and revival of Victorian painting is provided by the arch-Victorian, William Powell Frith. His huge genre scenes, such as 'Derby day', were the joy of the printseller. His series of four pictures, 'The road to ruin', were sold in 1878 for £6,300 ($30,618), in 1886 for £1,575 ($7,655) and in 1919 for £460 ($2,235), but by 1962 they might have been considered cheap at £7,200 ($20,160).

The fashion for Victorian painting does not seem to be concentrated on any particular genre. The value of work by good nineteenth-century exponents of traditional types of painting, such as still lifes and landscapes, has risen sharply in price with the shortage of good seventeenth- or eighteenth-century examples, while the interest of American collectors in any particular artist can lead to spectacularly high prices. Shayer's peasant landscape scenes appear frequently in the sale room, and as much as £6,800 ($33,048) has been paid for a particularly fine example. A valid comparison can be made between his 'Cornish beach with fisherfolk', sold in 1968 for £1,150 ($5,589), and another of his

179

ENGLISH PICTURES
OF THE EIGHTEENTH
& NINETEENTH
CENTURIES

'A Spanish *contrabandista*' by
J. F. Lewis, sold in 1968 for
£294 ($705); his Spanish scenes
are not highly regarded.

pictures of a very similar scene that was sold in 1950 for £30 ($84). Ladell's still-life pictures can now fetch over £2,000 ($4,800); in the early 1950s £100 ($280) was their maximum price. Tissot was the most expensive painter of this group in 1950; his friendship with Degas and Whistler rubbed off on his own style and made his work less Victorian in spirit. His 'Henley regatta' made as much as £945 ($2,646) in 1950. Few good pictures by him have come up for auction in recent years, although over £11,000 ($26,400) has been paid for a painting decidedly less interesting than the one sold in 1950.

Among the leaders of the dramatic rise in prices is J. F. Lewis, whose Arab scenes, both in watercolour and oil, proved extremely expensive in the 1960s; his Spanish scenes, however, are not as popular. In 1967, an oil-painting, 'The Reception', made £5,200 ($14,560); it had been sold in 1960 for £840 ($2,352). But 1968 saw the same price paid for a watercolour, 'A Frank encampment in the desert of Mount Sinai', which had passed through the sale room in 1955 for £80 ($224). Ruskin had said of this drawing '. . . it will one day be among things that men will come to England from far away to see, and will go back to their houses saying "I have seen it" . . .'. The underbidder on the picture was a famous American collector.

The prices that may be paid for Victorian paintings are unpredictable. They remain largely in private hands, having long been ignored by museums and collectors alike. However, books on Victorian painting are beginning to appear in increasing

180

numbers—an encouragement to the market, for collectors feel safer entering well-documented fields. The Victorians' reassessment is well under way, but the canon of relative importance—and thus of financial value—is not yet fully established. It is a fascinating field to study and one which offers excellent opportunities for backing one's own judgement. High prices are still the exception rather than the rule.

WHAT COSTS WHAT

The finest examples of English eighteenth-century painting are extremely hard to come by. With the spread of museums and public galleries, the longer a school or artist has been highly regarded, the more difficult it is to obtain good examples of their work. Thus eighteenth-century painting is expensive and well documented, and fine pictures of the period are now hard to come by. While the nineteenth century is a newcomer in popular taste and works of the period are far cheaper; fine pictures are much more readily available.

The great masters of English art are naturally the most expensive, though there is a very wide difference in prices, according to period and subject. Despite the price of £130,000 ($364,000) paid for Gainsborough's 'Mr and Mrs Andrews' in 1960, his small Bath period portraits, simple, repetitive, and without landscape backgrounds, which come into the sale room quite frequently, can sell for less than £2,000 ($4,800).

Turner is a much more 'modern' artist than Gainsborough, not

'A Frank encampment in the desert of Mount Sinai' by J. F. Lewis. This cost £80 ($224) in 1955 and £5,200 ($12,480) in 1968. Lewis's scenes of the Middle East are now far more popular than his paintings of Spain.

ENGLISH PICTURES
OF THE EIGHTEENTH
& NINETEENTH
CENTURIES

Turner's 'A view of Ely Cathedral' painted before 1800 in much the same style as that of Dayes. It fetched £200 in 1965.

Turner's 'The mouth of the Teign', painted in 1813; a masterly work, but showing no break with the tradition of realism. It fetched £1,100 ($3,080) in 1960.

only in date but also in spirit. His wild, almost abstract, storm scenes rarely appear in the sale room, but they could probably top Gainsborough's record if any of them were to do so. The highest price yet paid for a Turner at auction is £88,000 ($246,400), paid in 1965 for his 'Ehrenbreitstein', a superb painting of 1835. With Turner, prices are very closely linked to the date of the picture. As he climbed his way from being a conventional watercolourist to being a great individual master, his style developed and flowered. A watercolour in the style of his early instructor, Dayes, which was painted before 1800, was sold for £200 ($480) in 1968 – a reasonable price, since the picture might well have been painted by his modest instructor himself. The watercolours of the early 1800s,

182

Turner's 'Vesuvius in eruption', painted about 1817; this was a pointer to his later impressionistic work. It fetched £3,800 ($10,640) in 1961.

Turner's 'View of Lake Zug', painted in 1843, during his last and greatest period. In 1959 it fetched £11,025 ($30,870).

when Turner's mastery of the medium was becoming apparent, though he had not abandoned a fairly strict realism, can make a few thousands in the sale room. As his impressionistic approach develops, his prices mount steadily, until they reach a peak with pictures painted in the late 1830s and 1840s.

Turner and Gainsborough are probably potentially the most expensive of the English masters. Heaven knows what Hogarth's 'Rake's Progress' or 'Marriage à la Mode' would fetch if either series were ever to come up for sale. Such of his paintings as do infrequently reach the sale room are probably rather depressed in price by the very rarity of his work. The most expensive Hogarth painting in recent years was his 'Portrait of Daniel Locke', sold for £52,500 ($147,000) in 1965. A year earlier one of his minor works was sold for only £350 ($980).

Hogarth contrasts sharply with Stubbs. With the new international vogue for sporting pictures, it was virtually impossible in the mid 1960s to buy any work by Stubbs for less than £6,000–£7,000 ($16,800–$19,600). The highest price ever paid for one of his paintings in the sale room – £75,600 ($211,680) paid in 1966 for 'Goldfinder with mare and foal' would look cheap by present standards.

Constable is potentially one of the most sought after of the English masters but no important works have recently been seen in the sale room. Luckily for him, he was born just late enough to find a market for his brilliant landscapes in the last eighteen years or so of his life, between 1819 and 1837. Although he was widely imitated in England in the nineteenth century, it was the French Romantic painters and the Impressionists who first appreciated his emotive treatment of light and carried on in spirit his approach to landscape painting. Constable's influence on these schools makes it all the more surprising that since 1951 no picture by his hand has fetched more than £10,000 ($28,000) in the sale room, a figure at which it would be virtually impossible to find a reasonably good Impressionist work.

'Morning – cloud before the sun', a small picture, but one which gave a clear foretaste of Impressionism, made only £550 ($1,540) in 1964. In recent years, pleasant landscapes by Constable have frequently been sold for £2,000–£3,000 ($4,800–$7,200) but his most expensive picture auctioned since the war, 'The young Waltonians', was sold at Christie's for £44,100 ($123,480) in 1951. Although, by comparison with the sort of prices paid during the 1960s, this sounds a relatively modest sum, it constituted a milestone in post-war sale-room history; no painting of any school again matched this price in the sale room until 1957, when a Gauguin still life was sold for £106,000 ($297,143) in Paris.

It is obvious from what has been said that prices for works by the great masters of British art may vary between a few hundred pounds and many thousands. It is equally difficult to pin-point the cost of various genres of painting that flourished in Britain during the eighteenth and nineteenth centuries. Perhaps it may help to look back at the summary of these markets given at the beginning of this chapter.

The great portrait school and the school of marine artists were seen as traditional collecting fields. Works by artists of the portrait school are undoubtedly the most expensive. Since the war, the highest price paid at auction for a painting by Romney is £12,000 ($58,320), for a Hoppner £9,000 ($43,740), for a Lawrence £23,000 ($64,400), and for a Reynolds £25,000 ($70,000). Fine examples of the work of all these artists could certainly fetch higher prices, but very fine portraits are now rarely seen in the sale room. Minor works are quite frequently on the market and prices below the £1,000 ($2,400) mark are still quite possible, though £2,000–£3,000 ($4,800–$7,200) is a more normal price range.

Reynolds's 'James Boswell' at £25,000 ($70,000) shows how the historical importance of the sitter can affect the price of a picture. On aesthetic grounds, portraits of ladies or appealing children,

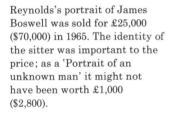

Reynolds's portrait of James Boswell was sold for £25,000 ($70,000) in 1965. The identity of the sitter was important to the price; as a 'Portrait of an unknown man' it might not have been worth £1,000 ($2,800).

'The Angerstein children' (*left*), sold for £23,000 ($64,400) in 1967, is an example of Lawrence at his best.

'The Countess of Charlemont and her son' (*right*), which reached £750 ($2,100) in 1966, is too sentimental and not one of Lawrence's successes.

are generally more expensive than those of gentlemen. Though Reynolds's portrait is finely painted, Boswell was a portly and far from handsome figure and if listed as a 'Portrait of an unknown man' it might have fetched less than £1,000 ($2,400). Lawrence's picture of 'The Angerstein children', on the other hand, which fetched the same price, was an appealing work to which an historical interest attached, the children being those of John Angerstein, founder of the National Gallery. (Ironically, his descendants were unsuccessful bidders at the sale.)

Similarly, prices for marine paintings of the British school can go up to £10,000 ($28,000) or even £15,000 ($42,000), as they did during the 'Brooking boom', and minor works regularly fetch £100–£200 ($240–$480). Brooking, Monamy, Dominic, and J.T. Serres are generally the most expensive artists, with Brooking out in front. A few thousands pounds is quite a normal price for an interesting picture by any of these artists. On the other hand, Thomas Luny, or William Anderson usually fetch four-figure prices in the sale room only for their very best works.

Sporting pictures are in fashion. This means that there is tremendous competition when a really fine example comes on the market, and even modest examples are expensive. This was underlined in 1968 when Ben Marshall's 'Alexandre le Pelletier de

186

(*Above*) Thomas Luny at his
best, a picture that cost £1,050
($2,940) in 1967. (*Right*) A
decidedly less successful work
which went for £231 ($646) in
the same sale.

Molimide', an outstanding canvas, was sold for £58,000 ($139,200), or almost three times as much as any example of his work had previously fetched at auction. Even more surprising at the time, 'A kill at Ashdown Park' by James Seymour, made the same price within a week of the Marshall. Seymour, an early almost primitive

Ben Marshall's 'A spaniel in a landscape' (*left*), sold for £2,400 ($5,760) in 1968.

The same artist's 'A light bay hunter', a much more interesting painting, sold for £7,350 ($17,640) in 1968.

exponent of the school, had not up to this time attracted much interest in the sale room. Ferneley, Herring, Alken, and Pollard have all fetched prices close to £20,000 ($48,000). It is increasingly difficult to find even the poorest example of their work for less than £1,000 ($2,400) and values of around £5,000 ($12,000) to £6,000 ($14,400) are quite normal. The parallel already drawn between this market and that of the Impressionists lies in the fact that

Ben Marshall's 'A portrait of Alexandre le Pelletier de Molimide' (*left*), sold for £58,000 ($139,200) in 1968. For a really fine picture such as this, bidding becomes intensively competitive. This price was three times higher than any previously paid at auction for Ben Marshall's work.

John Varley's 'The Thames at Millbank', sold for £450 ($1,080) in 1968. In the late 1950s it would have been expensive at £50 ($140).

'Outside the Red Lion' by William Shayer, sold for £6,800 ($16,320) in 1968.

189

Samuel Palmer's 'Cow lodge with a mossy roof'. This is an 'exceptional' watercolour, dating from his visionary years, and cost £7,200 ($20,160) in 1963.

they are both so popular that not only the finest works are expensive–fine works of every school are expensive–but even their minor works cost a good deal.

Watercolours and Victorian pictures are still available to private collectors in very large numbers and a good many interesting pieces can be had for less than £100 ($240). At the same time museums and richer collectors are now actively chasing the finest examples which can be bid up to several thousands.

Pre-Raphaelite paintings are particularly prized. By 1969 the highest price paid for Rossetti was £5,250 (around $14,700), and for Holman Hunt £9,975 (around $27,930), while a portrait by Millais had reached £25,500 ($71,400). An increasing number of paintings were fetching four-figure prices, but examples of the work of any Pre-Raphaelite artist could still be had for a few hundreds.

Among Victorian painters, apart from this movement, the most notable prices by 1968 had been achieved by J. F. Lewis, Shayer, Frith, Tissot, and Etty; Solomon, Alma-Tadema, Ladell, G. F. Watts, and F. W. Watts were close behind with their better pictures fetching around £2,000 ($4,800). But this pattern could easily

John Robert Cozens's 'The Galleria di Sopra above Lake Albano', sold for £2,950 ($8,260) in 1962. Cozens is one of the most highly prized of English watercolourists.

be upset if one particularly fine painting by another artist came up for sale—one very high price tends to bring the value of the artist's less important works sharply higher.

Only exceptionally fine watercolours fetch more than £1,000 ($2,400). Samuel Palmer's Shoreham period pictures are extremely rare and £7,200 ($20,160) was paid for a 'Cow lodge with a mossy roof' as early as 1963. However, over the last ten years, there has been a major increase in interest in his visionary years and by 1968 a tiny watercolour landscape of this period made £14,000 ($33,600).

Other watercolourists whose work has fetched exceptionally high prices in the sale room include Paul Sandby with 'North terrace, Windsor Castle' at £8,925 ($24,990) in 1965, John Sell Cotman with 'The white cloud' at £5,600 ($15,680) in 1965, Alexander Cozens with 'A rocky wooded landscape' at £3,800 ($9,120) in 1968, and his son John Robert with 'A grotto in the campagna' at £4,200 ($10,080) in the same year. These are all 'top' prices in the sale room and are by no means typical for watercolours as a whole. Attractive landscapes are still more likely to fetch around £200–£300 ($480–$720), and minor examples less than £100 ($240).

191

CHAPTER 8

The Impressionists

The break with academic traditions which was so fundamental a feature of the Impressionist movement set in train the search for new means of visual expression, a succession of painterly experiments and theories, which has characterized a hundred years of artistic development and is still with us today. This is clearly a major reason for the esteem in which the Impressionist painters are now held and the fact that paintings of this school are among the most consistently expensive and sought after in today's art market.

The popularity of this school is underlined not only by the very high prices paid for important works–the 1960s saw two early paintings by Renoir and Monet fetch over half a million pounds apiece at auction–but also by the large sums for which the most modest works are exchanged. The slightest sketch from a master's hand seldom fetches less than £4,000–£5,000 ($9,600–$12,000) at auction.

It is underlined not only by the very high prices paid for the work of the great Impressionist and Post-Impressionist painters, but also by the competition for the paintings of their precursors or artists even loosely connected with the movement.

Impressionist paintings are sought after by museums and private collectors all over the world. It is, however, the enthusiasm of private people with ample means that ensures the consistently high prices paid for the very large number of paintings and drawings of this period that come on the market every year.

There are, of course, many factors which contribute to the popularity of Impressionist paintings among collectors. They are attractive and easy to understand–no break has yet been made with the figurative tradition. Their bright colours have an immediate appeal. The availability of paintings, particularly those of quality, makes it a more exciting field for collection than that of the more sparsely represented old master painters. Further, there are very few problems of attribution; a collector is much safer in spending large sums. Nearly all the works that come on the market are fully documented and the large majority are reproduced in *catalogues raisonnés*–the complete catalogues of an artist's work.

The current popularity of Impressionist artists is in contrast with their own struggle for acceptance and financial security. Manet and Degas, cushioned by private fortunes, enjoyed a relatively privileged position. This did not, however, help them in obtaining official recognition. Monet, Renoir, Pissarro, and Sisley all went through periods of desperate financial difficulty, at times not knowing where the next meal would come from, let alone the next canvas. Their unshakable faith in a new approach and the revolution in Western art forms that it has brought in its train were dearly bought.

The Impressionists, a highly diverse group of artists, were bound together by their refusal to conform to the current academic conventions. Already Delacroix, Courbet, and the Barbizon painters had sought to loose themselves from these chains by getting out of the studio and taking a new look at nature, ignoring what were considered worthy subjects for a painting, and drawing their compositions from scenes of everyday life.

The Impressionists took this new realism a stage further. They recognized that what we see does not necessarily coincide with what we know we are looking at. The eye is struck by a pattern of

Renoir's 'Le Pont des Arts' of 1868, a very important early work. It was sold for £646,000 ($1,550,000) at Parke-Bernet in New York in 1968 and now belongs to the Norton Simon Foundation. This is the highest price ever paid at auction for an Impressionist picture.

colours and tones, in which not all the components are clearly defined. Light, especially sunlight, can play tricks with the formal laws of perspective, presenting as flat planes of colour, objects that we know to be three-dimensional, or distorting distance by the contrast of light and shade.

The movement sought to challenge the stale conventions of traditional painting. The accent was laid on reproducing the immediate impressions made on the eye as it takes in a scene, and on a disregard for dignified subject-matter; anything and everything that appealed to the artist was worthy to be painted. This was a serious break with what the public had come to expect from a painter. It was the juxtaposition of well-dressed gentlemen and naked ladies which sparked off the public outcry that arose over Manet's 'Déjeuner sur l'herbe'–rather than nudity, which was perfectly acceptable in a Classical setting. Degas was pilloried for considering the racecourse, the café, and the ballet school as suitable subjects for art. Monet, Renoir, Pissarro, and Sisley were all criticized for painting landscapes simply as they saw them. Monet's 'Impression, sunrise', the picture that earned the group the then derogatory title of 'Impressionists', was dismissed with amusement as a crude unfinished sketch.

It is, of course, these very characteristics that give Impressionist pictures their popularity in the sale room today. To a generation sated with photographs, it seems a far higher aim to convey the impression of colour and atmosphere which strikes the eye than to go in for precise realism. The twentieth-century concept of art as a means of personal expression makes the story-picture seem stylised and old fashioned. At the same time, to catch a fleeting impression, to convey with pencil or brush the atmosphere of a moment, was not a very time-consuming matter; for this reason, most Impressionist artists were relatively prolific and the auction rooms are still well supplied with their canvases.

The Impressionist movement and the reaction of those who belonged to it to traditional artistic conventions began to make themselves felt in the 1860s. During this decade the Impressionists met and worked together for the first time, Monet, Renoir, and Sisley at Gleyre's studio; Manet and Degas began their sometimes stormy friendship after a meeting in the Louvre. Although all had pictures accepted by the Salon at least once, the decade was notable for the number of Impressionist masterpieces that were denied this official recognition. As a protest against the narrow-mindedness of the Salon's judges, the 'Salon des refuses' was organized in 1862. This included most of the works that had been rejected. Manet, Pissarro, Fantin-Latour, and Cézanne were among those represented. The exhibition, which was greeted by the public with mirth rather than serious appreciation, hardened the opposition of official art circles to the new movement. The continual rejection of the Impressionists' work by the Salon led, between 1874 and 1886, to eight successive independent exhibitions organized by the Impressionists and their friends.

In all, fifty-six artists exhibited at these shows. The list of names makes fascinating reading today and places the six artists who are generally thought of as the 'great' Impressionists, Manet, Degas, Renoir, Monet, Pissarro, and Sisley, into the more complex and diverse context of the Parisian art world that they knew. There were a few artists of the old guard, such as de Nittis, who, though accepted at the time, exhibited with the Impressionists out of friendship for one or other of the group and who, it was hoped, would add an air of seriousness and respectability to the exhibition. De Nittis's work is now seldom seen but, when it is, it is beginning to fetch high prices in the sale room. A few others who exhibited, such as Boudin and Lépine, are thought of now as forerunners of the movement and their work is particularly valued on that account. There were also a number of other adherents of the Impressionist movement whose work is also appreciated today, among them Caillebotte and Berthe Morisot, and in addition the great Post-Impressionists, Cézanne, Gauguin, and Seurat. The full list of exhibitors follows with, wherever possible, the highest sale-room price recorded for each artist since the Second World War. The pursuit of works by those artists, who

A fine pastel by Federico Zandomeneghi, 'Le thé' sold for £7,000 ($16,800) in 1968. When a very successful work by one of the lesser associates of the Impressionists comes on the market it can fetch a very high price.

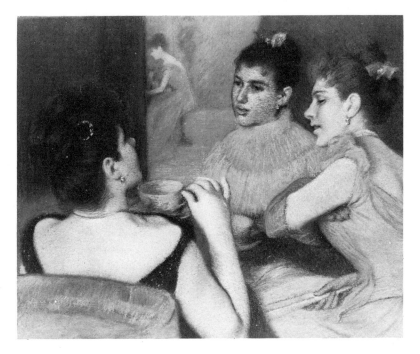

THE IMPRESSIONISTS have virtually disappeared from the sale-room catalogue, might make an interesting speculative venture for anyone with a certain amount of time and money on his hands.

Astruc, Zacharie (1835–1907)
Attendu, Antoine-Ferdinand (exhibited 1870–1905)
Beliard, E.
Boudin, Eugène (1824–98), £52,000 ($124,000)
Bracquemond, Félix (1833–1914)
Bracquemond, Mme Marie
Brandon, Édouard (1831–97)
Bureau, Pierre-Isidore (1827–?)
Caillebotte, Gustave (1848–94), £11,153 ($29,370)–1969
Cals, Adolphe-Félix (1810–80), £158 ($378)–1969*
Cassatt, Mary (1845–1926), £58,333 ($140,000)–1969
Cézanne, Paul (1839–1906), £285,650 ($800,000)–1966
Colin, Gustave (1828–1910), £109 ($262)–1969*
Cordey, Frédéric-Samuel (1854–1911)
Degas, Edgar (1837–1917), £146,000 ($352,400)–1965
Desboutin, Marcellin (1823–1902)
Desbras, Louis
Forain, Jean-Louis (1852–1931), £16,500 ($40,320)–1968
François, Jacques
Gauguin, Paul (1848–1903), £130,000 ($364,000)–1959
Guillaumin, Jean-Baptiste-Armand (1841–1927), £41,250 ($91,148)–1969
Lami, Eugène (1855–1919)
Latouche, Louis (1829–84)
Lebourg, Albert-Charles (1849–1927), £7,770 ($18,600)–1969
Legros, Alphonse (1837–1911)
Lepic, Ludovic-Napoléon (1839–90)
Lépine, Stanislas (1835–1902), £6,500 ($18,200)–1967
Levert, Jean-Baptiste-Léopold
Maureau, Alphonse
Meyer, Alfred (1832–1904)
Millet, Jean-Baptiste (1831–1906)
de Molins, Auguste
Monet, Claude (1840–1926), £588,000 ($1,411,200)–1967
Morisot, Berthe (1841–1945), £46,000 ($125,582)–1968
Mulot-Durivage, Emilieu
de Nittis, Giuseppe (1846–84), £25,333 ($60,799)–1969
Ottin, Auguste-Louis-Marie
Ottin, Léon-Auguste
Piette, Ludovic (1826–77)
Pissarro, Camille (1831–1903), £108,333 ($260,000)–1968

Pissarro, Lucien (1863–1944), £2,835 ($6,800) – 1969

Raffaelli, Jean-François (1850–1924), £4,200 ($11,760) – 1967

Rédon, Odilon (1840–1916), £45,300 ($103,302) – 1968

Renoir, Pierre-Auguste (1841–1919), £645,833 ($1,550,000) – 1968

Robert, Léopold

Rouart, Stanislas-Henri (1833–1912)

Schuffenecker, Claude-Émile (1851–1934), £4,000 ($9,600) – 1969

Seurat, Georges (1851–91), £37,800 ($105,840) – 1965

Signac, Paul (1863–1935), £52,083 ($125,000) – 1968

Sisley, Alfred (1839–99), £85,333 ($202,552) – 1969

Somm, Henry (1844–1907)

Tillot, Charles-Victor (1825– ?)

Vidal, Eugène

Vignon, Victor (1847–1909), £750 ($1,800) – 1969*

Zandomeneghi, Federico (1841–1917), £7,000 ($16,800) – 1968

* Highest prices in 1968–69 season.

The 1870s are generally thought of as the great period of the Impressionist movement and the prices of Impressionist pictures painted during these years are likely to be higher than those of any other decade. The period 1885–95 belongs to the Post-Impressionists, Cézanne, Gauguin, Van Gogh, Seurat, and Toulouse-Lautrec, who with their sharply varying developments of the Impressionist approach opened the way for the experiments of the twentieth century. The importance of their work began to be recognized at the same time as that of the Impressionists themselves, or only shortly afterwards.

The speed at which new artistic developments are understood, accepted, and accorded a high financial status has steadily increased from the time of the Impressionists to the present day. This is a reflection both of the speeding-up of communications and the steady spread of interest in art. Hundreds of exhibitions are now held every year; hundreds of new art books come off the presses. And with the telephone, the aeroplane, and now the communications satellite, a new interest once kindled is quickly appreciated throughout the international art world. This speeding-up process has, however, been gradual. The struggle of the Impressionists was crucial in setting this development in train; theirs was the pioneering work in educating the public to see in experiment and innovation something exciting and desirable.

Although Manet first exhibited at the Salon in 1861, it was not until a few years before his death in 1883 that he began to receive the recognition he had sought throughout his life. A major exhibition the year after his death consolidated his position. In 1885, Gauguin told his wife to sell some pictures, as he was extremely hard up; he suggested a Degas, as he was one of the only artists who sold easily at that time. In 1888, Gauguin rejoiced in the sudden boom in Monets and commented in a letter that 'it is not too pricy to demand 400 francs for a Gauguin, in comparison to 3,000 for a Monet'. Renoir did not begin to sell well until 1892, when he had a highly successful exhibition. The sale of the 'Chocquet studio' in 1899 brought the final financial victory for the Impressionist movement.

Pissarro, in a letter to his son Lucien, described the sale as a 'great artistic event'. It included works by Renoir, Manet, and Pissarro himself, in addition to thirty-two paintings by Cézanne, and prices were uniformly high.

This was in Paris. The speed with which Impressionist pictures were accepted elsewhere varied from country to country. A crucial role was played by the art dealer, Paul Durand-Ruel, who helped to achieve acceptance for the Impressionists both at home and abroad. His first contact with the movement seems to have been in 1870 in London, whence he, Monet, and Pissarro had fled across the Channel to escape the Franco-Prussian War. He soon met other members of the group, and in ten exhibitions of French painting which he held in London between 1870 and 1875 the Impressionists were well represented. They elicited only a marginal interest, however, from English collectors.

Durand Ruel has gone down in history as the inventor of the modern artist-dealer relationship. With backing from bankers and rich collectors, he tried to obtain complete rights over an artist's paintings, buying up his early works and receiving a promise of future works against the guarantee of a monthly allowance. His idea was that by judiciously managing the market in an artist's work, he could steadily enhance its value and make a comfortable profit, both for the artist and himself. Owing to a series of misfortunes he never had much success, although his method has become an accepted practice in the twentieth century. In 1884, when Durand-Ruel was in difficulties, the American artist, Mary Cassatt, came to his rescue by buying Impressionist paintings and trying to interest collectors in them. She was the daughter of a leading Philadelphia family and had lived in Paris for many years as a close friend and associate of the Impressionists, particularly of Degas. With her wealthy connections in America, she did more than any other person to stimulate the interest of American collectors in the Impressionists. She helped to arrange Durand-Ruel's first exhibition in New York in 1886, which was

Manet's 'Le fumeur', sold for
£160,700 ($450,000) at Parke-Bernet
in 1965, is now in the collection of
Mr and Mrs Paul Mellon.

Monet's 'La terrasse à Sainte-
Adresse' painted in 1867, a very
important early painting. It was
sold for £588,000 ($1,411,200) at
Christie's in 1967 and is now in the
Metropolitan Museum of Art,
New York.

In contrast are the minimal
explorations of mood such as the
series of oil-sketches of Mont
Kolsaas at different times of day
made by Monet in the 1890s. This
version fetched £25,000 ($60,480) in
1968.

so successful that he opened an office there two years later. She also acted as an adviser to several wealthy and influential collectors, such as the Havermayers, whose paintings form the basis of the Metropolitan Museum's collection. The Impressionist school thus became popular in America at an early date.

In Germany also there were some enthusiastic collectors before the turn of the century. However, it was between 1900 and the First World War, when Durand-Ruel pursued the idea of a travelling exhibition and visited many countries, that international acceptance of the Impressionists began to be assured. The English were perhaps the slowest to accept the message. Durand-Ruel held an Impressionist exhibition in London in 1905, not daring to titillate the conservative British palate with later developments in French art. The exhibition met with little success. It was followed in 1910 by another, which he called 'Manet and the Post-Impressionists', which was itself followed in 1912 by a Futurist exhibition, and finally came Roger Fry's 'Second Post-Impressionist Exhibition'. The British had to swallow fifty years of important artistic development in one gulp. It was not properly digested until the 1920s, when a few serious collectors of the new French school, from the Impressionists to Picasso and Matisse, appeared on the English scene, led by Samuel Courtauld.

The years between the two world wars saw the importance of the Impressionists, the Post-Impressionists, and later developments of the school of Paris, firmly established among the cognoscenti both in Europe and America. The solid position carved out for the Impressionist school in the 1920s and 1930s by art historians, museums, critics, collectors, and artists, formed the basis of the virtual deification of these artists in the post-war years and was thus an important factor in determining values in the present-day market.

One point about this period should be underlined. It was still possible to buy the finest works by Impressionist and Post-Impressionist artists in fair numbers. This is well illustrated by the Courtauld collection. Sir Samuel Courtauld only began to collect nineteenth-century French pictures in the 1920s; in 1923 he made £50,000 ($238,500) available to the Tate Gallery for the purchase of paintings of these schools, which were at the time virtually unrepresented in the gallery. In addition to this, Courtauld himself bought a number of superb paintings, among them Manet's 'Bar at the Folies-Bergère', Monet's 'Gare Saint-Lazare', Renoir's 'La loge', while the Tate used his money to purchase Seurat's 'Une baignade', and many other Impressionist and Post-Impressionist paintings.

With very fine pictures still on the market, and interest in the

THE IMPRESSIONISTS school mainly limited to a few connoisseurs, less important Impressionist pictures were not expensive before the war. At the same time, important pictures could fetch high prices – £10,000– £20,000 ($48,600–$97,200) was not unusual for a Manet, a Monet, a Degas, or a Renoir – his 'Les Canotiers' is said to have been sold for over £50,000 ($238,500) as early as 1923; this is the equivalent of about £200,000 ($480,000) in present-day money. The Wall Street crash and the depression that followed lowered prices but the Impressionists were not as hard hit as the English school or their own friends and precursors, the Barbizon painters, whose land-scapes had reached the apogee of their popularity in the first two decades of the twentieth century.

As Europe was plunged into war in 1939 the collection of Impressionist and modern pictures belonging to Cornelius J. Sullivan was auctioned at the Parke-Bernet Galleries in New York. The results of this sale, which included some fine pictures, though no masterpieces, provides an excellent balance sheet of the financial rating of Impressionist and Post-Impressionist painters at the end of the 1930s. The following table lists a selection of the pictures, their prices, and a rough estimate of their value in 1969:

	1939	1968
Cézanne – 'Madame Cézanne'	£5,500 ($27,500)	£200,000 ($480,000)
Van Gogh – 'Portrait de Mlle Ravoux'	£3,800 ($19,000)	£125,000 ($300,000)
Toulouse-Lautrec – 'Femme dans le jardin de M. Forest'	£1,140 ($5,700)	£60,000 ($144,000)
Gauguin – 'Autour des huttes, Martinique'	£540 ($2,700)	£150,000 ($360,000)
Toulouse-Lautrec – 'Head of a Woman'	£420 ($2,100)	£20,000 ($48,000)
Van Gogh – 'Coin de verger'	£330 ($1,650)	£30,000 ($72,000)
Cézanne – 'Geraniums' (watercolour)	£325 ($1,625)	£30,000 ($72,000)
Pissarro – 'The Market Place' (gouache)	£170 ($850)	£25,000 ($60,000)
Cézanne – 'Rose dans la verdure' (watercolour)	£130 ($650)	£20,000 ($48,000)

200

	1939	1968
Renoir – 'Portrait of Jean' (pencil)	£155 ($775)	£4,000 ($9,600)
Degas – 'Danseuse' (charcoal)	£150 ($750)	£15,000 ($36,000)
Renoir – 'Child with Bonnet' (pencil)	£90 ($450)	£8,000 ($19,200)

The prices in this sale seem absurdly low by present-day standards. However, the Cézanne at £5,500 ($27,500) and the Van Gogh at £3,800 ($19,000) represented at the time a very substantial outlay for a picture and were expensive by any standards. More significant of the extent to which the situation has changed was the possibility of buying fine drawings, watercolours, and gouaches for between £90 ($360) and £200 ($800). Impressionist pictures had not yet become a province only for the very rich.

The whole art market was muted during the war years. Those with possessions held on to them if they could. After the wreckage in Europe had been cleared and life began to come back to normal in the early 1950s, a new collecting era opened. This period which has been the subject of detailed study in the Times-Sotheby Index, was an extraordinary time for collectors. More money than ever before was poured into the purchase of pictures, above all into purchasing the works by Impressionist, Post-Impressionist, and twentieth-century artists. It is as if the impact of the Second World War and the break-up of traditional patterns of society that it brought in its train suddenly evoked public sympathy for modern art. The break with traditional art forms inaugurated by the Impressionists and carried through by other artists with increasing momentum into the twentieth century seemed for the first time to be generally appreciated.

Many factors have helped to stimulate this new collecting interest. The spread of education, and especially art education, has contributed. The American tax laws have given it an added impetus. Exhibitions and art books have helped to spread the fashion. And the demonstrably rapid rise in art prices has itself encouraged collectors to feel safer in venturing large sums.

The Times-Sotheby Index shows that average prices for Impressionist pictures multiplied almost eighteen times between 1951 and 1969. The norm for a good-quality picture shifted from around £2,000–£3,000 ($5,600–$8,400) to around £30,000–£40,000 ($84,000–$112,000). The first major boom in prices came between 1952 and 1960. There was a pause for breath in the early 1960s, but

THE IMPRESSIONISTS

in 1967 and 1968, in an atmosphere loaded with economic gloom and currency squabbles, prices again began to move sharply upwards.

The first sign of this new situation came with the Cognacq sale in Paris in 1952. The most expensive work in the sale was by Cézanne, a still life, 'Pommes et biscuits', which was sold for £33,000 ($94,286) – more than twice as much any work by Cézanne was known to have fetched before. A charming but not top-ranking portrait by Renoir was the second most expensive picture at £22,500 ($64,285), a price that would have been unthinkable before the war. The work of Manet, Monet, Degas, Pissarro, and Boudin all seemed staggeringly expensive by pre-war standards.

However, this was only a foretaste of the boom in Impressionist prices. The Weinberg sale in London and the Lurcy sale in New York, both in 1957, brought two more outstanding collections on to the market, and the prices paid, e.g £71,300 ($200,000) for Renoir's 'La serre' – left those reached at the Cognacq sale far

Renoir's 'La serre', from the Georges Lurcy collection, was sold at Parke-Bernet in New York in 1957 for £71,300 ($200,000). A large subject picture by Renoir is a rarity on the market, though this was not of the quality of his most famous works.

behind. In the same year, the Greek ship-owner Stavros Niarchos bid £106,000 ($297,145) in Paris for a Gauguin 'Still life with apples', the first time more than £100,000 ($280,000) had been paid in the sale room for a painting of any period.

In 1958 an auction event occurred which set the seal on what was happening to Impressionist pictures. The Goldschmidt sale at Sotheby's, in which only seven paintings were included, all of very high quality, made over three-quarters of a million pounds. The pictures were:

Cézanne–'Garcon au gilet rouge'	£220,000 ($616,000)
Van Gogh–'Les jardins publiques à Arles'	£132,000 ($369,600)
Manet–'La rue Mosnier aux drapeaux'	£113,000 ($316,400)
Cézannes–'Les grosses pommes'	£90,000 ($252,000)
Manet–'Le promenade'	£89,000 ($249,000)
Renoir–'La pensée	£72,000 ($201,600)
Manet–'Self-portrait'	£65,000 ($182,000)
	£781,000 ($2,186,800)

The Goldschmidt sale was well publicized and the prices made big news. Suddenly the eyes of the world were turned on the sale room. The sale not only showed the prices that fine nineteenth-century French paintings could command, but encouraged collectors to chase them even higher in the years that followed. According to the Times-Sotheby Index, Impressionist prices multiplied almost six times during the period 1958 to 1969, though paintings of the quality of the Goldschmidt pictures would not necessarily have appreciated to this extent. When paintings of very exceptional quality, such as these, come up at auction they fetch very special prices; a trend in prices is only significant when comparable works appear regularly on the market. The Index trend is based on works of good to medium quality of which there are the greatest number available.

The same period saw many good collections of Impressionist pictures sold by auction, each time at prices higher than before. In 1967 and 1968 two particularly significant prices were paid, £588,000 ($1,411,200) for Monet's 'Terrasse à Sainte-Adresse', and £646,000 ($1,550,000) for Renoir's 'Pont des Arts'. The next highest sale-room price on record for an Impressionist picture was £286,000 ($800,800), paid in 1965 for a Cézanne landscape that is now in the Mr and Mrs Paul Mellon collection in Virginia.

Both the Monet and the Renoir were very early works painted before 1870 during the first flowering of the Impressionist movement. Monet's 'Terrasse', painted in 1867, is full of the warmth of

Cézanne's 'Garçon au gilet rouge', from the famous Goldschmidt collection, sold at Sotheby's in 1958. It fetched £220,000 ($616,000) and is now in the collection of Mr and Mrs Paul Mellon.

summer, bright flowers, blue sea, and sun, a pointer to his achievements in 'painting from nature' in later years. The Renoir, painted in 1868, shows this artist's virtuosity as a painter even in his early years, but has little in common with the style of his later pictures. That these two paintings, neither of them mature masterpieces, though both of exceptional importance in the history of Impressionism, should fetch over half a million pounds each, emphasizes the special position of the Impressionist school in the present-day art market. On the one hand, important Impressionist paintings can fetch prices quite as high as those paid for the occasional major works by the great old masters when they come up for sale on the other, the lesser prizes are also expensive because the Impressionist school shares the popularity of the 'moderns' among rich private collectors.

204

WHAT COSTS WHAT

The work of the great Impressionists, Manet, Degas, Renoir and Monet, with that of Cézanne, Gauguin, Van Gogh, and Seurat among the Post-Impressionists, is today potentially the most expensive in the sale room of those who were working at that period. The Post-Impressionists have a rather special position because of their influence of twentieth-century art. Cézanne's obsession with the breakdown of form in terms of tone and colour, Gauguin's primitivism, Van Gogh's Expressionist outpourings, and Seurat's analytical theory of colour (*Pointillisme*) have all been taken up again and explored to their furthest limits by twentieth-century artists. Indeed, they are the undisputed ancestors of the most important modern movements.

Cézanne's 'Garçon au gilet rouge' from the Goldschmidt collection now seems a bargain at £220,000 ($616,000), although it was already considered expensive when it was sold for £3,600 ($17,496) in 1913. It is a more important canvas than the

Gauguin's important Tahitian picture, 'Te tiai na ve ite rata' was modestly priced at £130,000 ($364,000) in 1959.

205

Van Gogh's 'Portrait de Mlle Ravoux', a good though not a major work, fetched £157,000 ($439,600) in 1966.

His 'Paysan bêchant' (*right*), fetched £10,500 ($29,400) in 1963. This was a particularly fine drawing, although it dated from the period before Van Gogh came to Paris. It would have proved considerably more expensive at the end of the 1960s.

half-million-pound Monet or the similarly priced Renoir sold in 1968. In 1959 a very important painting by Gauguin, 'Te tiai na ve ite rata' made £130,000 ($364,000), but by 1966 Van Gogh's 'Portrait de Mlle Ravoux', an interesting though not major work, could reach £157,000 ($439,600). No major *Pointilliste* oil-painting by Seurat had been auctioned since the war–he worked so slowly and died young–though half a million or even a million pounds would seem reasonable prices for such a painting by present-day standards. 'Une baignade', one of his most famous works (now in the National Gallery in London) cost the Tate only £3,917 ($18,684) in 1924. No significant price trends can be established for these artists because their work is not well represented at auction. In 1970, £100,000 ($240,000) would seem a reasonable price for a fairly ordinary picture by any one of them, and even early drawings tend to make around £6,000–£10,000 ($14,400–$24,000) or more– witness Van Gogh's 'Paysan bêchant', painted before he came to Paris, and sold for £10,500 ($29,400) as long ago as 1963.

Manet, who died in 1883 at the age of fifty-one, was not as prolific as the other Impressionist artists. This means that his work is not well represented at auction. Two fine works have reached the sale room in recent years, his famous 'La rue Mosnier aux

'Répétition de ballet' a very fine work by Degas, though in gouache and pastel, not oil, made £146,400 ($410,000) at Parke-Bernet in New York in 1965. It already seemed cheap by 1969.

drapeaux', sold for £113,000 ($316,400) at the Goldschmidt sale in 1958, and the less important 'Le fumeur' sold for £160,700 ($450,000) in New York in 1965.

Very high prices at auction for Degas's work are also unusual. This is not, however, a reflection of the rarity of his work, but on his choice of medium. His major oil-paintings are few in number. He preferred working in pastel or gouache—or a combination of the two—and devoted far more time and enthusiasm to drawings than his fellow Impressionists. One fine gouache and pastel, 'Répétition de ballet' made as much as £146,000 ($410,000) in 1965, while modest pencil or chalk drawings are generally sold at around £10,000 ($24,000) each. One attractive red chalk drawing of a dancer made as much as £18,500 ($45,200) in 1969.

Monet and Renoir, on the other hand, both lived to a ripe old age—Monet died at eighty-six and Renoir at seventy-nine—and both painted to the last. The sale rooms are still well stocked with their works, though they vary enormously in quality, particularly

A red chalk drawing of a dancer by Degas, sold for £18,500 ($45,200) at Sotheby's in 1969. Good drawings by the Impressionist masters seldom fetch over £10,000 ($24,000).

Renoir's 'Jeune fille de profil' (*below left*), painted in about 1888 and measuring only 12½ by 9¼ inches, was sold for £90,000 ($216,000) in 1968 – a tiny reminder of his greatest style.

'Petite baigneuse' by Renoir (*below right*), sold for £4,500 ($10,800) in 1968. Measuring only 7¼ by 4½ inches, it is a minimal example of the master's skill.

in the case of Renoir. Anything showing even a trace of his greatest period – that of 'Les parapluies' or 'La loge' – would be likely to fetch close on £100,000 ($240,000); a tiny but delicious portrait, measuring only $12\frac{1}{2} \times 9\frac{1}{4}$ inches was sold in Paris in 1968 for £90,000 ($216,000). Late rough sketches of no great merit by Renoir abound at auction, and they seem extremely expensive at their usual price of £5,000–£15,000 ($12,000–$36,000).

Renoir's values, according to the Times-Sotheby Index, have appreciated less than those of other Impressionist artists. Between 1951 and 1969 his average prices multiplied only eight and a half times, as compared to the almost eighteenfold increase achieved on average by the six artists covered by the Index. There seems to be two explanations for this. One, that the obvious charm and colour of Renoir's paintings has made them particularly popular throughout this century, so that they were already expensive in the early 1950s – 'Jeune fille au chapeau garni de fleurs de champs' made £22,500 ($64,285) at the Cognacq sale in 1952. Two, the flood of rough, though colourful, sketches from his hand that are always available make it relatively easy to buy 'a' Renoir. In the 1960s, however, the increase in the value of Renoir's work kept pace with that of the other artists, and in the last two years or so of the decade even these rough sketches, which may earlier have held back the average trend in prices, jumped sharply in price.

Monet, on the other hand, though one of the leaders of the Impressionist movement and highly regarded at the end of the nineteenth century, rather fell from favour by comparison with Manet, Degas, or Renoir in the pre-war period. However, he has made up ground in recent years, his prices multiplying, on average, twenty-nine times between 1951 and 1969. Monet was a more consistent artist than Renoir and a number of particularly good pictures by him have come on the market, which has helped to improve his standing among collectors. The sale room is well supplied with attractive minor landscapes whose prices fall more or less consistently in the £20,000–£50,000 ($48,000–$120,000) range; anything of greater quality or special interest can jump to over £100,000 ($240,000).

The work of Pissarro and of Sisley has never been as popular as that of the other great Impressionists, though both must be counted among the finest landscape artists of all time. The sort of price paid for an attractive landscape by either artist has moved from around £2,000–£3,000 ($5,600–$8,400) in the early 1950s to nearer £30,000–£50,000 ($72,000–$120,000) in 1970. Particularly fine pictures by both these artists have fetched close to or more than £100,000 ($240,000), but modest examples of their work can be bought for around £3,000–£5,000 ($7,200–$12,000), though not

'Louveciennes–effet de neige',
by Monet, a fine landscape
painted about 1867–74 made
£104,167 ($250,000) at
Parke-Bernet in 1968.

A less interesting landscape
(*right*), 'La plage à Sainte-
Adresse' dating from 1867, made
£41,000 ($114,800) in 1967.

'La mare aux canards à Montfoucault' by Pissarro, painted in 1875, similar in size to the Sisley shown facing page 213, was sold for £28,000 ($67,200) in 1968.

A distinguished later work by Pissarro, 'Le Pont-Neuf, Paris' (*below*) fetched £87,500 ($210,000) in 1968. It was signed and dated 1902 and measured 21½ by 25¾ inches.

without some difficulty, for the quality of their paintings was fairly consistent. There is far more contrast, for instance, between the quality of Renoir's finer paintings and his rough oil-sketches than between the best and the most modest works of Pissarro or Sisley.

The exorbitant prices paid in the 1960s for even minor works by the great Impressionists, combined with the shortage of really fine pictures by them, has led to a new interest in other artists connected with the movement, Fantin-Latour, an early friend of Manet's, who is largely represented in the sale room by attractive flower pictures—with which he achieved a remarkable range of

A modest but attractive composition by Fantin-Latour, 'Roses blanches et jaunes dans un vase haut' (17¾ by 12¾ inches) made £19,000 ($45,600) in 1968.

Renoir's 'Nu couché, vu de dos', a charming minor
oil-sketch of about 1897, measuring 9¾ by 18 inches,
made £21,000 ($50,400) in 1968.

'Gros vase de dahlias et fleurs variées', a very
grand flower composition by Fantin-Latour
(18¾ by 23¾ inches) made £36,000 ($86,400) in 1968.

'Bords de la Seine, environs de Saint-Cloud' by Alfred Sisley, signed and dated '79 and measuring a modest 15 by 18 inches, made £30,000 ($72,600) in 1968.

A very successful harbour scene by Boudin, 'Bassin de Commerce à Bruxelles', made £24,150 ($57,960) in 1967.

A modest work by Eugène Boudin 'Le bassin du Havre', fetched £6,400 (15,360) in 1968. An almost identical painting had been sold at Parke-Bernet in 1951 for £134 ($375).

variations, considering the limited scope of flower compositions –shared in the boom in prices for Impressionist paintings during the 1950s and 1960s. The Times-Sotheby Index shows their average value to have multiplied twelve times between 1951 and 1969.

The same goes for Boudin's seascapes and beach scenes, which so deeply affected Monet in the 1860s and 1870s. Though neither artist had the range or power of the true Impressionists, their popularity is undoubtedly closely linked to that of the Impressionist movement as a whole. In 1968 £54,000 ($129,600) was paid for a flower piece by Fantin-Latour, while in 1969 a similar price was paid for a Boudin 'View of Venice', both good pictures–but not masterpieces. Both artists are regularly represented in the sale room, their prices normally varying between £5,000 ($12,000) and £20,000 ($48,000). Fantin-Latour may have a slight edge over Boudin, but then flower pieces, irrespective of the date when they were painted, are always popular.

Among the precursors of Impressionism, Corot and Courbet are perhaps the greatest figures. Both believed strongly in painting from nature and in spite of official criticism succeeded in breaking important new ground in landscape painting. Courbet, the champion of Social Realism, was one of the first to do battle for the idea that scenes of everyday life, without moral overtones, were worthy subjects for the artist. During the first two decades of the twentieth century the art-market popularity of both Corot and Courbet reached its zenith; prices close to £20,000 ($97,200) were paid for their work in the sale room. At the time of the slump in 1929, however, both of them were already falling from favour.

213

'La solitude; étude d'après nature faite à Vigen' by Corot was sold for £5,040 ($12,100) in 1968. This rather romantic type of landscape was more popular at the turn of the century than it is today. This was a study made in about 1851 for the painting, 'La solitude', exhibited at the Salon in 1866.

Today their more modest works are not greatly in demand, though their importance to the artistic developments of the nineteenth century is done justice to by the very high prices paid for the occasional important work. In 1964, one of the two known major studies for Courbet's famous painting 'Les demoiselles des bords de la Seine' (now in the London National Gallery) was sold at Sotheby's for £62,000 ($173,600), and in 1967 a brilliant portrait study by Corot, of a young woman in red against a woodland background, 'Jeune femme au corsage rouge tenant une mandoline', made £110,714 ($310,000) at Parke-Bernet.

The painters of the Barbizon school, so-called after the village of Barbizon in the Forest of Fontainebleau, where they worked together painting woodland scenes and landscapes, also had their influence on the Impressionists. Their work, too, was highly regarded at the beginning of the century, but fell from favour in the 1930s. Only Millet has a fairly strong following in the sale room today; the prices paid for his work are roughly equivalent to those of Boudin or Fantin-Latour. For Daubigny, Harpignies, Rousseau, and Diaz, the tide has hardly turned, although they were all extremely gifted landscape artists. About £5,000 ($12,000) is the maximum that their work fetched at auction in 1969, and indeed several of their paintings fetched less than £1,000 ($2,400) each. Even these prices were, however, a major improvement on those of a year or so before.

Among other artists who can be considered as forerunners, although in later years they were friends of the Impressionists and exhibited with them, are Daumier, Jongkind, Lépine, and Monticelli. All rose sharply in value in the 1960s, with Daumier in the Fantin-Latour class, Jongkind a little less expensive, and Monticelli and Lépine less again–though still decidedly more popular than the Barbizon painters.

The biggest revaluation of the 1960s came among the immediate followers of the Impressionists: Berthe Morisot–Manet's sister-in-law and a very gifted artist in her own right; the American Mary Cassatt, particularly sought after by her own countrymen; and to a lesser extent, Guillaumin, who was a very prolific artist and painted a large number of very similar landscapes. Fine pictures by all three artists can now fetch prices around the £30,000–£50,000 ($72,000–$120,000) mark.

In the late 1960s there was also a sudden upsurge of interest in the *Pointilliste* school–the friends and disciples of Seurat. Seurat's scientifically evolved theory of colour, by which a painting was built up of small dots of colour which would blend in the viewer's eye or mind, had a powerful influence in the 1880s and was dubbed Neo-Impressionism. Pissarro for a short time embraced this new approach enthusiastically, but it was left mainly to Seurat's younger friends and contemporaries to explore the method fully –Seurat himself died in 1891 at the age of thirty-two, five years after he had exhibited his masterpiece, 'La Grande Jatte', at the last of the Impressionist group's exhibitions and stirred up both controversy and enthusiasm for his new method of painting.

Berthe Morisot's 'Le port de Fécamp' sold for £53,000 ($125,582) in Paris in 1968. This was the highest price paid at auction for any example of her work up to the end of the 1960s.

215

THE IMPRESSIONISTS

Important paintings by Seurat are almost unobtainable, though tiny preparatory sketches for his major compositions occasionally appear and can be worth around £50,000 ($120,000). The school is mainly represented at auction by the work of his followers, among whom Signac, a close friend and companion of his experimental years, is the most important. An exceptionally fine Paris view by Signac, 'Le Pont des Arts', painted in 1925, made £52,083 ($125,000) in New York in 1968, and good canvases can be expected to fetch prices in the £40,000–£50,000 ($96,000–$120,000) range. But in 1969 a masterpiece by Henri Edmond Cross, a less distinguished follower, set a new auction record for a *pointilliste* painting at £91,000 ($218,400). His 'Pointe de la Galère' of 1892 showed a vivid orange sunset over the Mediterranean with dusky blue pine trees and bushes in the foreground and sailing boats on the evening sea. Normally, a work by this artist can be expected to sell in the range of £20,000–£30,000 ($48,000–$72,000), while a fine early work by Luce, who takes perhaps third place among Seurat's followers, would sell for £10,000–£15,000 ($24,000–$36,000).

'Le Pont des Arts', a very fine *pointilliste* view of Paris by Signac, painted in 1925. It fetched £52,083 ($125,000) in New York in 1968.

CHAPTER 9

Twentieth-Century Paintings

At most periods in history a number of contemporary artists have been popular and highly paid for their work – though not necessarily those artists who have later come to be accepted as the great masters of the period. Modern art has always been expensive. This is particularly true today, and since much twentieth-century art is hard to understand, or relies simply on the viewer's emotional reaction, the degree of public appreciation accorded to individual artists – as measured in financial terms – is perhaps less selective than it has ever been. There are no longer any set criteria for judging an artist's competence; thus more artists than ever before succeed in making at least a temporary reputation as so many 'collectors' are trying to make a 'discovery'.

Today artists are, as always, professionals earning a living; but their relation to collectors, critics, and patrons is essentially different to what it was in the past. The public looks to the artist as a bridge-builder between everyday life and the world of the spirit and the emotions – or in less old-fashioned terms, the powerful and elemental forces that mould the subconscious. Most people can only manage to admit to this violent 'other' world through the medium of art, music, or literature.

Any means of expression adopted by the artist is acceptable to the public, for the human spirit, or subconscious, is so many-faceted that it may be expressed in an infinite number of ways. But this in its turn allows artists almost unlimited freedom to play on the gullibility of the public.

This is, of course, only one side of the coin. There are also more serious connoisseurs intent on following and understanding new developments in art than ever before, more museums determined to provide a full exposition of artistic developments in the twentieth century, and more private individuals who like to have good modern pictures on their walls – though preferring well-established names to those of the true *avant-garde*. The combination of these various strands of interest results in competitive sale-room bidding for modern pictures, and very high prices.

Modern art is a very general term and can be stretched or contracted at will. Modern pictures are not generally sold at auction until the artist is well established and widely appreciated. Therefore, pictures that pass at auction as modern paintings will often be found to have been painted in the last years of the nineteenth century and only occasionally include paintings by artists whose reputation has been made since the Second World War. Impressionist and modern pictures are today enthusiastically pursued and bought by rich private collectors throughout the world. Even the forerunners of Impressionism, such as the Barbizon painters, Corot, Boudin, Monticelli, and Delacroix, are sought after at auction for their early indication of the artistic revolution to come. Admittedly, a few artists of genuine originality, whose work is outside the main stream of development, may have gone out of fashion. All the same, seldom in the history of art has so long a period been looked on as 'modern' and highly valued for that reason.

This widespread popularity of modern art forms is a comparatively recent development. Towards the end of the last century, the art-loving public was suddenly faced with a revolutionary development that it found particularly difficult to accept. This was the Impressionists' break with tradition–the concept that colour, line, and form could be used more significantly to convey a mood or impression by interpreting rather than following nature. In our own century, the same public has been confronted with a development no less startling and just as difficult to understand –the move towards non-figurative art.

The traditions from which the Impressionists broke away had been in force since the Renaissance; it is not surprising that it took the public a long time to accept and assimilate a break with the approach to painting followed by artists for several hundred years. In the twentieth century, however, everything has been speeded up. The Impressionist experience taught people to look for experiment and innovation rather than to deride it. Improved communications make it easier for the public to keep in touch with what is going on in the world of art. It is fashionable to take an interest in contemporary painting and much hard work is put in by museums, dealers, and publishers to accommodate and encourage this interest.

By 1900 the Impressionists had achieved a certain financial respectability. Between the two world wars, interest in collecting their pictures remained virtually limited to connoisseurs and the intelligentsia; the wide popular appeal of the Impressionists is largely a post-war development.

The public has been much quicker to jump the hurdle presented by abstract painting, the possibilities of which have been explored in depth only since the war, though it has its roots much earlier in the century. In 1907, Picasso and Braque were making their first Cubist experiments. Acknowledging a heavy debt to Cézanne and his analytical breakdown of form and colour, the Cubists moved steadily further from nature. Meanwhile, Kandinsky in Germany was taking the first tentative steps towards complete abstractions. As Sir Herbert Read has said, 'Cubism . . . was always an interpretation of objective reality, of a given *motif*. The art that Kandinsky was to initiate was by contrast essentially and deliberately non-objective.'

By 1936 paintings of Picasso's Blue period were already extremely expensive, yet, according to a French authority, his new pictures were almost unsaleable. The Cubist movement had a devoted friend and promoter in the dealer Daniel-Henry Kahnweiler, who worked indefatigably in its cause from the inception of the movement to the beginning of the Second World War and still handles Picasso's works today. Even so, by 1939 the movement had achieved only modest financial recognition in sale-room terms. Kandinsky, too, was appreciated by only a narrow circle. This situation has now changed completely. In 1964 one of Kandinsky's paintings fetched £50,000 ($140,000) at auction. In 1968 Picasso's 'La Pointe de la Cité', a fine Cubist picture painted in 1912, was sold at auction for £125,000 ($300,000); Braque's superb 'L'Homme à la guitar' had made the same price at the Lefèvre sale in Paris in 1965.

It was suggested in the previous chapter that the break-up in the traditional patterns of society that followed the Second World War brought the public into closer sympathy with modern art. Almost all accepted standards and values have been challenged over the last twenty or thirty years; people have generally become more broad-minded and receptive to new ideas. The war certainly seems to have reinforced the trend towards abstraction among contemporary artists, as exemplified in particular by the work of the New York school and the school of Paris. Furthermore, the money that is poured into modern canvases year by year today far exceeds the amount spent annually on works by the great masters of the past. The Times-Sotheby Index of twentieth-century paintings, based on prices paid for the work of seven well-established artists, shows their values to have multiplied on average almost thirty times between 1951 and 1969. The artists chosen, all belonging to the school of Paris, were Picasso, Braque, Bonnard, Chagall, Vlaminck, Utrillo, and Rouault.

The high prices paid for strictly contemporary paintings probably help to support the value of influential earlier schools.

The idea of the dealer controlling the market in his artists' pictures, conceived by Durand-Ruel, has now become an accepted practice. In the early years, the system was adopted, with some financial success combined with periods of strain, by such great dealers as Vollard, Rosenberg, and Kahnweiler. Since the war, with the emergence of the Marlborough Fine Arts Company, with a list of painters on its books as long as your arm, the possible rewards of the living artist (and the dealer) have become very large. Moreover, the period of time in which a young artist may be able to achieve those rewards has become very short. Francis Bacon, whose importance began to be recognized around 1945, had achieved so wide a fame by 1968 that £60,000 ($144,000) was apparently being asked for one of his paintings in New York. Sculptures by Anthony Caro, first seen at the Kasmin Gallery in London in 1960, and then costing about £60–£65 ($168–$182), had touched the £10,000 ($24,000) mark by 1968. And this rate of increase is modest compared to the speed at which prices can rise in New York or Paris.

The present situation is in a sense a complete reversal of that which led to the apathy and derision that greeted the Impressionists' experiments a hundred years ago. The achievements of successive generations of painters show that an investment in the work of an *avant-garde* artist can bear fruit a thousandfold – if he can obtain an international reputation or a strong national following, with successive exhibitions of his work every two or three years and after ten or twenty years a 'retrospective' in a public gallery. There are a great many contemporary artists today who have achieved some success and recognition. When the 1960s have been relegated to a single chapter of art history, there will inevitably be a good number of drop-outs, but this does not deter enthusiastic connoisseurs and speculators from backing their fancies or their hunches.

There are, of course, many ways of collecting pictures, but the two main approaches can be combined in varying degrees. One is the approach of the connoisseur, who collects with knowledge and understanding; the other is to 'know what you like', to judge a picture by your own emotional reaction to it without bothering about its pedigree or particular place in art history. Both approaches are equally valid; in fact, many artists would argue that the second is preferable, because a collector with too intellectual an approach may tend to overlook the intrinsic emotional quality of a painting.

The intellectual hurdles posed by modern art – first, the retreat from photographic realism by the Impressionists, and second, the rejection of all figurative elements – proved too much for the

Kandinsky's 'Emphasized corners' of 1923 made £22,000 ($61,600) in 1964 in a sale of fifty paintings by the artist from the Guggenheim Foundation. The early abstract paintings proved the most expensive with the top price of £50,000 ($140,000) for his 'Improvisation' of 1914.

Kirchner's 'Zwei nakte Frauen im Walde' set a new auction record for this artist's work at £21,000 ($50,400) in 1969.

Chagall's 'Les fiancés', a large and
successful painting and a riot of
colours, sold for £73,500 ($176,400)
in 1968.

'know-what-you-like' type of collector during the first fifty years or so of the twentieth century. Collecting was left mainly to the intelligentsia; and with so limited a public, prices did not rise very high.

Whenever interesting contemporary collections of pictures, made in the first few decades of this century, come up for sale, they tend to have been formed by members of the professional classes, doctors, lawyers, writers, and so on, and have usually involved only a modest outlay.

As we have seen, the post-war years have brought a wide public over the hurdles erected by 'modern' art, and the know-what-you-like collectors have romped into the market. Abstract paintings have become popular and expensive, whether they are fully 'understood' by their purchaser or not, since collectors have been keen to demonstrate their sympathy with contemporary artistic innovations. Significantly, the signs of a returning interest in figurative painting among young artists in the 1960s was accompanied by a definite shift in collectors' interest towards more figurative works in the last few years of the decade. The enthusiasm of know-what-you-like collectors has forced prices up all along the line and at the same time has introduced an interesting new distinction between artists who are expensive because of their art-historical importance and those that are expensive simply because they are decorative. Thus, it would be mainly museums that would compete to secure a 'Composition in red, yellow, and blue' by Mondrian, with its unrelentingly geometrical rectangles and squares, in order to document his influence on post-war abstract art. A pair of lovers rising out of a bunch of flowers with a crescent moon, painted in Chagall's glowing and romantic colours, might prove even more expensive in the sale room, although in art-historical terms Chagall is a less important figure than Mondrian.

Most successful of all, of course, is a combination of the decorative with art-historical significance. This has been achieved most notably by Picasso. He is, however, something of a phenomenon, and an analysis of the gradual build-up of his tremendous reputation will one day make a fascinating study. Meanwhile, his roughest pen and ink sketch can be expected to fetch around £2,000 ($4,800) in the sale room. An early Blue period painting, 'Mère et enfant de profil', made £190,000 ($532,000) at Sotheby's in 1967, and a work of particular importance could be expected to fetch a good deal more.

During a long life – Picasso was born in 1881 – his style has altered radically many times. After his early Blue and Pink periods, he plunged into the experiments that led to Cubism. Out of this

Picasso's masterly Blue period 'Mère et enfant de profil', which was sold at Sotheby's for £190,000 ($532,000) in 1967, the highest auction price recorded for his work.

period has grown his individual and mature style, though he has never lost his penchant for experiment. His stature as an artist is now so great that museums must seek to document his stylistic development *per se*, whether or not a particular phase can be said to have influenced other artists. At the same time, 'a Picasso' is

222

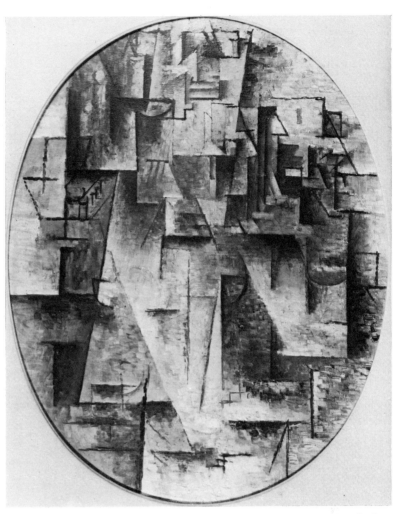

Picasso's 'Pointe de la Cité', a Cubist painting of 1912, was sold for £125,000 ($300,000) at Sotheby's in 1968.

generally easily recognizable and is a splendid status symbol to have hanging on the wall. This means that there is intense competition for his work in the sale room, whether it be for an important canvas which several museums and serious collectors feel they must have in order to document a particular turning-point in his career, or for a more modest work which many private collectors covet either for its artistic quality or for the glory of owning 'a Picasso'.

The importance of Picasso's work was already beginning to be recognized in the 1930s, but his deification is definitely a post-war phenomenon. The Times-Sotheby Index shows the average prices paid for his work multiplying more than thirty-seven times between 1951 and 1969. This indicates a slight slowing down in the 1960s, but prices in 1969 were roughly five times higher than in 1960.

The speed at which prices have increased since the early 1950s

Braque's 'Hommage à J.S. Bach' was painted in 1912 and fetched £115,000 ($266,400) in 1968 in the same sale at which £125,000 ($300,000) was paid for Picasso's 'Pointe de la Cité'.

is, however, particularly notable, for Picasso is a prolific artist and a large amount of his work remains in circulation. Paintings of his Blue or Pink periods are by far the most expensive, but in the 1960s the interest in Cubism increased tremendously, as is shown by the price of £125,000 ($300,000) paid for 'La Pointe de la Cité' in 1968.

While Picasso towers like a giant above all other artists of his time, at least in financial terms, two other artists, Braque and Matisse, share to some extent his great master status. Braque, together with Picasso, was a progenitor of the Cubist movement, but unlike Picasso he never quite abandoned this style. He used it mainly as a technique for giving more meaning and depth to the basically figurative style of painting which he adopted from about 1920 up to the time of his death in 1963. He has been described as 'an artist's artist' and today his work does not have the wide popular appeal of Picasso's though it is greatly sought after by serious collectors. Prices paid for his work have, however, steadily increased at more or less the same rate as those of his old companion. The Times-Sotheby Index shows the average value of

224

Braque's pictures that have come up for auction, multiplying twenty-two times between 1951 and 1969. This trend was reinforced in the 1960s, as Cubism began to break into the 'know-what-you-like' collector's field. In 1966, 'La Mandore', a painting dating from his important Early Cubist phase, was sold for £34,000 ($95,000) and in 1968, a rather more important work, 'Hommage à J. S. Bach', was sold for £115,000 ($266,400).

Matisse is a much easier artist to appreciate. He was a leader of the Fauve movement and never abandoned their vivid and exciting colours. His work always remained figurative. He himself wrote that he wished his art to be 'like a good armchair in which a man might rest from physical fatigue, in which he might find a little pleasure, luxury, and happiness'. And indeed the decorative quality of his work was rapidly appreciated and pursued by connoisseurs, though it was still not expensive in the 1930s. He achieved an early popularity, particularly in America and Russia, and was anyway not a prolific artist. Thus important examples of his work rarely come up for sale. No Matisse canvas of major importance has been auctioned since the war.

Matisse has undoubtedly shared in the dramatic rise in popularity of the Paris school in the post-war years. However, with no master works on the market, his most expensive picture at auction remains 'Intérieur au parquet gravé', a late attractive picture, sold for £38,000 ($106,400) in 1962. His remarkable Fauve 'Portrait of Derain', bought by the Tate Gallery for £7,035 ($19,698) in 1954, looks incredibly cheap by the standards of the late 1960s. Fauve paintings by Derain himself, a less important artist, have fetched as much as £60,000 ($144,000). The 1954 price of the Matisse was, however, a major advance on his pre-war levels, the portrait having been sold in 1928 for only £280 ($1,361).

Picasso, Braque, and Matisse are now established as the great masters of twentieth-century art, but their direct influence on present-day artistic developments is limited. Much more important as the precursors of post-war Abstract Expressionism are Kandinsky, Klee, and Mondrian. The blossoming interest in contemporary abstract art, the jump over that non-figurative hurdle by a wide public, has sent the prices of these artists spiralling upwards. Kandinsky, with his riot of colour, is perhaps the easiest to appreciate, and the £50,000 ($140,000) paid in 1964 for his 'Improvisation 1914' remains the highest price paid in the sale room for a work by any of these three artists. Klee's work began to be appreciated by the new collecting public in the 1960s, and since then his small canvases, pregnant with symbolic meaning, have shot up in price. A new record was set in 1968 when his 'Südische Garten' was sold for £36,000 ($86,400). Mondrian

TWENTIETH-
CENTURY PAINTINGS

Mondrian was not a prolific artist and important paintings by him are seldom seen at auction. This 'Large composition in red, blue, and yellow' made £21,400 ($60,000) in New York in 1966.

remains the most difficult of the three to appreciate, his strict geo-metrical patterns and clear colours appeal to a rather academic taste. There are, however, plenty of museums and serious collectors who would pay a very high price for a really important example of his work, but the £27,000 ($64,800) paid in 1969 for his 'Composition 1' (1920) is the highest price so far recorded for his work at auction.

These three artists opened up a new and important direction of artistic development and the financial value accorded to their canvases is a just recognition of their influence. Despite this, the prices fetched by their works is only just on a par with that of some of the early school of Paris artists, whose art-historical importance is less clearly defined. Bonnard, Derain, Chagall, Vlaminck, and Modigliani, whose work is easier to understand and more obviously decorative, all fetch the same sort of prices at auction as Kandinsky, Klee, and Mondrian.

The school of Paris is the best-represented twentieth-century school at auction, and the most popular. It is, indeed, remarkable how consistently and how rapidly prices for works by members of the school have risen in the post-war period, for the seven artists whose values have been analysed in the Times-Sotheby Index represent a wide variety of styles and backgrounds.

Only Picasso, Braque, and Bonnard fetched prices over £1,000 ($2,800) with any regularity in the early 1950s. In 1959, a Picasso went for £12,000 ($33,600), a very important Cubist Braque for the exceptionally high price of £36,000 ($100,800), and a sunlit Bonnard still life with a cat for £25,000 ($70,000). At that time these were the highest prices ever paid for works by these artists at auction. But by 1968 the highest auction prices for the three of them were, respectively, £190,000 ($532,000), £125,000 ($315,981), and £86,000 ($206,400).

Bonnard, though of lesser stature in art-historical terms than either Braque or Picasso, has kept pace with their upward trend in price. The work of all three artists was between twenty and forty times more expensive in 1969 than in 1951. The sunlit calm of Bonnard's paintings of family life – especially of the childish female figure at her toilet or in the bath – have an irresistible charm which makes him one of the most expensive of twentieth-century painters. It is his sensitive feeling for light and colour that are his greatest painterly qualities and it is this that makes his work so highly prized. His early Nabi pictures are generally less expensive at auction.

Chagall, whose work seldom fetched more than £300–£400 ($840–$1,120) in the early 1950s, is now almost as highly prized as Bonnard. His Russian love of colour and his lyrical mysticism make him a decorative painter *par excellence*. Although he fell under Cubist influence for a period – and painted at this time by far his finest works – he never abandoned figurative painting. The first of his pictures to fetch over £1,000 ($2,800) at auction was 'Midsummer Night's Dream' in 1955; in 1960 a flower piece made almost £12,000 ($33,600), and a year later a superb painting, 'Les amoureux', made a new record at the Parke-Bernet Galleries, at £27,679 ($77,500). But in 1968 £73,000 ($176,400) was paid for 'Les fiancés'. The Index shows the average value of his paintings as being fifty times higher in 1969 than in 1951.

Chagall was never closely connected with any school or movement and it is the sheer decorative appeal of his canvases that has given his work the most rapid financial appreciation among the seven Index artists. The same can be said of Utrillo, though the rise in the value of his work has been more modest. His simple, sometimes almost childish views, have a ready appeal and the

TWENTIETH-CENTURY PAINTINGS

clearly recognizable style is an advantage to purchasers who are in search of a status symbol. In the early 1950s the paintings of Utrillo and of Chagall fetched roughly the same prices at auction. Though Utrillo has now been outpaced by Chagall, the average price of his work is some sixteen times higher than it was then.

Vlaminck also started on a par with Chagall and Utrillo in the early 1950s; by 1969 he took second place in popularity among the three. He was a very prolific artist and it is the landscapes and flower pieces of his later period that are pursued by the majority of collectors – and there are plenty to satisfy the demand. Again, he has a highly individual and easily recognizable style, with thick paint laid on in sweeping brush strokes. Prices of his later landscapes had risen in value from £200–£300 ($560–$840) in 1950, to £10,000–£20,000 ($24,000–$48,000) by 1969. Paintings of his Fauve period are now easily the most sought after; £87,000 ($208,800) was paid for his particularly fine 'Le pont sur la Seine à Chatou' in 1969, when the average value of his work was thirty times higher than it was in 1951.

Out of the seven Index artists, Rouault's work has advanced least in price. His dark, heavy style, particularly in the later

Vlaminck's 'Le pont sur la Seine à Chatou', a rare Fauve work painted in about 1906, was sold for £87,000 ($208,800) in 1969.

religious pictures, is perhaps too sombre for it to find a ready market. Nevertheless, prices for his work soared from the hundreds to well into the thousands between 1951 and 1969, and on average were fourteen times higher. His work was rather uneven and the steady pattern of prices is broken on the rare occasions when something of real quality comes on the market. For instance, a distinguished and amusing watercolour, 'Clown à la rose', made the outstanding price of £36,000 ($88,110) in Paris in 1968. It was painted in 1908 on behalf of a small friend who wanted to give his father a painting for his birthday; Rouault painted the picture, but signed it with the child's name.

WHAT COSTS WHAT

Modern pictures and new money tend today to go together. Many of the 'old rich' are encumbered with stately homes, where modern pictures would seem out of place. But the new rich can arrange the décor of their homes as they think fit. Large colourful canvases can be mingled with primitive sculptures, tubular furnishings, fur rugs, and anything else that attracts their fancy. And as modern pictures are fashionable, many people feel they must have them. Thus modern pictures are generally expensive. However, it is not simply that prices are higher—very high prices can be paid for outstanding pictures of any period. It is the sheer number of good, bad, and indifferent modern pictures which flow through the sale room at prices between £5,000 ($12,000) and £10,000 ($24,000) that demonstrates the fashionable popularity of buying twentieth-century paintings.

It is one thing, however, to buy the work of a painter who has a wide international following and regular exhibitions, and quite another to buy the work of one who is only just emerging on the scene. It is in New York, in Paris, and London–but especially New York–that the greatest interest in and potential rewards for new artists lie. That there is usually an element of speculation in the collector's motivation must be accepted–the idea of getting in on a future 'famous painter' before the market has discovered him. The work of new artists is, however, normally handled by a dealer, who also fixes the prices on a fairly rough-and-ready basis, not yet having a clear idea of how marketable the artist's work will turn out to be.

The process of establishing a reputation can carry the value of an artist's work from an arbitrary figure chosen by his dealer– when he has been lucky enough to find one–to perhaps tens of thousands of pounds when the importance of his paintings is internationally accepted. The auction room tends only to see the later stages of this process. It has thus not been possible to cover here the schools which have sprung into prominence in the post-war years, though the work of many new artists has been quite regularly seen in the sale room since 1960.

This does not mean that their works cannot match the prices of those of earlier schools. The post-war years have seen for the first time the growth of an American school of painting whose importance and world-wide influence can equal any European counterpart. Pollock, Rothko, Motherwell, de Kooning, and others have achieved strong international reputations and their work can fetch up to £50,000 ($120,000) or £60,000 ($144,000). Equally, the major figures of the English school are now internationally known and sought after and the work of both Francis Bacon and Henry Moore can make these sort of prices; while among Parisian artists Dubuffet, de Stael, and Giacometti are now as well known and expensive as many of their predecessors. These comparative newcomers did not, however, fall within the scope of the Times-Sotheby Index.

The international reputations of artists of the pre-war European schools are now very solidly founded. This means that from a financial point of view the purchaser feels himself secure. A delighted appreciation of the artist's vision can be combined with the comfortable knowledge that the value of his work is much more likely to go up than down.

The logic of this is fairly simple. Year by year, the number of wealthy people is increasing, as is their total wealth. Thus the amount of money potentially available to spend on modern pictures is steadily increasing. At the same time, museums, by their purchases of modern art, are continually removing good paintings from the market. It is natural in this situation that the value of most accepted artists' work should continue to rise and that new artists should be 'discovered' in order to provide enough 'art' to go round.

There is a fairly well established pecking order among modern schools of painting; as good paintings of one school become scarce, those of another tend to become popular. This type of market in modern pictures is a post-war phenomenon. In the 1950s it was the work of the Impressionists that established the current pattern of collecting. By about 1960 their paintings were becoming very expensive and fine examples very scarce. Eyes began to turn to their followers, those who initiated the important developments of the school of Paris between about 1880 and 1915. It was the turn of artists such as Picasso, Braque, Matisse, Bonnard, Vuillard, and Chagall.

It is the auction record for artists of this period that has been

230

Klee's 'Südische Garten', painted in 1936 and measuring only 10½ by 12¼ inches, was sold for £36,000 ($86,400) in 1968. This is the highest auction price recorded for his work.

traced by the Times-Sotheby Index. Matisse and Vuillard have not, in fact, been included, but three rather more minor but representative figures, Vlaminck, Rouault, and Utrillo, were chosen to balance the greater masters. In terms of hard cash the early school of Paris artists still prove the most desirable at auction among twentieth-century painters.

The early school of Paris, however, became an extremely expensive collecting field in the second half of the 1960s and other schools of painting began to attract attention. A new interest in German Expressionism had been set in motion by a major exhibition at the Museum of Modern Art in New York in 1958. Dealers began to search out those collectors who had bought Expressionist works in the early days, but it was not until the mid 1960s that paintings of this school began to come through the sale room in considerable numbers.

By 1969, German Expressionist paintings had reached the sort of price levels that were common for early school of Paris paintings at the beginning of the 1960s. As has been mentioned already, Kandinsky and Klee have reached as much as £50,000 ($140,000) and £36,000 ($86,400) respectively at auction and a price between £50,000 ($120,000) and £100,000 ($240,000) would come as no surprise if a particularly rare and important work by either artist appeared in the sale room. In 1969 a good painting by Kirchner, 'Zwei nakte Frauen im Walde' made £21,000 ($50,400) and Emile

Nolde's 'Tropenglut' made £18,750 ($45,000). A double-sided portrait in harsh and vivid colours by Jawlensky made £25,500 ($61,200) at the end of 1968. These are all top auction prices for these artists, but less notable works were coming regularly through the sale room in 1969 at prices around £5,000–£10,000 ($12,000–$24,000).

At the end of the 1960s, the artists of the Surrealist school of the 1920s and 1930s seemed set to repeat this pattern. Their sudden rise in popularity in 1968–69 at auction was probably a reflection of the returning interest in figurative painting; for one of the fascinations of Surrealism lies in the use of figurative elements introduced out of context. Several artists, such as Magritte and Dali, had previously been poorly represented at auction and the more abstractly inclined members of the group, such as Max Ernst, Joan Miró, and Yves Tanguy, had been in the ascendant. Max Ernst is the most consistently represented in the sale room and one of his undoubted masterpieces, 'Arbres solitaires et arbres conjugaux', made £11,000 ($30,800) in 1963. A fine work by Yves Tanguy, 'Je vous attend', made £13,200 ($36,960) in 1966, but his work is rarely on the market and very sought after. In 1969, however, a good, though not exceptional, work by Ernst, 'Le poulpe', went for £18,000 ($43,200), and the more figuratively inclined exponents of the school began to fetch very high prices. In December 1968, a painting by Magritte had made a new auction record at £6,500 ($16,000) in Paris, but in July 1969 'L'avenir' (1934)

'Arbres solitaires et arbres conjugaux' by Max Ernst may by counted among his most brilliant paintings, but it fetched only £11,000 ($30,800) in 1963.

was sold at Sotheby's for £19,000 ($45,600). Similarly, Salvador Dali's 'Cannibal nostalgia' caused a surprise in the London market when, in December 1968, it was sold at Christie's for £6,825 ($16,380). Three months later, his admittedly finer painting 'Ossification matinale du Cyprès', made £34,646 ($83,046) in Paris. At the end of 1969, auctions of modern pictures were notably better stocked with the work of Surrealist artists.

There are, of course, other twentieth-century schools of painting ready to be discovered, or re-discovered. The Italian Futurist movement, for instance, has had little share of the limelight for several years. Few paintings of this school are seen in the sale room. No painting by de Chirico has so far fetched more than £11,250 ($27,000) at auction, and the top price recorded for Giacomo Balla is £7,500 ($21,000). The financial interest accorded to the various schools of the twentieth century, as for certain individual artists, will no doubt continue to shift from year to year.

'Mercurio passa davanti al sole visto con cannochiale', painted in 1914 by the Futurist artist, Giacomo Balla. His work is rarely seen in the sale room and £7,500 ($21,000) which was paid for this picture is the top price so far paid for his work at auction.

In 1969, however, in Paris, Salvador Dali's 'Ossification matinale du Cyprès' made £34,646 ($83,046), the highest price ever recorded for any Surrealist painting at auction.

233

TWENTIETH-CENTURY PAINTINGS

The continuing pre-eminence of the artists who shared in the development of the school of Paris in the early years of this century is, however, well assured, as can be seen from the prices that were recorded in the late 1960s for the work of the artists considered by the Times-Sotheby Index.

Picasso's signature alone is enough to raise the value of even his most modest drawing to four figures. In general, it is his early paintings, from the Blue and Pink periods of the early 1900s and the Cubist pictures, that command the highest auction prices. This was clearly shown when in 1967 his superb Blue period painting, 'Mère et enfant', fetched £190,000 ($456,000), and in the following year when his Pink period 'Paysage de Gosol' made £180,000 ($432,000) and his Cubist work, 'Pointe de la Cité', went for £125,000 ($300,000). These were highly important paintings of his most admired periods and naturally they fetched exceptional prices. The amounts paid for two more modest works give an idea of the value of his less important pictures. A small painting, measuring only $13 \times 7\frac{3}{4}$ inches, 'Verre, as de trêfle et poire coupée', was sold for £21,000 ($50,400) at Sotheby's in July 1969. It dated from 1914, the period when he was veering away from Cubism, but still using its formal and simplified structures, though with more freedom and a brighter palette than when the movement started. A larger work of this period would have fetched a far higher price.

A large picture painted by Picasso in 1964, 'Nu couché', measuring $25\frac{1}{4}$ by $39\frac{1}{2}$ inches. This was sold in 1968 again for £21,000 ($50,400).

'Le canal Saint-Martin', dating
from Braque's short Fauve period,
made £54,000 ($131,040) in 1968. It
was painted in 1906 and measured
$19\frac{3}{4}$ by 24 inches.

'Rue de Mont-Cenis avec la maison
de Berlioz', a White period painting
by Utrillo (1914), was sold for
£31,400 ($64,029) at the Galerie
Motte in Geneva in 1969. This is
the highest price that has been
paid for Utrillo's work at auction.

'Verre, as de trèfle, et poire coupée' by Picasso (*right*) a composition of 1914 in *papier collé*, charcoal, and gouache. Measuring only 13 by 7¾ inches, it fetched £21,000 ($50,400) in 1969.

'Papier collé' by Braque, sold for £17,000 ($40,800) – a collage with charcoal, dating from 1912 and measuring 24 by 18½ inches.

A much bigger picture (25¼ × 39½ ins), though not so large as to present a hanging problem, and dating from 1964, a period which is not generally so popular among collectors, fetched the same price in 1968 at Sotheby's. This was 'Nu couché', a picture of a rather overweight nude on a bed with a blue background.

The value of Braque's paintings is always a little below that of comparable works by Picasso. His important Cubist painting, 'Hommage à J.S. Bach', dating from 1912, was sold for £115,000 ($276,000) in 1968 in a sale which also included Picasso's 'Pointe de la Cité' at £125,000 ($300,000). This again was a painting of major importance and it commanded an exceptional price. A few years earlier, Braque had experimented with the new approach of the Fauve movement, working simply from nature in brilliant colours. A good Fauve work of his, 'Le Canal Saint Martin', was sold at Christie's in 1968 for £54,600 ($131,040). A modest collage with charcoal, 'Papier collé', of 1912, comparable perhaps in quality with Picasso's small 'Verre', was sold for £17,000 ($40,800) in a sale in the same year. Again, Braque's work proved slightly less expensive than that of Picasso.

Bonnard's 'La glace haute ou la glace longue' (*left*) dating from about 1914, made £55,357 ($155,000) in 1965. It measured 49 by 32½ inches, and distilled all the qualities for which Bonnard's painting is loved. This remained a record auction price for his work for only three years; in 1968 his 'Nu debout dans un intérieur', a work of similar quality, made £86,000 ($206,400).

A more modest work (*right*) by Bonnard, 'Jeune fille en robe verte', painted in 1910 and measuring 23¼ by 15¼ inches. It was sold for £13,650 ($32,760) in 1968.

These are the two most important artists whose work was considered for the Index. However, the value of the more notable paintings of Bonnard and Chagall comes close to theirs. Bonnard's superb 'Nu debout dans un intérieur', distilling the essence of what is sought after and loved in his work, was sold for £86,000 ($206,400) in 1968. Even a modest portrait, 'Jeune fille en robe verte', (23¼ × 15¼ ins) made £13,650 ($32,760) at Christie's in the same year. Similarly, Chagall's 'Les fiancés' was sold for £73,500 ($176,400), and an entertaining and colourful village

237

'La mariée et l'âne' by Chagall (*above*), made £7,500 ($18,000) in 1969. It was painted in about 1953 and measured only 10½ by 8¼ inches.

scene, 'Scène de village avec pendule'–a smaller but less outstanding work–made £21,875 ($52,500). A tiny and less successful painting, 'La mariée et l'âne', measuring only $10\frac{1}{2} \times 8\frac{1}{4}$ inches, was sold in 1969 for £7,500 ($18,000).

The work of Vlaminck, Rouault, and Utrillo passes through the sale room fairly frequently, though paintings by them that are of real quality are rare. All three artists have highly individual styles which make their work easily recognizable, and this gives them a special value for those who wish to be seen to have expensive pictures on their walls.

One very remarkable Fauve canvas by Vlaminck, 'Le pont sur la Seine à Chatou', was sold in 1969 for £87,000 ($208,800). This was, however, a great painting; the artist's work is not normally rated so highly. Apart from this, no single canvas by Vlaminck has yet fetched more than £40,000 ($96,000) at auction. Most of his paintings that flow through the international sale rooms are the landscapes that he painted in the 1920s and 1930s, with strong, sweeping brush strokes. One exceptionally fine early example, 'Les toits' of 1912, was sold in New York for £26,250 ($63,000) in 1968. A modest example, 'La récolte', a lightly sketched harvest-field with a windmill, made £8,333 ($20,000) a year later.

238

'Scène de village avec pendule'
by Chagall (*left*), painted about
1952 and measuring 25¼ by 21
inches–an attractive work
which fetched £21,875 ($52,500)
in 1968.

A minor but typical Vlaminck
landscape, 'La récolte' (21½ by
25½ inches) (*right*) made £8,333
($20,000) in 1969.

Vlaminck's colourful view, 'Les
toits' of 1912, was sold in
New York in 1968 for £26,250
($63,000).

TWENTIETH-CENTURY PAINTINGS

A typical later work by Utrillo, 'Église de Provence', of 1925, was sold at Sotheby's for £15,000 ($36,000) in 1969.

A large early watercolour by Georges Rouault, 'Clown à la rose', made £36,000 ($87,333) in Paris in 1968. It was painted in 1902 and measures 39½ by 25½ inches.

When it comes to Utrillo's work, it is the paintings of his White period that are particularly sought after. So far, the highest auction price recorded for a work of this period is £31,400 ($64,029), paid at the Gallerie Motte in Geneva for his 'Rue de Mont-Cenis avec la maison de Berlioz', painted in 1914. A more normal price for an attractive though not outstanding work was the £15,000 ($36,000) paid at Sotheby's for his 'Église de Provence', of around 1925.

The dark passions that take shape on Rouault's canvases have perhaps more in common with the German Expressionists than with the school of Paris. A large early watercolour, a colourful and unusual example of his work, made £36,000 ($86,400) in Paris in 1968, but again a more normal price is the £15,000 ($36,000) paid at Sotheby's in the same year for his 'Reine de cirque', an attractive though not outstanding work.

A fairly typical later work by Rouault, 'Reine de cirque', brought £15,000 ($36,000) at Sotheby's in 1968. It was painted in about 1952 and measures 23¼ by 16¼ inches.

The Times-Sotheby Index

During the 1960s it became increasingly obvious that the prices paid for works of art were rising very rapidly. On the occasions when a painting or *objet d'art* was sold twice at auction within a matter of a few years, the price was often two or three times higher on the second occasion. But no means existed of measuring the extent to which prices were rising or had risen in the art market.

It was in order to fill this gap that *The Times* newspaper and Sotheby and Company, the London auctioneers, decided to combine forces in 1967 to compile an index by which the rise in art prices could be measured in much the same way as *The Financial Times* index or the Dow Jones Average measure changing price levels in the stock market. The aim was to deduce the extent to which prices had changed, on average, in various different fields of the art market.

A stock market index may combine an oil share which has changed modestly in price and a gold-mining share which has doubled or tripled in value – and others which have changed in varying degrees – and thus arrives at an average measure of how prices generally have moved. Similarly, the Times-Sotheby art index has taken into account some paintings which have multiplied tremendously in value and others which have changed to only a modest extent, and the final result is an average measure of how art prices have changed over the years.

It was decided that the Index should cover twelve different fields including, in addition to pictures, books and other works of art. The index for each field would be calculated annually, using prices recorded at auction in all the world's major sale rooms. The results in each field were to be published in *The Times* once a year, together with an analysis of market trends. The first index covering the rise in value of Impressionist paintings was published in November 1967, and since then the Index results have been published monthly. The twelve fields covered by the Index are: *Impressionist paintings, Old Master prints, English silver, Old and Modern books, English glass, Old Master pictures, Twentieth-*

century paintings, French furniture, English pictures of the eighteenth and nineteenth centuries, Oriental ceramics, Old Master drawings, English porcelain.

A special article comparing the record of all twelve fields is also published at the end of each sale-room season.

Inevitably, the computation of a price index posed slightly different problems in each field. Thus, although the method of compilation is essentially the same in all fields, there are slight variations in the approach adopted in each case.

Method of computation and degree of accuracy
The construction of an art-price index presents many special problems which do not arise with a share index. In the first place, many works of art that appear on the market are unique and a basis must be established for deciding when prices are comparable and when they are not. In the second place, many of the factors which contribute to an auction price rely on subjective judgements, the quality of a painting, for instance, or the extent to which its effect is marred by condition. The size of a painting can also affect its price, though not in so straightforward a way that the dimensions can be directly linked to the value.

Subjective judgements had, thus, to be built into the method of compiling the Index. Since, in the nature of things, one person's feelings about a painting will vary from those of another, the Index cannot pretend to any precise degree of accuracy. It measures orders of magnitude rather than small variations.

The method of compilation is best described by taking a specific example. The Impressionist index, for instance, is based on the work of six artists: Monet, Renoir, Sisley, Pissarro, Fantin-Latour, and Boudin. The aim was to choose a number of artists representative of the movement as a whole, and whose paintings appeared regularly enough in the sale room to provide a basis for computation. Thus Monet and Renoir, two of the greatest figures of the movement, were chosen, together with the great landscape artists Pissarro and Sisley, and two lesser figures, Fantin-Latour and Boudin, part forerunners and part companions of the Impressionists. The aim was to index the movement in price for the works of each artist seperately and then to combine them into an over-all index.

There remained the problem of the wide variation in quality, size, period, etc. of each picture sold. However, it seemed reasonable to suppose that for any individual picture these characteristics did not change with time; a good picture will always be a good picture, a poor one always a poor one, a large one always large, and so on. It should thus be possible to divide the complete *œuvre* of an artist into groups of paintings of equal 'intrinsic' value determined by these characteristics. Two paintings would be assigned to the same group if their size, period, quality, etc. implied that they would be likely to fetch roughly the same price at auction.

Records were collected of all the paintings by Renoir sold at auction between 1950 and 1967 and these records were duly divided into groups of roughly equal 'intrinsic' value. This is the point at which a subjective judgement is incorporated in the Index calculations. The paintings were divided into groups on the basis of the judgement of an expert, namely, the Director of Sotheby's Impressionist department. It was assumed that a comparison of the prices paid in different years for two pictures from the same group would provide a measure of the rise in price of Renoir's work between the two dates of sale.

One further important assumption had to be made—that while the value of Renoir's work was changing, the relative value of one picture compared to another remained constant. In other words, if one picture had cost twice as much as another in 1950, it would cost twice as much as the other if both paintings came up for sale at any other date. This assumption implies that among the groups of pictures of equal 'intrinsic' value, the prices paid for pictures in one group would remain in a constant proportion to those paid for pictures in another.

Once this simplifying assumption has been made and the ratio between the value of paintings belonging to one group and those belonging to each of the others has been established, the price of any painting by Renoir could be compared with the price of any other. Suppose the pictures in group A were four times as valuable as those in group B, then if a picture in group B were sold in one year, its price would be multiplied by four and compared with that of a picture in group A sold in another year, in order to obtain a measure of how prices had risen between the two years.

This is the basic principle on which the Index calculations are based. In practice, records of all the paintings sold at auction between 1950 and 1967 that were illustrated in their respective sale catalogues were gathered together. They were then divided into groups by Sotheby's Impressionist expert and each group was allotted a theoretical 1967 price—the expert's estimate of what any painting from the group could be expected to fetch at auction in 1967. The ratio between the 'intrinsic' value of one group and that of another was calculated on the basis of these 1967 prices. If the pictures in group A seemed likely to fetch around £20,000 ($56,000) in 1967, and those in group B about £5,000

($14,000), it was assumed that the pictures in group A had been worth four times those in group B throughout the period.

One group was then selected as the basis for computation. The price of every picture that had been sold was scaled either up or down to an equivalent price for this group, using the ratios already established on the basis of 1967 prices. For each calendar year the equivalent prices for every painting sold were averaged. The change in this average value from year to year was taken as the measure of the change in value of Renoir's work. In mathematical terms this may be expressed as follows:

$$I_t = \sum_i P_{it}\, r_i\, q_{it} \times 100 / P_{n_0} \sum_i q_{it}$$

where I_t = index number in year t.

P_{it} = average price of picture in group i in year t.

q_{it} = number of pictures in group i in year t.

r_i = ratio (1967 price of group n)/(1967 price group i).

P_{n_0} = average price of group n in 1950–52.

(Unweighted mean for 1950, 1951, and 1952 of the average 'equivalent group n price' of all the pictures sold in each year).

Using this formula, an annual index of the value of Renoir's work could be calculated between the base year 1950–52 and 1967. Using exactly the same method, price indices were established for the other five artists. The over-all Impressionist index for any single year was obtained by taking an arithmetical average of the index values for each of the six artists. The Index is brought up to date each year by taking the paintings by each artist sold at auction, slotting them into their appropriate groups, and calculating the index as for earlier years.

It is impossible to devise an entirely satisfactory method of measuring the change in art prices and this method, like any other, has some obvious faults. The assumption that the value of one example of an artist's work remains a constant fraction or multiple of the value of any other is a major simplification. In practice, one type of painting or period may suddenly become more popular, while another goes out of fashion. Further, it appears to be a fairly general rule that the more a painting costs in absolute terms, the more slowly it climbs proportionately in price.

In a year when a large number of paintings come on the market representing a wide spectrum of quality, the Index is a fairly faithful reflection of changing price levels. In a year when the artist is sparsely represented at auction, one very expensive or very cheap picture can affect the level of the Index to an unrealistic extent.

Paintings of very exceptional quality, on the rare occasions when they come on the market, are not used in the Index calculations. There is no 'right price' for a masterpiece and no sensible basis can be evolved for comparing the figure it reaches at auction with the price of any other work.

THE COMPOSITION OF THE INDEX

Old Master pictures

The works of older artists come on the market much less frequently than those of the Impressionist or twentieth-century schools. There is thus not enough material available to calculate a price index for individual artists. The Old Master index is, therefore, based on various schools or types of painting. In selecting the artists whose work should be grouped together to complete an index the overriding consideration was whether their work had enough in common to make it probable that their popularity would fluctuate in parallel. In preparing each index the work of each school was treated in the same way as the work of a single artist in calculating the Impressionist index. It was important that those paintings which were grouped together as of equal 'intrinsic' value in 1967 should remain of roughly equivalent value as time went by. When the Index was originally published in 1968, seventeen different types of painting were included. The work involved in keeping all seventeen indices up to date was found to be too extensive and for later publications only seven selected types of painting were used, namely, Italian primitives, Northern primitives, flower pictures, Dutch landscapes, historical portraits, Seicento, and the Italian eighteenth-century vedutisti. The full list of schools of painting originally used in calculating the Old Master painting index is given below, together with examples of artists whose work is included in the index.

Northern primitives: Ambrosius Benson, Adriaen Isenbrandt, Herri met de Bles, Master of the Magdalen Legend, Joachim Patenier.

Brueghel School: Jan Brueghel the Elder and Younger, Pieter Brueghel the Younger, Paul Bril, Joos de Momper.

Dutch and Flemish flower pictures: Jan Brueghel the Elder, Balthasar van der Ast, Ambrosius Bosschaert, Roelandt Savery, Simon Verelst, Abraham Mignon, Jean-Baptiste Monnoyer, Pieter Casteels, Willem van Aelst, Daniel Seghers.

Dutch and Flemish still-lifes: Abraham van Beyeren, Jan Davidsz. de Heem, Cornelis de Heem, Willem Claesz Heda, Pieter Claesz, Frans Snyders, Melchoir d'Hondecoeter, Jan Weenix, Jan van Os.

Dutch landscapes: Jan van Goyen, Jacob van Ruisdael, Salomon van Ruysdael, Aert van der Neer, Philips Wouwermans.

Dutch marine pictures: Willem van der Velde, Abraham Storck, Abraham Willaerts, Jan van Goyen.

Dutch genre: Gabriel Metsu, Nicolaes Maes, Frans van Mieris, Jacob Ochtervelt, Gerard Dou.

Dutch peasant scenes: Adriaen van Ostade, Isaac van Ostade, David Teniers, Jan Steen, Adriaen Brouwer.

Dutch architectural painters: Pieter Saenredam, Gerrit Berckheyde, Emanuel de Witte, Jan van der Heyden.

Historical portraits: Antonio Moro, Frans Pourbus, Daniel Mytens, Simon Verelst.

Italian primitives: Sano di Pietro, Followers of Giotto, Lorenzo di Niccolo Gerini, Giovanni del Biondo, Bernardo Daddi, Jacopo del Casentino, Lorenzo Monaco.

Early renaissance: Botticelli and workshop, Filippino Lippi, Lorenzo Costa, Pesellino, Bartolommeo Montagna, Lorenzo Mazzolino.

Late renaissance: Vincenzo Catena, Garofolo, Giorgio Vasari, Locovico Lana, Paris Bordone, Marco Basaiti.

Seicento: Salvator Rosa, Guido Reni, Pietro da Cortona, Francesco Solimena, Ippolito Scarsellino, Guercino, Orazio Gentileschi.

Italian eighteenth-century vedutisti: Antonio Canaletto, Francesco Guardi, Bernardo Bellotto, Michele Marieschi, Antonio Joli, Giovanni Francesco Panini, Paolo Zuccarelli.

French eighteenth-century masters: Nicolas Lancret, Francois Boucher, Jean Honoré Fragonard, Jean-Baptiste-Joseph Pater.

French eighteenth-century view painters: Hubert Robert, Claude-Joseph Vernet, Lacroix de Marseille.

Old Master drawings

As in the case of Old Master pictures, the index for Old Master drawings is based on schools rather than on individual artists. Just as the Dutch schools are particularly well represented in the Old Master pictures index, since they play so important a part in present-day sale-room turnover, the Italian schools are concentrated on for drawings, since they provide a large share of most sales of Old Master drawings. Five different types of drawing were indexed separately:

Italian sixteenth century: Luca Cambiaso, Francesco Parmigianino, Agostino, Lodovico and Annibale Carracci, Polidoro da Caravaggio, Taddeo and Federico Zuccaro.

Italian seventeenth century: Guercino, Giovanni Benedetto

Castiglione, Salvator Rosa, Pietro da Cortona, Stefano della Bella, Carlo Maraita.
Venetian eighteenth century: Giovanni Battista Tiepolo, Domenico Tiepolo, Marco Ricci, Francesco and Giacomo Guardi, Canaletto.
Dutch and Flemish sixteenth and seventeenth century: Willem van de Velde the Younger, Jan van Goyen, Paul Bril, Jan Brueghel the Elder, Lambert Doomer, Jacob de Gheyn, Hans Bol, Abraham Blomaert, Albert Cuyp, Pieter Molyn, Allart van Everdingen, B. Breenbergh, C. van Poelenbergh.
French eighteenth century: Antoine Watteau, François Boucher, Jean-Honoré Fragonard, Nicolas Lancret, Hubert Robert, Moreau le Jeune, Moreau l'Ainé, H. D. and J. G. van Blarenberghe, Gabriel de Saint-Aubin.

English pictures of the eighteenth and nineteenth centuries
The index for English pictures is based on six different types of painting and not on the work of individual artists. This again reflects the limited number of paintings that come on the market by any one artist. The list of schools and examples of the artists included are:
English portraits: Gainsborough, Hoppner, Lawrence, Reynolds, Romney.
English sporting pictures: J. F. Herring, senior, Ben Marshall, James Pollard, John Ferneley, senior, Henry Alken, senior, George Stubbs.
English marine pictures: William Anderson. Charles Brooking, Thomas Luny, Peter Monamy, Dominic Serres, J. T. Serres.
Pre-Raphaelite paintings: Ford Madox Brown, Holman Hunt, Millais, Rossetti.
Victoriana: Alma-Tadema, Etty, Frith, Landseer, Edward Ladell, Lord Leighton, J. F. Lewis, William Shayer, Tissot.
English watercolour landscapes: Cotman, A. Cozens, J. R. Cozens, Copley Fielding, Girtin, Edward Lear, Samuel Palmer, Rowlandson, Sandby, Francis Towne, Varley.

Old Master prints
This index is based on original prints made by five artists and two other very distinct 'types' of print. The artists whose graphic work is considered separately are Dürer, Rembrandt, Canaletto, Piranesi, and Goya. In addition, indices are calculated for prints published by Hieronymus Cock after the drawings of Pieter Brueghel the Elder, and for fifteenth-century German, or Gothic, prints. The method of computation of these two indices is identical to that described for the work of an individual artist, except that

248

each group of prints of equal 'intrinsic' value may contain the work of several different artists or engravers.

Impressionist paintings
The index is based on oil-paintings by six artists, Monet, Renoir, Pissarro, Sisley, Boudin, and Fantin-Latour. Manet and the great Post-Impressionists, Cézanne, Van Gogh, Gauguin, and Seurat could not be included because their work is not well enough represented at auction. Degas was also omitted, since he is usually represented in the sale room by pastels and drawings.

Twentieth-century paintings
The index is based on the work of seven artists: Picasso, Braque, Bonnard, Chagall, Vlaminck, Rouault, and Utrillo. It is in the main based on oil-paintings, though occasionally important works in mixed mediums are taken into account. The choice of artists to use in the calculation of this index was limited to those whose work had been fairly consistently represented at auction from 1950 onwards. In the early years, the German Expressionists were hardly seen in the sale room and the important post-war schools of New York, Paris, and London only began to be seen regularly in the sale room in the 1960s.

The following charts show the course of the over-all price indices for each of the six fields covered by the Times-Sotheby Index, together with the price indices for the individual artists or schools from which the over-all indices are built up. They are drawn on a semi-logarithmic scale; this means that the same percentage increase in price from one year to another is shown by the same jump on the graph, whatever the absolute value of an index. For example, if the index for Picasso's paintings rises from 1,500 to 2,000 while the index for historical portraits rises from 150 to 200, the changes in price as measured on the vertical axis of the graphs are identical because the percentage increase in price is the same in each case. If an ordinary arithmetic scale were to be used, the impression would be given visually that Picasso's paintings had risen in value far more than historical portraits.

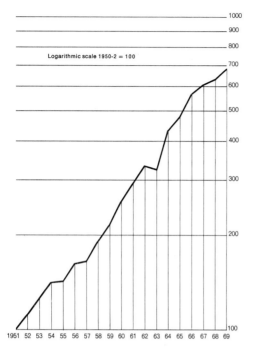

OLD MASTER PAINTINGS over-all
  index: up 7 times log scale: 1950–52
  =100

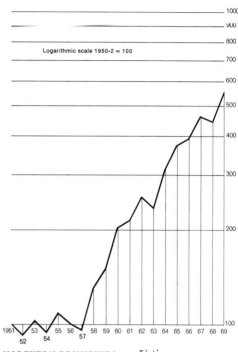

NORTHERN PRIMITIVES: up 5½ times

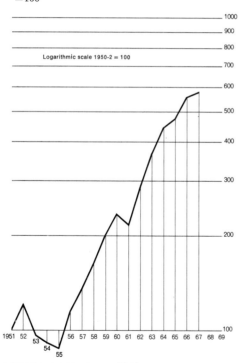

BRUEGHEL SCHOOL: up 5½ times
  (calculated up to 1967 only)

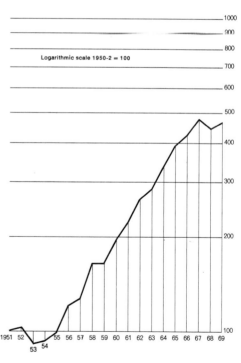

DUTCH AND FLEMISH FLOWER
  PICTURES: up 4½ times

250

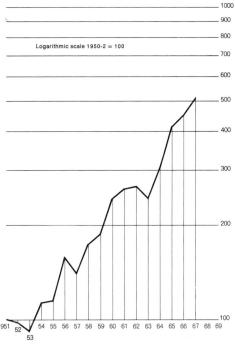

Logarithmic scale 1950-2 = 100

DUTCH AND FLEMISH STILL-LIFES: up
5 times (calculated up to 1967 only)

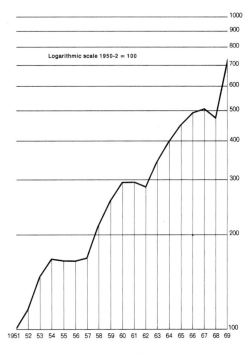

Logarithmic scale 1950-2 = 100

DUTCH LANDSCAPES: up 7 times

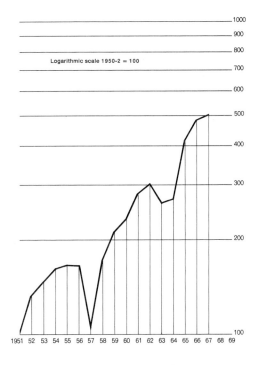

Logarithmic scale 1950-2 = 100

DUTCH MARINE PICTURES: up 5 times
(calculated up to 1967 only)

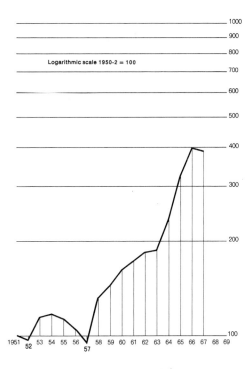

Logarithmic scale 1950-2 = 100

DUTCH GENRE PAINTINGS: up 4 times
(calculated up to 1967 only)

251

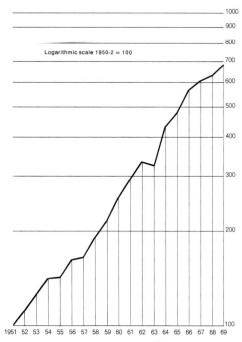

OLD MASTER PAINTINGS over-all
index: up 7 times log scale: 1950–52
=100

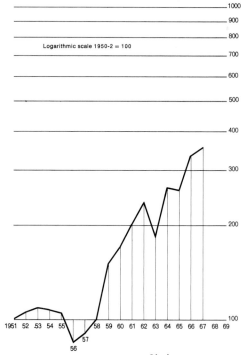

DUTCH PEASANT SCENES: up $3\frac{1}{2}$ times
(calculated up to 1967 only)

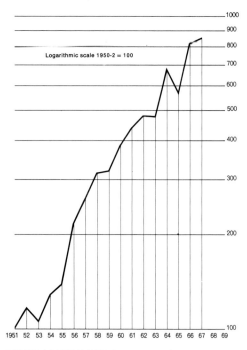

DUTCH ARCHITECTURAL PAINTINGS:
up $8\frac{1}{2}$ times (calculated up to 1967
only)

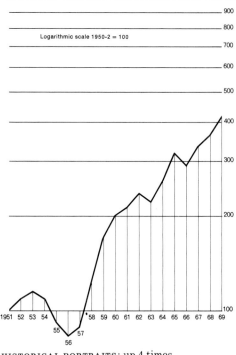

HISTORICAL PORTRAITS: up 4 times

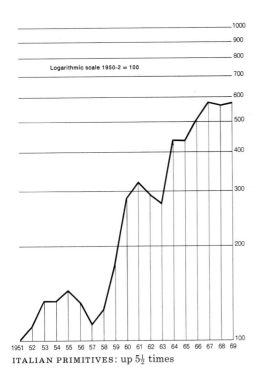

ITALIAN PRIMITIVES: up 5½ times

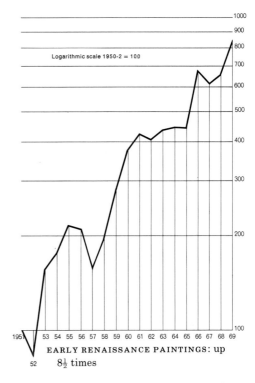

EARLY RENAISSANCE PAINTINGS: up 8½ times

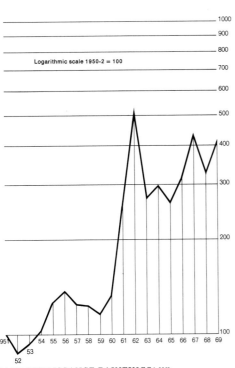

LATE RENAISSANCE PAINTINGS: up 4 times

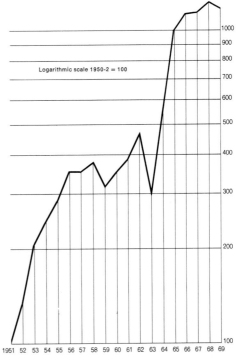

SEICENTO PAINTINGS: up 11½ times

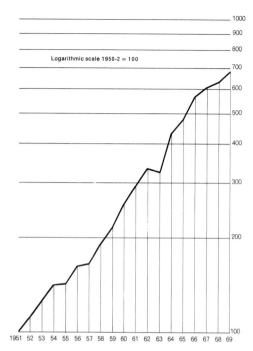

OLD MASTER PAINTINGS over-all
   index: up 7 times log scale: 1950–52
   =100

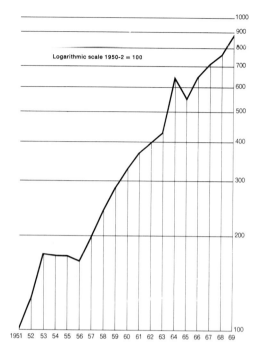

ITALIAN EIGHTEENTH-CENTURY
   VEDUTISTI: up $8\frac{1}{2}$ times

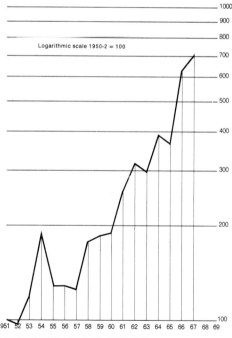

FRENCH EIGHTEENTH-CENTURY
   MASTERS: up 7 times (calculated up
   to 1967 only)

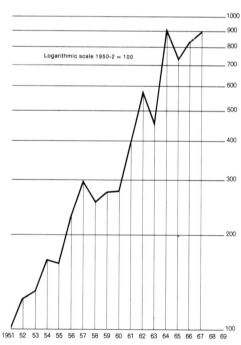

FRENCH EIGHTEENTH-CENTURY VIEW
   PAINTERS: up 9 times (calculated up
   to 1967 only)

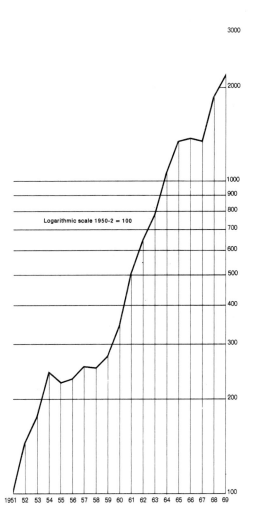

5000

4000

3000

2000

Logarithmic scale 1950-2 = 100

1000
900
800
700

600

500

400

300

200

100

1951 52 53 54 55 56 57 58 59 60 61 62 63 64 65 66 67 68 69

5000

4000

3000

2000

Logarithmic scale 1950-2 = 100

1000
900
800
700

600

500

400

300

200

100

1951 52 53 54 55 56 57 58 59 60 61 62 63 64 65 66 67 68 69

OLD MASTER DRAWINGS over-all
  index: up 22 times

ITALIAN SIXTEENTH-CENTURY
  DRAWINGS: up $30\frac{1}{2}$ times

255

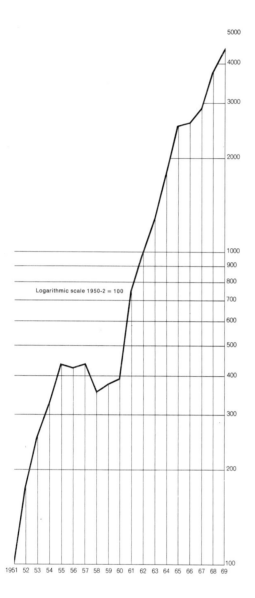

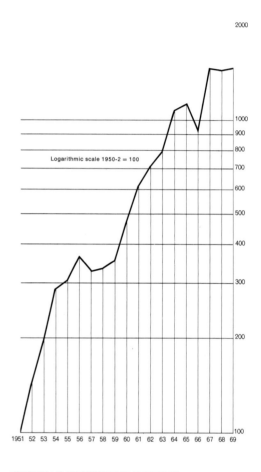

ITALIAN SEVENTEENTH-CENTURY
DRAWINGS: up 45 times

VENETIAN EIGHTEENTH-CENTURY
DRAWINGS: up $14\frac{1}{2}$ times

256

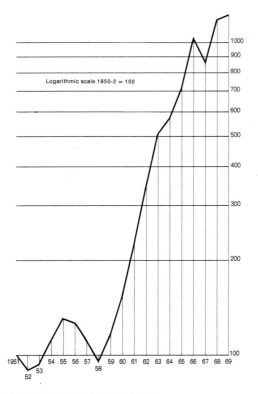

Logarithmic scale 1950-2 = 100

SIXTEENTH AND SEVENTEENTH-
CENTURY DUTCH AND FLEMISH
LANDSCAPE DRAWINGS: up 12 times

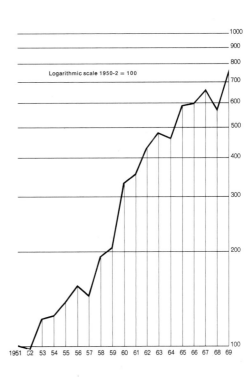

Logarithmic scale 1950-2 = 100

FRENCH EIGHTEENTH-CENTURY
DRAWINGS: up $7\frac{1}{2}$ times

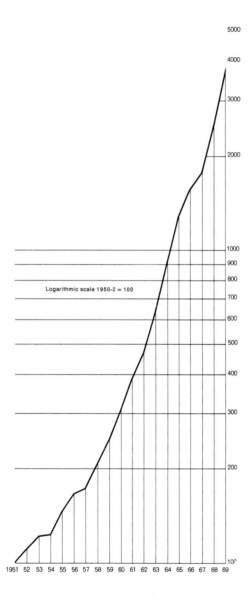

OLD MASTER PRINTS over-all index:
up 38 times

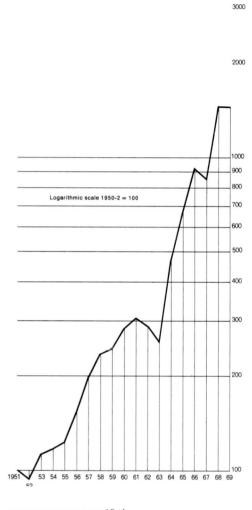

GOTHIC PRINTS: up 15 times

258

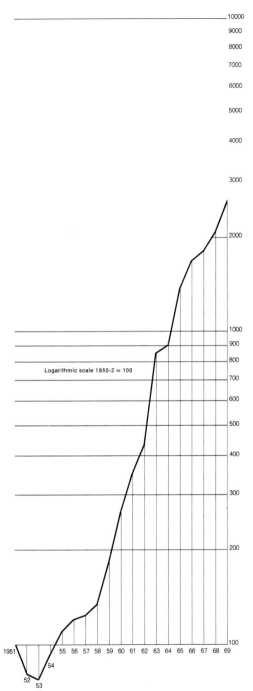

DÜRER PRINTS: up 26 times

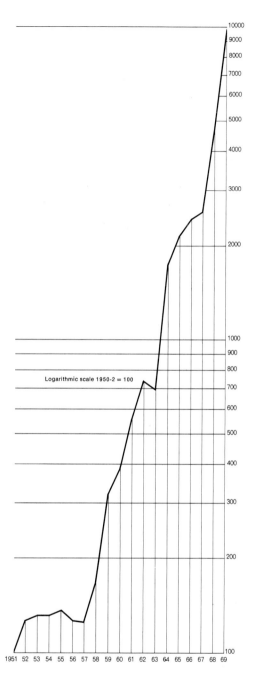

PRINTS AFTER PIETER BRUEGHEL: up
97 times

259

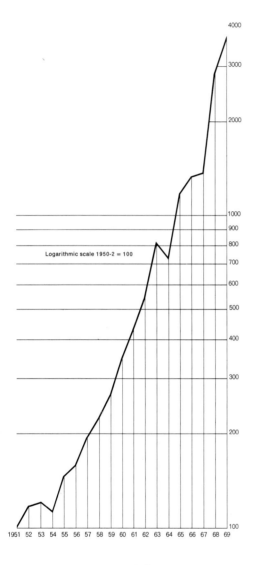

REMBRANDT PRINTS: up 40 times

CANALETTO PRINTS: up 30 times

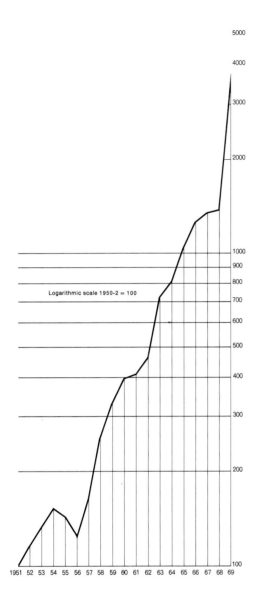

PIRANESI PRINTS: up 33½ times

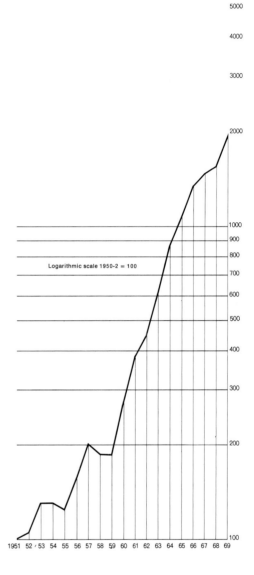

GOYA PRINTS: up 19½ times

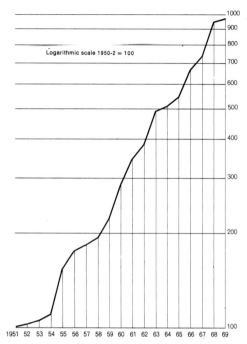

ENGLISH PICTURES over-all index:
up $9\frac{3}{4}$ times

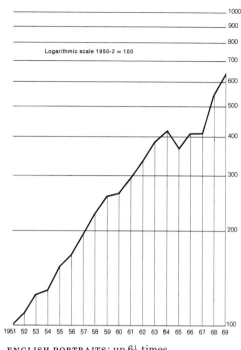

ENGLISH PORTRAITS: up $6\frac{1}{2}$ times

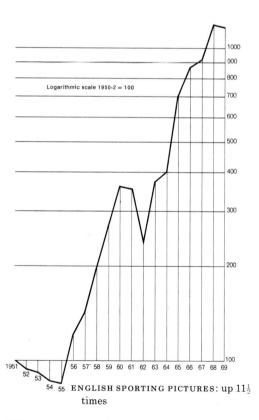

ENGLISH SPORTING PICTURES: up $11\frac{1}{2}$
times

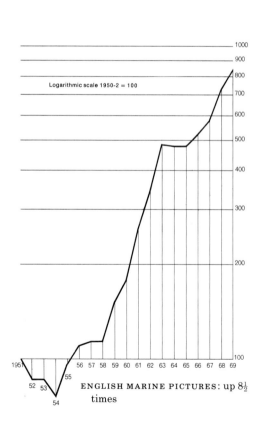

ENGLISH MARINE PICTURES: up $8\frac{1}{2}$
times

262

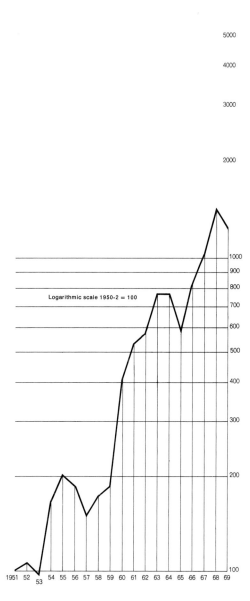

PRE-RAPHAELITE PAINTINGS: up 12½
   times

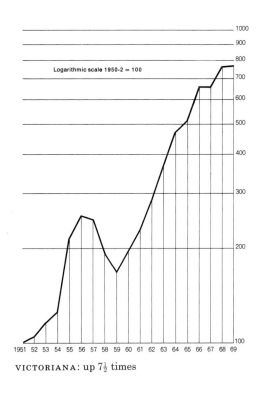

VICTORIANA: up 7½ times

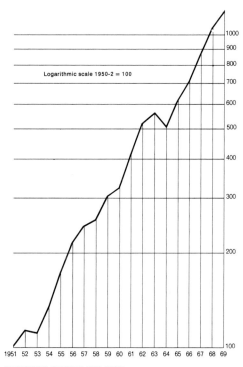

ENGLISH WATERCOLOUR
   LANDSCAPES: up 12 times

263

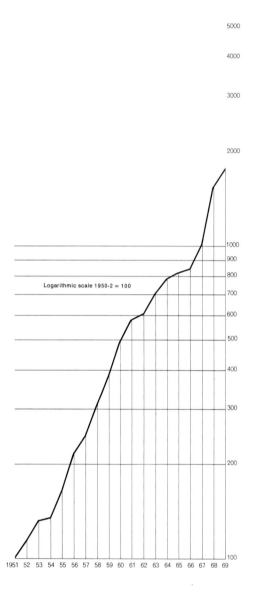

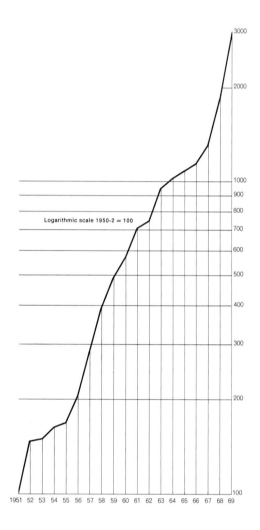

IMPRESSIONIST PAINTINGS over-all
   index: up 17½ times

MONET: up 29½ times

264

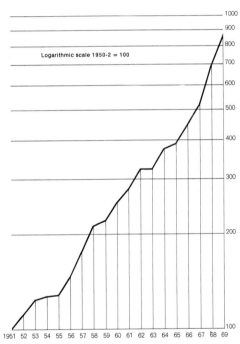

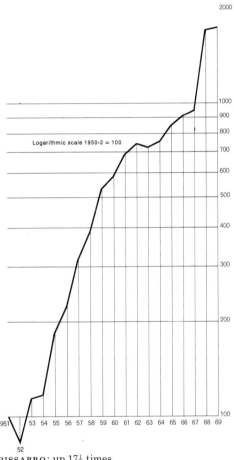

RENOIR: up $8\frac{1}{2}$ times

PISSARRO: up $17\frac{1}{2}$ times

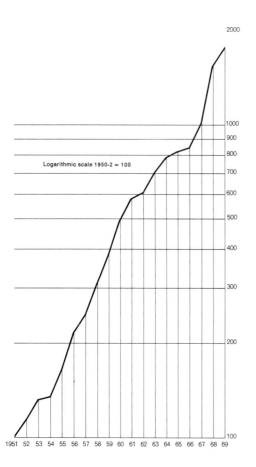

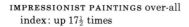

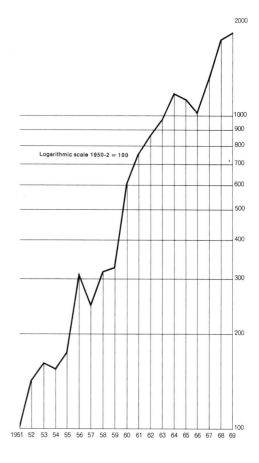

IMPRESSIONIST PAINTINGS over-all
   index: up 17½ times

SISLEY: up 18½ times

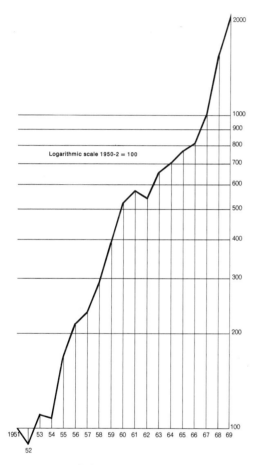

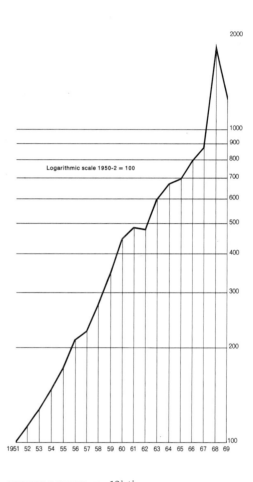

BOUDIN: up 20½ times

FANTIN-LATOUR: up 12½ times
(*Note:* One extremely expensive picture pushed the index unrealistically high in 1968; the fall in 1969 is not significant.)

267

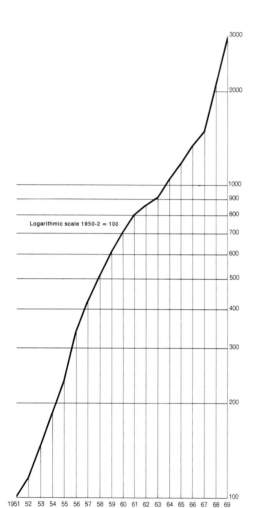

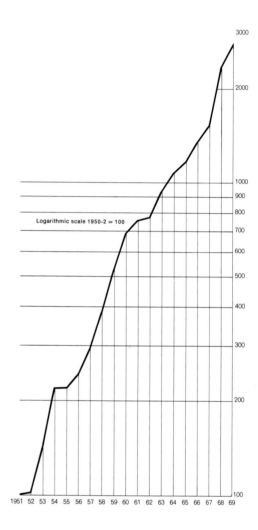

5000

4000

3000

2000

1000
900
800

Logarithmic scale 1950-2 = 100

700

600

500

400

300

200

100

1951 52 53 54 55 56 57 58 59 60 61 62 63 64 65 66 67 68 69

5000

4000

3000

2000

1000
900
800

Logarithmic scale 1950-2 = 100

700

600

500

400

300

200

100

1951 52 53 54 55 56 57 58 59 60 61 62 63 64 65 66 67 68 69

TWENTIETH-CENTURY PAINTINGS
over-all index: up 29 times

PICASSO: up $37\frac{1}{2}$ times

268

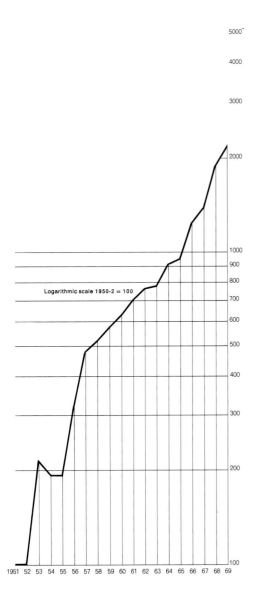

Logarithmic scale 1950-2 = 100

BRAQUE: up 22 times

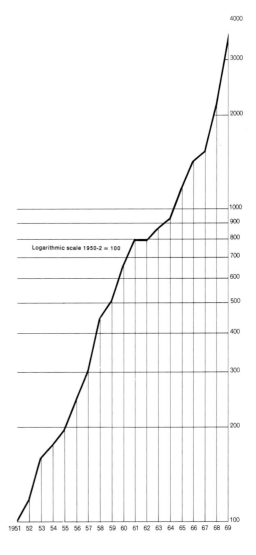

Logarithmic scale 1950-2 = 100

BONNARD: up 35 times

269

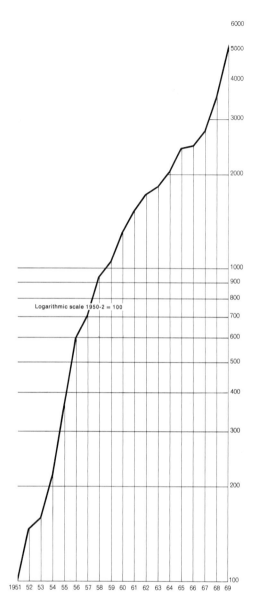

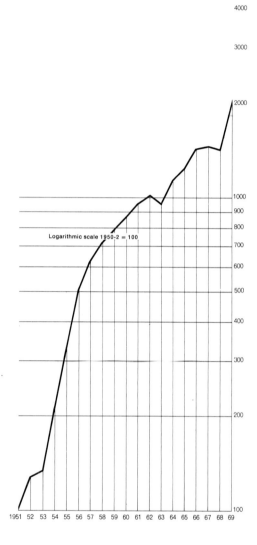

CHAGALL: up 50½ times

VLAMINCK: up 30 times

270

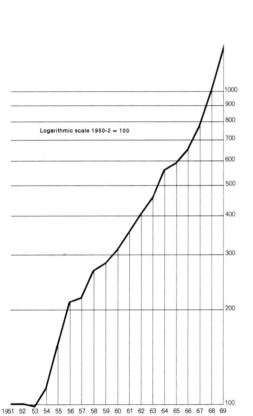

Logarithmic scale 1950-2 = 100

5000
4000
3000
2000
1000
900
800
700
600
500
400
300
200
100

1951 52 53 54 55 56 57 58 59 60 61 62 63 64 65 66 67 68 69

ROUAULT: up 14 times

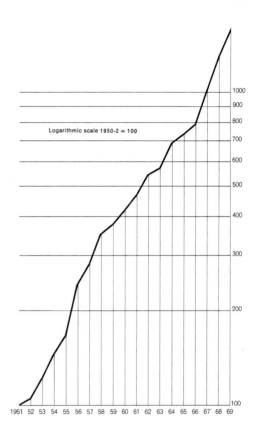

Logarithmic scale 1950-2 = 100

5000
4000
3000
2000
1000
900
800
700
600
500
400
300
200
100

1951 52 53 54 55 56 57 58 59 60 61 62 63 64 65 66 67˙ 68 69

UTRILLO: up 16 times

271

Bibliography

Jean Gimpel: *The Cult of Art*, Weidenfeld and Nicolson, 1969.

Raymonde Moulin: *Le Marché de la Peinture en France*, Les Editions de Minuit, 1967.

Gerald Reitlinger: *The Economics of Taste*, vol. 1: the rise and fall of picture prices 1760–1960, Barrie and Rockliff, 1961.

Maurice Rheims: *Art on the Market*, Weidenfeld and Nicolson, 1961.

Francis Henry Taylor: *The Taste of Angels*, Hamish Hamilton, 1948.

F. L. Wilder: *How to Identify Old Prints*, G. Bell and Sons, 1969.

Robert Wraight: *The Art Game*, Leslie Frewin, 1965.

Index

NOTE: numbers printed in italic indicate illustrations.

markets, 27; sales tax on works of art, 27–8; position *vis-à-vis* London, 28; structure of society, 35; and *avant-garde* artists, 34; interests in art history, 54, 56; influence of great museums, 57; reduced mobility of pictures, 58; collector-monarchs, 65–6, 67–8; old masters in museums, 70–1, 72; papermaking, 110

Evedingern, Allaert, landscape drawings, 118

Evelyn, John, and art-market speculation, 22

Eworth, Hans, 167

Export of Works of Art, Reviewing Committee and, 44

Expressionism, German, 231–2

Eyck, Jan van, absence from sale rooms, 58, 67, 76; attribution, 78

Fabriano, paper mills, 110

Fantin-Latour, Ignace, 194, 212; prices, 212–13; price rise, 263; 'Roses blanches et jaunes', 212

Fashion, factors influencing, 42; effect on prices, 42, 140–1; and minor works, 42; mirrored in art market, 47, 48, 49; rapid changes, 49–50

Fauve movement, 225, *228*, 235

Ferneley family, sporting pictures, 171, 173, 189

Ferrara, d'Este family, 65

Fischer, Harry, 31

Flanders, rival to Italy, 22, 76; old master schools, 52, 60, 69–70, 76, 78; bourgeois collectors, 67; price rises, 94–5; old master drawings, 117–18, 129; 'The Martyrdom of St Hippolytus', 76, *77*

Florence, 20, 63, 64, 75; period of unrest, 21; Medicis and, 21, 65; a Renaissance centre, 21; Mannerist school, 68; school of drawing, 115, of etching, 150

Florentine engravers, 'A bear hunt', *139*

Fontainebleau, studio of engravers, 147

Fopsen van Es, Jacob, still life, *97*

Forgery, of works of art, 20

Fragonard, Jean Honoré, 23, 150; prices fetched, 63, 103–6, 119, 133, 136; drawings, 119, 133, 136; availability, 133; 'La liseuse', 103, *104*, *105*, 106; 'Le repos de Diane', 103

France, 33; eighteenth century art market, 22–3; position of artist, 23;

influence on major arts, 23; post-Revolution spoils, 23; position of auctioneers, 28; export of masterpieces, 28; sales tax, 43, 45; lack of capital gains tax, 44; pre-emptive right of museums, 45; and international market, 45; export restrictions, 45–6; appreciation of decorative and fine arts, 49; interest in eighteenth century works, 52, 60, 63, 102–3, 133; devaluation of franc, 55; source of works of art, 61; and old masters, 61; Romantic painters, 63; royal collections, 66; eighteenth century innovations, 71–2, 82; old master drawings, 119, 133–6; old master prints, 147, 149

Franckenstein, Jonkheer van, collector of drawings, 112

Friedländer, Max, attributions, 67, 83, 87, 90

Frith, William, decline and revival, 179; prices, 190; 'Derby Day', 179; 'The road to ruin', 179, *179*

Fry, Roger, 'Second Post-Impressionist Exhibition', 199

Futurism, 1912 exhibition, 199; Italian, 233

Gainsborough, Thomas, 165, 168; mezzotints after, 150; landscapes, 169, 173; portraits, 169, 181; prices, 170, 171, 184; 'Blue Boy', 170; 'Cottage Door', 170; 'Mr and Mrs Andrews', 170, *171*, 181

Gambart, dealers, 176

Gauguin, Paul, 195, 197; prices fetched, 30, 73, 184, 198, 200, 203, 206; primitivism, 205; 'Autour des huttes, Martinique', 200; 'Still life with apples', 203; 'Te tiai na ve ite rata', *205*, 206

Genoa, 68

Genre painting, beginnings of, 69–70, 84; availability, 70; in European museums, 70–1; marine pictures, 78; portraits, 86, 102; flower pieces, 96; still life, 96–7

Gentilleschi, Orazio, 'Lot and his Daughters', 116

German Little Masters, 146

Germany, art collecting, 25, 55, 61, 72; devaluation of Deutschmark, 55; source of works of art, 61; court artists, 67; influence of Dürer, 146; woodcuts, 155; and Impressionists, 199; Expressionism, 231

Ghirlandaio, Domenico, 65

Molyn, Pieter, landscape drawings, 117, 129; prices, 129–30; 'Coastal landscape', 129–30, *130*; 'Winter landscape', 129–30, *130*

Momper, Joos de, 70; 'A river landscape', 98, *98*

Monaco, Lorenzo, 84; 'King David playing the psaltery', *83*, 84

Monamy, Peter, marine artist, 168; prices, 186

Mondrian, Piet, abstract artist, 221, 225–6; prices, 225, 226; 'Composition 1', 226; 'Large composition', *226*

Monet, Claude, 193, 194, 195; prices fetched, 25, 192, 198, 200, 202, 203, 205, 206; greatest period, 40; in London, 198; 'painting from nature', 204; availability, 207–9; price multiplication, 209, 260; 'Gare Saint-Lazare', 199; 'Impression sunrise', 194; 'Louveciennes', *210*; 'La plage à Sainte-Adresse', 210; 'Terrasse à Sainte-Adresse', 203–4

Montagna, Bartolomeo, 'St Bartholomew and St Augustine', *86*, 87

Monticelli, 215, 218

Moore, Henry, 230

Moreau l'Aîné, gouaches, 119, 136

Moreau le Jeune, ink and wash drawings, 119, 133, 136; prints, 150; 'La soirée de Saint-Cloud', *132*, 136

Morisot, Berthe, 195; reassessment, 215 'Le port de Fécamp', *215*

Morris, William, 176, 178

Motherwell, Robert, 230

Mummius, pillage of Corinth, 20

Munnings, Sir Alfred, 39, 173

Museums, increased numbers, 18, 33, 34, 57–8; American spending, 26, 43, 50, 110; English benefactions, 26; tax-free gifts to, 26–7, 43; and art collecting, 33–4, 110; artistic function, 34; dealer-curator relationship, 37; and prices of masterpieces, 38; sales to avoid death duties, 44; pre-emptive right of purchase, 44, 45; effect on prices, 51; interest in old masters, 52, 57, 61, 93; perpetual ownership, 58; and scarcity value, 58–9; competition between, 59; Dutch genre paintings, 70–1; interest in drawings, 109–10, 113, 117; and old prints, 140, 142; search for Impressionists, 192; and modern art, 221, 230

Nancy, print-making school, 149

Naples, 68

Napoleon, theft of art works, 19, 58

National Gallery, London, 76, 80, 206, 214; foundation, 58, 186

National Gallery of Art, Washington, 58, 78; prices paid, 73, 77

National Portrait Gallery, 167

Nazarenes, the, 64

Netherlands, 22; war with Spain, 70; influence of Dürer, 146; print-making, 148; woodcuts, 155

New York, 31; and contemporary artists, 24, 229; sales tax on works of art, 27; art market, 28, 30

New York Public Library, sale of pictures, 1956, 29

Niarchos, Stavros, buys a Gauguin, 30, 203

Nicolson, Ben, 31

Nolde, Emile, 'Tropenglut', 231–2

Northern school, art speculation, 22; scholarly taste, 52, 67; availability, 60, 62, 67, 70, 76, 78; portraits, 67; lack of documentation, 83–4; price range, 84; shift in taste to Bosch, 90; engravers, 144

Northwick Park, Spencer-Churchill collection, 90, 93, 94

Nowell-Usticke Rembrandt collection, 158

Old Master Drawings, price multiplication, 1951–69, 32, 48, 51, 109–10, 116, 118, 251–3; investment buying, 34, 51; split between museums' and collectors' market, 34; art-historical interest, 52, 109, 110–11, 116, 117, 119, 120, 122, 125; and paper-making, 110; earliest collections, 111–13; availability, 113, 114, 116; prices fetched, 113–14, 116, 118, 119, 120–37 *passim*; pre-1500, 114; seventeenth century Italian, 116–17; Dutch and Flemish, 117–18; eighteenth century, 119–20; use of watercolours, 119

Old Master Paintings, investment buying, 34; effect of reserve prices, 35; and catalogue illustrations, 36; forecasting prices, 38–9; attribution, 40–1; price multiplication, 1951–69, 48, 51, 61, 246–8; no major increase in interest, 51, 61; price range, 38, 57, 72 ff., 116; museums and, 52, 57, 70–1; effect of European prosperity on market, 56; sale room use of term, 57; limited supply of important works, 57; availability in

INDEX

sale rooms, 58, 61; business based on lesser works, 59–60; importance of condition, 60; peripatetic life, 60–1; international market, 61; present day market, 63 ff.; declining interest, 68; eighteenth century innovations, 71–2; main price-determining factors, 81–2

Old Master Prints, price multiplication, 1951–69, 32, 48, 51, 53, 138, 254–9; investment buying, 34, 51, 138; split between collectors' and museums' market, 52; art-historical interest, 52, 138, 152; early collections, 112–13; prices fetched, 138, 139, 140, 143–5, 147–53 passim, 153–64; variety of techniques, 138, 144; early dating, 138, 144; manufacture of paper and, 138–40; availability, 138–40, 141–2, 146–7; museum interest, 140; influence of fashion, 140–1, 143–4; factors affecting value, 141–2, 153–7; of famous works of art, 142–3, 147, 152; sales centres, 144; publishing ventures, 147; collecting interest, 152

Ostade, Adriaen van, 100; etchings, 149; 'Interior of an inn', 101

Palmer, Samuel, 174; prices, 175, 190, 191; 'Cow lodge', 190, 191

Panini, Giovanni Paolo, 60, 72; price rises, 63

Paris, Cognacq sale (1952), 29, 202; art sales, 30; dealers' methods, 31, 37; auction prices, 42–3; Court Artists, 67, 72; the Salon, 72; modern School, 227, 230, 231, 234

Parke-Bernet, N. York, 193; Rembrandt sale, 25, 158; Lurcy sale, 30, 202; taken over by Sotheby's, 30; sale of Impressionists, 200

Parmigianino, Francesco, drawings, 117, 124, 126; prices, 126; etchings, 148; 'The death of Dido', 126; 'The finding of Cyrus', 127

Patenier, Joachim, genre painting, 70

Pater, John Baptiste Joseph, 60, 72; price rises, 63, 103

Pencz, George, engraver, 146

Perugia, 121

Philip the Good, patron, 67, 69

Picasso, Pablo, 199, 230; price variation, 39, 48, 219, 221, 222, 234–5; status symbol, 52, 222–3; etchings, 152; and Cubism, 219, 221, 234; Blue and Pink periods, 219, 221, 224, 234; combination of decorative and his-

torical art, 221; range of styles, 221–3, 224; sale room competition, 223; price multiplication, 1951–69, 223–4, 227, 264; 'Mère et infant de profil', 221, 222, 234; 'Nu couché', 234, 235; 'papier collé', 235; 'Paysage de Gosol', 234; 'La Pointe de la Cité', 219, 223, 224, 235; 'Verre', 234, 235, 235

Pierpont Morgan Library, 117

Pillement, Jean Baptiste, drawings, 136

Piranesi, Giovanni Batista, 49, 150; prints, 144; etchings, 150, 161; prices, 153, 161, 163; 'Carceri d' Invenzione', 150, 161, 162; 'Verdute di Roma', 161–2, 163

Pisanello, 'Nobleman carrying a falcon', 115

Pissarro, Camille, 193, 194, 195, 198; in London, 198; prices fetched, 200, 202, 209–12; landscape artist, 209; price rise, 261; 'The Market Place', 200; 'La mare aux canards', 211; 'Le Pont-Neuf, Paris', 211

Pointillisme, 205, 206, 215–16; prices, 216

Pollaiulo, Antonio, print 'The battle of naked men', 144

Pollard, James and Robert, sporting pictures, 171, 173; prices, 189

Pollock, Jackson, abstract painter, 230

Porcelain, English, boom in Bow and Chelsea figures, 28; price multiplication, 1951–69, 48

Porcelain, French, 23

Post-Impressionists, 192; great masters, 195; great period, 197; exhibitions, 199; influence on modern art, 205

Poussin, Nicolas, 68; availability, 58

Prado, the, 58, 93

Pre-Raphaelites, 64, 176–7; Brotherhood, 176, 178; prices, 177–8, 190; effect of Impressionism, 178; rediscovery, 178–9; availability, 190

Press, the, reporting of art sales, 25

Prices, 17; multiplication since 1950s, 24–5, 32, 34; new records, 25; postwar slump, 28; revival in 1940s, 28; effect of 'reserves', 35; of illustrations in catalogues, 36; difficulty of assessing, 38; effect of rarity, 38, 42, 75–6; of masterpieces, 38, 72 ff.; determined by merit and reputation, 39; wide spectrum, 39; effect of size and medium, 39; art-historical interest element, 40, 82; effect of attribution, 40–1, 81–3; provenance and, 41, 82, 87; condition and, 41–2, 71, 78, 82, 87; fluctuations in fashion, 42, 49–50; importance of buyer and seller and, 42; external factors, 42–3; 1969 levels, 50–1; limited to museums and millionaires, 50, 51; effect of too rapid reappearance, 54; future prospects, 56; influence of a great name, 78, 185–6; element of chance, 81; and elusive 'quality', 82; effect of completeness, 165–6, 170–3; present day acceleration, 197, 229

Primaticcio, Francesco, engraver, 147

Private collectors, comparison between their and museum pictures, 39–40; lavish spending in America, 43, 54–5; and prices of masterpieces, 38; effect of tax laws, 44; increase due to Affluent Society, 50; varying range of taste and income, 50–1; domination of Impressionist and modern market, 52; and old masters, 52, 57, 58; and investment in fine art, 54; interest in documentation, 56; competition with museums, 59; in fifteenth century Italy, 65; and decorative paintings, 95; and old master drawings, 109, 110, 113, 116, 133; and English pictures, 166; and Impressionists, 192, 218; post-World War II period, 201; and twentieth century art, 217, 218, 220; two methods of approach, 220–1

Raeburn, Sir Henry, changing prices, 1929–69, 47; portraits, 169

Raimondi, Marcantonio, engraver, 142, 143–4, 147; 'Cleopatra', 143; 'Massacre of the Innocents', 144

Raphael, 60, 64, 67; continuing fame, 68, 91; drawings, 109, 114, 117, 120–2; prices, 121–2; prints, 143, 147; 'Cleopatra' (engraving), 143; 'St Jerome punishing the heretic Sabinianus', 81, 81; study for 'The Entombment', 114, 120–1, for 'Madonna and Child with Infant St John', 114, 121–2, 121

Religion, influence on art market, 26, 33, 54; replaced by art patronage, 26–7, 50

Relining, damage done by, 41–2

Rembrandt, Harmensz van Rign, prices fetched, 25, 74, 75, 78, 94–5, 117, 123, 148, 153, 158–60; greatest period, 40, 75, 123; definitive catalogue of drawings, 40, 117; 'school' of, 40; availability, 58, 74–5, 114, 123; collector of drawings, 112; his drawings, 114, 118, 123; etchings, 123, 138, 142, 143, 148, 158–60; prints, 140, 142, 144, 148, 152; 'Aristotle contemplating the bust of Homer', 25, 74, 75; 'Christ healing the sick', 148, 149, 159; 'Landscape with a cottage', 159–60, 160; 'The mocking of Christ' (drawing), 123, 123; portrait (small), 75, of Hendrickje Stoffels, 118, of his son Titus, 59, 75; 'school of Rembrandt' drawings, 23, 118; 'The three crosses' (print), 140, 148, 158, 159; 'Three trees' (print), 144

Reni, Guido, 68; reassessment, 62

Renoir, Auguste, 195; prices fetched, 25, 29, 30, 192, 200, 201, 202, 205, 206, 208, 209; broad spectrum, 39; greatest period, 40; unsaleable period, 47, 194; status symbol, 52; recognition, 198; virtuosity, 204; availability, 207–9; average price multiplication, 209, 261; 'Les Canotiers', 200; 'Child with Bonnet', 201; 'Les deux soeurs', 29; 'Jeune fille aux chapeau garni', 29, 209; 'Jeune fille de profil', 208; 'La loge', 199, 209; 'Les parapluies', 209; 'Petite baigneuse', 208; 'Portrait of Jean', 201; 'La Serre', 30, 202, 202

Restoration, 18; damage done by, 41; effect on prices, 41, 60, 82

Reynolds, Sir Joshua, 165; collector of drawings, 112, 126; mezzotints after, 150; financial rewards, 169; prices, 185; 'James Boswell', 185, 185–6; 'The Tragic Muse' (price paid), 170

Rheims, Maurice, 24–5

Ribera, José de, etchings, 150

Ricci, Marco, drawings, 120, 137; etchings, 150; 'Tobias and the Angel', 119

Robert, Hubert, prices fetched, 63, 108, 133, 136; drawings, 133, 136

Rome, 31, 63, 67, 68, 72; in Classical period, 19–20; at the Renaissance, 21; sack of, 18; print publishers, 147

Romney, George, 165; mezzotints after, 150; portraits, 169; prices, 185; 'The Misses Beckford' (price paid), 170